To Grace,

with all best wishes,

[signature]

September 4, 2018

COLOR AND CHARACTER

PAMELA GRUNDY

COLOR AND

CHARACTER

West Charlotte High and the American Struggle over Educational Equality

THE UNIVERSITY OF NORTH CAROLINA PRESS

Chapel Hill

This book was published with the assistance of the Z. Smith
Reynolds Fund of the University of North Carolina Press.

Manufactured in the United States of America

The University of North Carolina Press has been a member
of the Green Press Initiative since 2003.

Jacket illustration: detail of West Charlotte High School class of 1987 from the
school yearbook, *The Lion*. Courtesy of the Robinson-Spangler Carolina Room,
Charlotte-Mecklenburg Public Library.

All student portraits appearing on chapter-opening pages from the West Charlotte
High School yearbook, *The Lion*. Courtesy of the Robinson-Spangler Carolina Room,
Charlotte-Mecklenburg Public Library.

LIBRARY OF CONGRESS CATALOGING-IN-PUBLICATION DATA
Names: Grundy, Pamela, author.
Title: Color and character : West Charlotte High and the American struggle
over educational equality / Pamela Grundy.
Description: Chapel Hill : The University of North Carolina Press, [2017] |
Includes bibliographical references and index.
Identifiers: LCCN 2017015392| ISBN 9781469636078 (cloth : alk. paper) |
ISBN 9781469636085 (ebook)
Subjects: LCSH: West Charlotte High School (Charlotte, N.C.) — History. |
Educational equalization — North Carolina — Charlotte — History. | School
integration — North Carolina — Charlotte — History. | African Americans —
Education (Secondary) — North Carolina — Charlotte. | Charlotte (N.C.) —
Race relations.
Classification: LCC LC213.23.C4 G78 2017 | DDC 373.09756/76 — dc23
LC record available at https://lccn.loc.gov/2017015392

MIX
Paper from
responsible sources
FSC® C013483

To everyone who loves

WEST CHARLOTTE HIGH SCHOOL

For further information on this book,

visit www.colorandcharacter.org.

CONTENTS

FIGURES AND MAPS

MAPS

COLOR AND CHARACTER

Before the 1930s, many of Charlotte's African American residents lived in the downtown Second Ward neighborhood known as Brooklyn. As the city expanded, African American families moved west to growing neighborhoods such as Greenville and Biddleville. Official Map of Charlotte, 1954. Courtesy of the Robinson-Spangler Carolina Room.

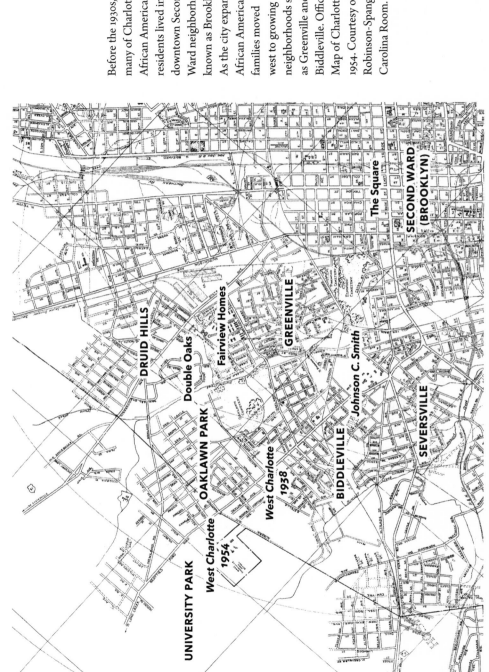

INTRODUCTION

When you feel as if you belong, as if you have a reason for being
there, you feel protected. You feel encouraged. Thriving, existing,
living vibrantly—you feel encouraged to do that. And that's what
I think West Charlotte provided for so many people. . . . You have
evidence of people belonging to something, and being a part of
something, and not having to make excuses for it. And you can see
how the human spirit thrives.

JOHN LOVE JR., class of 1980

The end-of-school buzzer sounds, and West Charlotte High School's students emerge into the early-summer heat. Clusters form as they wait for
buses and for rides, cell phones in hands, muted conversations broken now
and then by laughter. A handful of girls teases a tall boy standing in their
midst; another boy, eyes on the giggling group, leans down to wipe a fleck
of dirt from the white leather of his two-tone sneakers. A stone lion, mane
swept back from an impassive face, presides over the scene. A lion has been
West Charlotte's mascot since the school opened its doors in 1938, a time
when the banking mecca of Charlotte, North Carolina, was a midsized textile center, and ambitious African Americans from across the region flocked
to the segregated neighborhoods on the city's west side in search of jobs and
opportunity.

The history of West Charlotte High School tells a dramatic story of
triumph and struggle. During its first three decades, it served the African
American families who built Charlotte's west side neighborhoods. Despite
the constraints of Jim Crow segregation, it gave shape to a striving commu-

nity's ambitions, becoming a space in which a corps of skilled and dedicated teachers groomed young people to rise higher and go farther than their parents ever could. In the 1970s, when Charlotte embarked on a court-ordered school busing plan that would make its schools the most desegregated in the nation, West Charlotte emerged as the new system's celebrated flagship, embodying a multiracial determination to move beyond the inequalities of segregation, and to educate black and white students for life in an increasingly prosperous city.

But as the twentieth century neared its close, and a new court order eliminated race-based busing, it became clear that Charlotte's celebrated economic growth had left many neighborhoods behind. This was especially true on the west side, which had been battered by urban renewal, highway construction, suburbanization, and a set of policies and practices that discouraged investment in historically black neighborhoods across the nation. Charlotte schools resegregated along lines of class as well as race, and West Charlotte became the city's poorest, least stable, and most academically troubled high school. For the first time in its long, distinguished history, its shortcomings seemed to outnumber its achievements.

Within that history lies a profoundly American story of education, community, democracy, and race. In a nation where success and failure are deemed to stem from individual merits or shortcomings, schools have become a centerpiece of democratic promise, cast as places where aspiring students can acquire the skills and knowledge to rise above their station and realize their dreams. In reality, however, this promise has often been denied. Schools have been tightly enmeshed in the societies around them, routinely designed to prepare specific groups of students for designated social roles, whether picking cotton, cleaning houses, tending textile mill looms, or directing state affairs. The separate and decidedly unequal schools of the Jim Crow South were a flagrant example of deliberately stunted possibilities — one reason why the long legal campaign against de jure segregation began with schools.

West Charlotte High School's journey through segregation, desegregation, and resegregation illuminates the many challenges involved in creating schools that provide *all* students with the knowledge and equal opportunities they deserve. In its eight decades of existence, West Charlotte has been shaped not only by staff, students, and community, but by a civil rights movement, a conservative resurgence, a transforming economy, and a profoundly reconfigured urban landscape. Government policies, market economics, legal decisions, popular culture, educational philosophies, political struggles, and shifting concepts of race and community have all come into play. The school's story contains a vivid and instructive portrait of human possibility, found in the ways successive generations of teachers, students, lawyers, political leaders, and community members fought the inequalities of Jim Crow segregation, worked to realize the promises of integration, and devised strategies to help young spirits thrive. It also serves as a cautionary tale, a reminder that social change unfolds in multiple patterns along many intersecting paths, and that no progress is guaranteed to last.

As cities, states, and nation wrestle with the inequalities that present-day West Charlotte so dramatically embodies, the stories that students and teachers tell about their school hold many meanings. Memories can easily become nostalgia. But nostalgia, carefully examined, can be doubly illuminating—it highlights aspects of past lives that assume new significance when viewed in the slanting light of present challenges. Stories of West Charlotte's segregated and desegregated eras touch on many common strengths, among them a strong and stable corps of teachers, multiple arenas for growth and self-expression, and the determination to nurture body and soul as well as mind. Perhaps most significantly, students from those eras felt not only encouraged but also valued; they believed that their efforts and achievements were central not only to their own lives, but to the future of the community that surrounded them.[1]

West Charlotte's experience with integration also highlights the work required to put the rhetoric of equal opportunity into practice. Desegregation's advocates had high hopes. Many believed that encouraging children from different backgrounds to learn together would produce multiple benefits for individuals and for society as a whole. In the hard-edged realm of policy, integration also served another, more practical purpose. Families and communities play key roles in American public schools, and the combination of time, money, and influence they are able to expend has typically magnified the educational advantages enjoyed by students in better-off communities. Integrating schools both racially and economically thus promised to even out the influence of politically and economically powerful families, creating a genuinely level educational playing field. In practice, however, the weight of history, of race, and of the housing markets that shaped urban growth meant that while such a balance could indeed be struck, as it was for a brief time at West Charlotte, maintaining that equilibrium remained a constant challenge, within individual schools and in the district as a whole.

Finally, West Charlotte's recent struggles underscore the shortcomings of policies that address schools apart from their historical and social context.

By the 1990s, when a new generation of judges began to lift desegregation orders, a new approach to educational equality arose. This movement, often dubbed "corporate reform," broke with educational practices of the past and experimented with ideas drawn from the business world, concepts like "choice," "competition," "efficiency," "productivity," "return on investment," and "creative destruction." In theory, the power of choice, competition, and determined individual effort—augmented by the "accountability" made possible by an expansion of standardized testing—would create schools that provided an excellent education regardless of their racial or economic makeup. West Charlotte became a high-profile arena for exploring many of these ideas. Results, however, have fallen far short of promises.[2]

This is not the story I set out to tell. In 1998, when I began this project, a still-integrated West Charlotte remained a symbol of individual and community success. Graduates from both the segregated and desegregated eras told richly detailed stories of their experiences, shot through with warmth, laughter, and thoughtful reflection. The portrait of the school conveyed in those oral history interviews, while imperfect in many ways, was inspiring. At that point I intended to depict the strengths of the segregated West Charlotte, the battle to end Jim Crow, and the work that extended the civil rights movement into the final quarter of the twentieth century, as black and white Charlotteans labored to make a landmark Supreme Court ruling into reality. That narrative shone with possibility, with the value of courage, sacrifice, and long-term dedication. Then busing ended. Despite its remarkable history, despite the loyalty of its alumni, West Charlotte fell farther and faster than anyone had imagined. The entire community was forced to confront hard questions about the meaning of an accomplishment that did not last. I did not know what to do.

More than a decade passed before I returned to the project. By then, new themes had emerged—the contingency of progress, the story of people and places left behind, the folly of trying to rebuild an institution and its culture without drawing on the lessons of the past. The shift also underscored the flexible tenacity of racial hierarchies, the way in which, for example, a prosperous, majority white city could elect its first black mayor at the same time that public neglect, the drug trade, a growing income gap, and mass incarceration were hollowing out many of its historic African American communities.

Today, at a time when economic and political transformations have starkly widened gaps between the top and bottom rungs of American society, and when racial, ethnic, and cultural diversity is greater than it has ever been, cities across the nation face questions about the values their public schools should embody. One popular approach promotes a framework of choice and competition, placing the decisions made by individual families front and center even when that strategy heightens racial, economic, and educational divides. Another seeks to bridge those gaps through a renewed commitment to racially and economically integrated schools. The latter path requires more work, provokes more controversy. The history of West Charlotte High School highlights its worth.

This book's title, *Color and Character*, attempts to capture the connections between schooling and community values. Speaking to the March on Washington in 1963, Martin Luther King Jr. famously imagined a world where his children would "not be judged by the color of their skin, but by the content of their character." In choosing the word "character," King invoked not only mental accomplishment but also moral responsibility—an approach that meshed with the long-held belief that one of the many tasks of public schools is to build character, to nurture both accomplished individuals and responsible citizens.[3] In subsequent decades, however, King's soaring words were often flattened into the argument that equality should be defined as "colorblindness"—a theory that undergirded the dismantling of desegregation programs such as Charlotte-Mecklenburg's. Nothing could have been further from King's dreams.

The power of the Jim Crow system, as the history of West Charlotte so dramatically demonstrates, lay not only in the laws the Supreme Court overturned but also in the multitude of day-to-day experiences that wove the tenets of white supremacy into every area of life, forging habits of mind and action that have taken far longer to transform. The teachers of the segregated era understood this well and worked to build the kind of character that would allow their students to resist the encompassing web of racial inequalities. When schools desegregated, they drew a wider range of teachers and students into that project, becoming places where young people from many backgrounds could develop the knowledge and determination required to acknowledge the realities of race, to fashion new ways of living, and to turn the idea of equality into on-the-ground reality. That task was never finished, and many would argue that much of the progress made has been reversed. But two decades of commitment to desegregated schools shaped the character of Charlotte, made it a better, fairer city.

West Charlotte High School's history also challenges the notion that simply creating schools designed to nurture the talents of individual students can remedy our society's inequalities. This is a popular concept for many reasons, among them the extraordinary difference that education can make in a young person's life and the way this model champions individual effort and determination rather than requiring wholesale social or economic change. But the education West Charlotte provided had its broadest impact when its students entered a world where other work—whether legal, political, or economic—had created opportunities that young people committed to fairness and justice were able to seize on and expand. When the task of transformation fell almost exclusively to West Charlotte and its students, its successes proved more limited. This history calls on all of us to take a broad view of educational endeavors, to acknowledge how closely schools are tied to the communities they serve, and to see school improvement as a necessary but far from sufficient part of a broader push for equality and justice. I hope this work will help make that point, and contribute to that cause.

AN
AFRICAN
AMERICAN
SCHOOL

On the morning of September 6, 1938, several hundred nervous but excited African American teenagers set off for the first day of classes at the newly built West Charlotte High School. Scatterings of students grew into clusters as they made their way past the neat rows of bungalows and cottages that filled the streets of Charlotte's west side neighborhoods, while adults watched carefully from windows and front porches. Their paths converged at Beatties Ford Road, the two-lane thoroughfare that ran through the west side and out into the country. The imposing new building awaited them — a three-story, red-brick structure that held twelve teachers, sixteen classrooms and a library. Ten wide, concrete steps led to a set of double doors that opened onto the future.[1]

West Charlotte High School would spend its first three decades as an African American school, serving the children who lived in the west side's African American neighborhoods. From the day it opened its doors, the school and its staff became an integral part of west side life, anchored in the surrounding community while also serving as a bridge to a wider world. In an era marked by the uncertainties of war, a changing economy, and an expanding civil rights movement, West Charlotte's staff worked steadily at the challenging task of preparing adolescents to play multiple roles in their community and to navigate the shifting currents of the society around them.

West Charlotte opened in an auspicious time and place. The students who climbed the school's front steps came from a community on the move, in which ambitious migrants were fashioning vibrant cultural and economic institutions. Charlotte's population had nearly doubled in the prosperous 1920s, and continued to grow at a steady pace during the Depression. Earlier in the century, most of the city's African Americans had settled in the heart of town, many of them in the all-black Second Ward neighborhood called Brooklyn. By the 1920s, however, the city's burgeoning population began to push beyond its original four wards. Black families began to set their sights on the city's west side, on a network of neighborhoods anchored by the elegant brick buildings on the campus of Johnson C. Smith University, a prestigious Presbyterian school founded in 1867 to educate newly freed African Americans.[2]

Charlotte's pattern of racial and class arrangements had solidified early in the twentieth century. Throughout the nineteenth century, when social distinctions were maintained by a rigid code of hierarchical deference, Charlotte's residents had clustered on a grid of center-city streets — black next to white, rich next to poor. But that arrangement had proved short-lived. In the heady decades that followed the end of slavery, Charlotte's African Americans established schools, built successful businesses, and plunged into poli-

An African American School

West Charlotte's first building, completed in 1938. *The Lion*, 1963.
Courtesy of the Robinson-Spangler Carolina Room.

tics. In the 1890s, North Carolina's black voters joined with rural whites to seize control of state politics. Faced with this challenge to their economic and political power, wealthy whites launched a violent white supremacy campaign that broke up the black-white Fusion coalition, stripped African Americans of their hard-won right to vote, and began to craft the elaborate legal and cultural structures of Jim Crow segregation. They then withdrew to suburban enclaves in the southern part of town, most notably the vaunted Myers Park, where curving streets ran past towering trees and large homes occupied well-landscaped lots. A combination of housing prices, restrictive covenants, and unspoken agreements relegated working-class whites to the company-owned housing that clustered around the city's textile mills, or to inexpensive developments nearby. African Americans were steered west.[3]

The African American west side began at the Johnson C. Smith campus, where Trade Street turned into Beatties Ford Road. Around the upper edge of the campus stretched the community of Biddleville — so named because it dated from the days Smith had been known as Biddle University. A few blocks up Beatties Ford Road, at the intersection with Oaklawn Avenue, a cluster of shops and businesses adjoined the neat wooden bungalows of Washington Heights, built in the 1910s at the last stop on the city trolley line. To the east, Oaklawn Avenue ran down to Greenville, a nineteenth-century black settlement that was quickly filling with new homes. While white neighborhoods were increasingly divided by economic class, the limited space available to African Americans meant that they clustered closer together. The attractions of suburban life and the amenities of an expanding Johnson C. Smith drew some of Charlotte's most prominent African Americans — doctors, teachers, ministers — out to the new neighborhoods. But most of the area's residents were recent arrivals from rural areas in North and South Carolina, families who purchased or rented modest houses and apartments, and who found work in trades such as gardening, housekeeping, and construction.

Future city councilman Malachi Greene, whose family came to Charlotte from rural Chester County, South Carolina, noted that his father had a simple explanation for the move: "The prospects for Negroes were better in Charlotte." Charlotte was first and foremost a business town, in which the practical demands of making money led residents to look to the future rather than the past. While Jim Crow segregation remained firmly in place, this business-focused outlook fueled an ongoing economic boom that expanded the number and quality of jobs available to African Americans, as well as opportunities for black-owned businesses that served an all-black clientele.

Like their urban counterparts around the state, Charlotte's African Americans were also beginning to cautiously reenter the political arena, often led by residents who could operate from the relative safety of the city's growing number of independent African American institutions. By the mid-1930s, more than 600 African Americans were registered to vote, and in 1937, three African Americans ran for city offices. Mary McCrorey, the wife of Johnson C. Smith president Henry McCrorey, conducted what the *Charlotte Observer* called "a lively contest" for the Charlotte Board of Education. Funeral home proprietor Zechariah Alexander and businessman A. E. Spears competed for city council seats.[4]

Charlotte was far from paradise for African Americans. Hours were long and often irregular, pay was low, and police brutality was common.[5] Black residents, no matter how capable, faced the indignity of official segregation and strict limits on their opportunities. High school students were not spared these hardships. "We had young men and women who didn't know where the next meal was coming from, or whether someone was going to come by and have them put the furniture out in the yard this month," recalled Charles McCullough, a tall, lanky boy who would become a national high-jump champion and then return home to spend three decades coaching West Charlotte's basketball team. McCullough, who was raised by his grandmother, knew these economic pressures well. "I had to work," he said. "I was working at the bowling alley and I was caddying at the golf course. Later on, I had to cook for my brother, because my grandmother got sick. So I was doing all those things along with trying to play football, basketball, baseball, and what have you."

Hard work, limited health care, and environmental hazards made sickness and death regular features of life. The Greenville community, for example, sat next to the Southern Asbestos plant, which made fire-resistant asbestos fabric. Thereasea Clark Elder, whose family had left South Carolina to settle in a three-room home on Hamilton Street, recalled that in the summers workers would open the plant windows, releasing a fine, white dust that settled on porches and crept through window screens. Children played in the piles of asbestos waste heaped around the plant. Two of Elder's siblings died before they reached the age of three, and her lungs became scarred from asbestos exposure. "They were defeated long before they had a chance to enjoy life," she wrote of her siblings, noting that the pain of losing them contributed to her decision to go to nursing school, and then spend decades caring for Mecklenburg County residents.[6]

Some members of the community sought refuge from hardship in drugs or drink, and children knew to steer clear of the "cafe" one Greenville woman ran inside her home. More often, however, community members cushioned difficulties by helping one another. Families shared food from their gardens, helped with neighbors' home improvement projects, and exchanged plenty of advice. "Everyone cared about everyone," Elder recalled. "Everybody was aware of everything in that community. If anyone was sick, the community cared for that whole family. They provided wood, coal, food, whatever." If a family was quarantined with tuberculosis, neighbors left food on the porch. One night Elder's sister, Mae Clark Orr, was ill with tonsillitis, and both parents had to go to work. Mae woke up in the middle of the night to find a neighbor sitting by her bed, using ice to keep her cool. "That's how close we were," she said.[7]

Deaths in the neighborhood hardly had to be announced. "Every church had their bell, and when that bell toned, you knew that whoever was very sick in that church had died, and you would know where to go to carry the food," Elder explained. "You would know that would be Nazarene bell, or that would be Second Calvary's bell or that would be Brandon, whatever church." Community members often stayed with a bereaved family for weeks. "There was always somebody there to fill that void."

Newspaper staff (top) and journalism class. *The Mirror,* 1946. Courtesy of the West Charlotte High School National Alumni Association, Inc.

Community gatherings teemed with games, laughter, and food. Families and churches held picnics and fish fries where children and adults played games together. Young people gathered to listen to radios, strum guitars, and dance. When Charles McCullough was growing up in Fairview Homes, a public housing complex built on Oaklawn Avenue in 1940, adults organized games that ranged from horseshoes to bid whist. "These were people who knew if they didn't have something for us to do, we were going to find something to do," McCullough said. "We were going to be on top of those buildings . . . Or we were going to be up under the building, with the rats." Green-

An African American School

ville children spent their summers going to Bible school at first one church and then another, and swimming in the all-black swimming pool the city had built on the grounds of the old waterworks nearby. "We had plenty of activities to keep us busy, and it was all in the community," Elder explained. "We didn't have to go anywhere. We were entertained all day long."

Children's wanderings also brought them a wide range of experience. The constraints of segregation meant that most of Charlotte's African American neighborhoods housed residents with many levels of income, education, and experience: the parents of students in one class at Biddleville Elementary School had education levels that ranged from third grade to Ph.D., and jobs that included janitor, elevator operator, undertaker, cook, hotel worker, railroad worker, painter, merchant, teacher, minister, farmer, and barber.[8] Two of Greenville's older residents had been born in slavery, and Mae Orr was endlessly fascinated by the stories they told about that dark era. Schoolteacher Jesse Bingham gave Sunday afternoon "tea lessons," for which she got out her good china, served tea and cookies, and instructed neighborhood children in the niceties of pouring, setting tables, and genteel conversation. "She had a little whistle like a bird," Orr recalled, and children converged on her house whenever they heard it.[9]

As west side children roamed their neighborhoods, played games, and socialized, they were rarely free from watching eyes. The social fabric their parents had created included a clear-cut set of expectations for young people, as well as a sense of shared responsibility for their behavior. It was an old-fashioned ethos, built around strict curfews, good manners, and respect for adults. If children strayed out of line—became unruly, disrespectful, or too loud—adults quickly stepped in. "They took care of us," recalled Amanda Graham, who grew up on Fairmont Street in Biddleville. "If a parent would talk to a child, when you were doing something wrong, you had to stop doing whatever you were doing because that parent would tell your mother. That's what happened in those days."

Still, community members were as quick to praise as to scold, and children found themselves surrounded by warm encouragement. "Everybody took time for a child," Elder explained. "You were nurtured in education, in religion and yourself. . . . I was always told that I was really important, that I was loved. 'You keep that good work up.' 'I'm so proud of you.' 'You look so good today.'" At Fairview Elementary, Greenville residents packed the school to overflowing for school plays, recitations, and graduation ceremonies. "Everybody in the community went to everything that school put on," Elder explained. "They would be hanging out of windows and everywhere, because the auditorium would be *packed*. . . . When the school and the church put on any program, they were there."

Between 1923 and 1938, most of the west side's high school students had to make their way downtown. Charlotte's first black public high school—Second Ward High—was built in 1923, at a time when most of Charlotte's African American residents lived in the center city. West side students walked or took the trolley to school, and students from rural areas often boarded with city families during the week.[10] By the mid-1930s, however, population growth had led to massive crowding in schools across the city. In 1936, despite the challenges of the Depression, Mecklenburg County voters approved a million-dollar bond issue designed to relieve the overcrowding and, in the words of the Mecklenburg County Commissioners, "to give the city of Charlotte, and the rural sections of the county, school systems second to none in North Carolina." The bond allocated approximately $100,000 for a new black high school, designed to educate students from seventh through twelfth grades.[11]

County commissioners initially sought to save money by planning to build the new high school on a crowded piece of city land that had once held the municipal waterworks. Charlotte's African American leaders sprang immediately into action. Charlotte's black citizens were as entrepreneurial as its white ones, and they knew that the new school's location would have a significant effect on community development, as well as the value of the property surrounding it. They also understood the message the placement would convey. Two different community groups appeared before the commission to argue against the proposed site, which sat close to a railroad line, a machine shop, a foundry, and other industrial buildings. Such an unfavorable spot, contended longtime Johnson C. Smith professor E. A. Chisholm, would be "depressing to a high order of school work."[12]

Nor did black leaders rely on the commissioners to pursue a change. Acting in a long tradition of African American educational self-help, they quickly located an alternate site: ten acres of farmland right on Beatties Ford Road, just a few blocks above the bustling Beatties Ford–Oaklawn intersection. The owner, prosperous African American barber Thad Tate, gave the city a good price, a decision that both aided the community and raised the value of his remaining land. Construction on the new school began in the spring of 1938. Charlotte native and longtime Second Ward teacher Clinton Blake became the school's first principal.[13]

The dictates of white supremacy meant that West Charlotte opened with far fewer resources than Charlotte's white high schools. The school had been built without a lunchroom, auditorium or gymnasium. It had a handful of social studies maps, a few biology supplies, and some library books, but no radio, no projector, and no lab equipment for chemistry, physics, general science, or home economics. The situation was no longer quite as bad as it had been in the 1910s, when North Carolina spent nearly twice as much on white students as on black students, or in the 1920s, when the state spent ten times as much on white school buildings as on black, but the difference remained significant.[14]

What West Charlotte did have was teachers. The growth of high school and college opportunities in the 1920s had expanded North Carolina's pool of young, well-educated African Americans, and teaching was one of the few professions to which they could aspire. Longtime English teacher Elizabeth Randolph, a Shaw University graduate who came to West Charlotte in 1944, had wanted to be a teacher since she was a little girl. But, she explained, she also had little choice. "I can't think of anything else I could have done," she said. "If you didn't get a job teaching, you went to the post office or you did something that was menial."[15] As principal of an urban high school, Clinton Blake could lure prospective teachers with the amenities of city life, as well as a city-funded supplement to the state salary. He had no shortage of talented individuals to choose from.

Many West Charlotte teachers brought experience with wider worlds. Math teacher and athletic coach Jack Martin had attended Johnson C. Smith for both high school and college, because his hometown of Chester, South Carolina, had no high school for blacks. After captaining the Johnson C. Smith football team, he had headed to New York University for a master's in physical education before returning to Charlotte to teach. Industrial arts teacher Leroy "Pop" Miller, who grew up in Salisbury, had been drafted by the Army days after he graduated from North Carolina A&T, and served as part of the "Red Ball Express" that supplied American troops as they fought their way across France and into Germany. He brought home a wealth of mechanical and logistical knowledge, as well as four Bronze Stars. Durham native Johnny Holloway, who became West Charlotte's music director in 1950, had done his wartime service in the 337th Army Band and pursued graduate work in music at Ohio State. He spent summers in New York City playing his tenor saxophone with the nation's jazz greats.[16]

These teachers had a demanding job. Preparing young people for a world that would be both competitive and discriminatory required a multi-

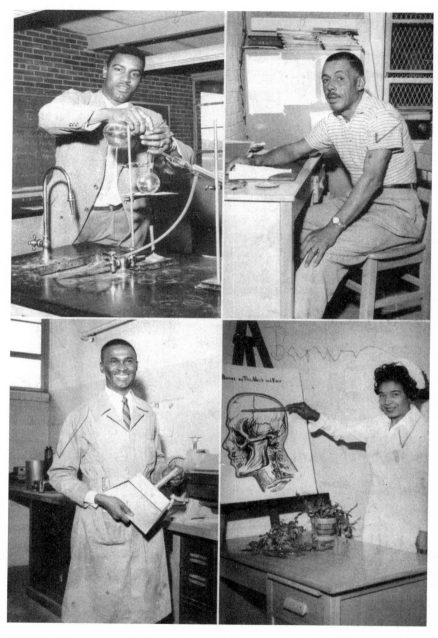

West Charlotte teachers. Clockwise from top left: science teacher Evon McNair, physical education teacher Thomas "Jack" Martin, cosmetology teacher Lilliesteen Moore, and industrial education teacher Leroy "Pop" Miller. *The Lion*, 1958. Courtesy of Marie G. Butler.

faceted approach, one that started with teaching students to think for themselves. The *North Carolina Teachers Record*, the journal of North Carolina's black teachers' organization, stated the case bluntly in 1936: "The successful teacher is not the one who feeds his pupils on facts, but the one who inspires them to test every fact, however ancient or moss-covered it may be. There is no evidence that North Carolina is in need of an additional supply of rubber stamps."[17] The endeavor also involved building students' confidence. "We were really taught," recalled Sarah Moore Coleman, who went on to a long career in social service, school administration, and political organizing. "They taught us to have so much dignity and self-assurance. And not to be afraid."

Nurturing this kind of independent fortitude required a multiplicity of efforts, and teachers rarely missed an opportunity. Saundra Jones Davis's favorite teacher was Lilliesteen Moore, a poised cosmetology teacher who had strict standards for both learning and ladylike behavior. Davis laughed as she recalled the year that two members of the football team signed up for cosmetology. "You know most people think when you say cosmetology, they think you come in and just learn to do hair a little," she said. "But you've got to learn everything about the body. You've got to know what to do for burns and everything else. She just stayed on them all the time. They thought it was a play thing, but she made them learn."

Staff members also sponsored a wide range of activities that fed body and soul, as well as mind. Sarah Coleman particularly loved the ballroom dancing classes taught by English teacher Samuel Moore. "We used to dance to music like the Viennese waltz," she recalled. "And they used to swing us up in the air. It was just so beautiful. I never will forget it." Pop Miller was renowned for his devotion to school rules, enforced by liberal use of his ever-present wooden paddle. But he also believed that high school should be a joyful time. "My high school days were the happiest days of my life," he explained. "I didn't have a care in the world. And I always wanted the same thing for all of the students. That's the time when you start looking at girls. You start dancing and doing the things that you enjoy out of life. And I think you prepare for life, and I think every youngster should have that experience."[18]

Teachers had no illusions about the obstacles their students would face. Elizabeth Randolph, who grew up in Raleigh, had learned a hard lesson about the differences between urban and rural life during her first teaching job, in rural Rutherford County. "Franklin Roosevelt was running for his second term," she explained. "And I was just all excited. I said, 'Oh I'm going to get a chance to vote for President Roosevelt.' Well, when I talked about it at school, the teachers were saying, 'You're going to do what?' I said, 'I'm going to vote for President Roosevelt.' And so they said, 'You aren't going to vote for anybody. . . . They don't let black people vote up here.' Well, I didn't believe them so I went to register. They would not allow me to register and told me that I could not vote, that they could not allow black people to vote."[19] During his time in the Army, Pop Miller dealt with plenty of prejudice on the part of white soldiers and commanders. "At times, we had to fight them just like we did the Germans," he noted.

Teachers were also thoroughly aware of the resources they lacked. They saw it in the second-hand books, sent to West Charlotte when the white schools were finished with them, and in the hand-me-down athletic and band uniforms that came from all-white Harding High School. They saw it during the summers they spent studying outside the region—because no black North Carolina schools offered graduate degrees in education, black teachers who wished to further their studies had to travel outside the state. "We weren't satisfied," stated Pop Miller, who did his summer graduate work at Pennsylvania State University. "You knew what was taking place at good schools. At Penn State we'd go out to the high school and see all the nice things that those kids had."

Still, they also knew that work and determination could pay off, even in difficult circumstances. Many had grandparents who had been enslaved, and many were from the first generation of their families to attend college. Obstacles became an incentive to work harder. "We cannot choose the things that will happen to us," Jack Martin once wrote. "But we can choose the attitude we will take toward anything that happens. . . . Make up your mind that you are going to have an attitude that is happy, confident, zestful, optimistic, positive, courageous, sympathetic, loving, kind."[20] Barbara Davis, who taught English, focused on what she and her students could do for each other. "The lack of things sort of frustrated us as teachers," she explained. "But I tell you there was so much warmth and love in teaching the youngsters with what you had. There was so much cooperation and response and admiration from those youngsters that you taught from the heart. . . . I gave of myself what I thought they should have had."

Neither West Charlotte nor its staff was wholly free from the status hierarchies that pervaded African American communities. Mae Orr, who came from working-class Greenville, vividly recalled the day she discovered that the school taught typing. "One day I went up to the second floor, and

An African American School

I heard these typewriters — tap, tap — in the library," she said. "And I went and I looked in the window. And there they were in there typing, a whole typing class. And then the next thing I noticed was who the students were. They were professors', doctors', lawyers' children. We didn't even know a typing class existed. . . . It was a different kind of segregation." Gerald Johnson grew up in middle-class Oaklawn Park, but he hung out with what he called a "pretty rough crowd," and as a result it often took his parents' intervention to get him into advanced classes, despite his high test scores. "None of the teachers thought I was too bright," he said. "And of all the advanced classes that came up, I always was the last kid to get put into those classes. People just didn't think I belonged because I didn't run with the crowd that they were used to seeing going into this."[21]

Students knew they were often shortchanged on resources — "I never got a new book, never," Mae Orr noted — and no one had to tell them that they faced a challenging future. But their teachers' focus and determination gave them confidence that they could move ahead. "Our teachers handled each textbook as if it was the most up-to-date material ever seen," Thereasea Elder recounted. "We were taught to ignore the scribbling on the worn paper and to embrace the truth of knowledge that was before us."[22] Malachi Greene fell in love with science at West Charlotte, and was sure the school provided him with everything required to succeed. "Mr. Blake would do things like find money to get us white rats and all that kind of stuff, so we could do our experiments," he explained. "And if a piece of equipment was needed, he would make sure that it was there." As Madge Hopkins looked back at her years at the school, she saw gaps she had not noticed at the time. "We were separate and we were not equal," she noted. "But I didn't know it, and I'm glad they didn't tell me."

West Charlotte's staff built this sense of possibility with a combination of exhortation, action, and personal example. Clinton Blake, who would lead the school for almost thirty years, set the tone. Blake's own background embodied the promise that work, sacrifice, and education could bring. His father, born at the start of the Civil War in rural South Carolina, had come to Charlotte as a railroad mail clerk, a job dominated by African Americans because whites considered it too dangerous — the specially built mail cars in which clerks sorted the mail between stops were made of wood rather than steel, which meant almost certain death if a train crashed. The income from the risks Caesar Blake took allowed the family to build a large home in Second Ward, and to send their children both to Johnson C. Smith's high school and to college. After leaving Smith, Clinton Blake studied at Talladega Col-

CLINTON L. BLAKE, A.M., Principal

Spontaneous helpfulness, a major attribute of Mr. Blake's personality has made him an ideal principal of West Charlotte High School. In all the duties of a principal and as a civic leader he has maintained with much courage and willingness a spirit of usefulness. May the progress of West Charlotte High School during the intervening years become increasingly evident.

The Mirror   1947

West Charlotte's founding principal, Clinton Blake, led the school for nearly three decades. This yearbook description captures the affection and respect he earned from students and community members. *The Mirror*, 1947. Courtesy of the West Charlotte High School National Alumni Association, Inc.

lege and Atlanta University, and eventually acquired a master's from Columbia in New York.[23]

Blake brought great expectations and enormous energy to West Charlotte. He insisted on strict order at the school, and traversed the halls with a paddle sticking out of his back pocket, ready to mete out punishment on the spot if needed. "Everybody saw that paddle," noted Amanda Graham. "Nobody wanted it." He knew most of the students' parents—many of whom he had taught at Second Ward. "He used to tell us, say, 'Well, go home and tell your parents that I whipped you. I probably whipped them too at some time,'" laughed Rudolph Torrence, who would eventually become one of Charlotte's most prominent black police officers. "He was very respected in the community. If Mr. Blake said it, that was the law." Blake's impeccable dress and palpable pride in himself and his school inspired teachers and students alike. He also thrived on competition—a zeal he passed on to his students. "We won the state basketball championship my senior year," Torrence noted. "That year we had a pretty good team, and we did a lot more traveling than we had done in previous years. Because we were winning. And our principal loved to win. And when you won he would make sacrifices so that you could go to the next level. But by the same token, if you lost, he'd say 'I ain't spending a *dime* on you.'"

Blake's competitive drive combined with a cheerful, generous spirit. Mae Orr occasionally defied Blake's decrees, but described him as a "jolly" man who "wanted the best for his students."[24] He ran a catering service that served black and white clients, and he loved to cook for students, staff, and his church. He hosted yearly meetings for members of his Alpha Kappa Alpha fraternity. He let students drive his car. On the occasion of West Charlotte's first graduation, in 1941, students felt comfortable enough with Blake to gently tease him. "To our Principal, Mr. Blake, who has been our faithful guardian for these years, we give the extreme pleasure of getting rid of us," the graduating class wrote in their humorous "Last Will and Testament." "May he never have another class as trying as this one. May he also have a long life in which to gloat over the superiority of the next generation of pupils over ours."[25]

"Mr. Blake was something," explained Thereasea Elder. "He demanded the best. He would pull out of you whatever it was to pull."

In addition to enforcing discipline and academic standards, Blake oversaw the development of an extensive arts and extracurricular program that offered students opportunities for self-expression, cooperative endeavor, travel, and performance. While black schools often struggled to find funding for extra activities, teachers and administrators stressed their significance, especially in the realm of character. "In extra-curricular activities come many social situations, ethical choices, and emotional states that inherently affect character," Leonard Smith Jr. of the Greene County Training School noted in the *North Carolina Teachers Record* in 1937. "If it be true that the objective of modern education is good citizenship and that the school must increasingly supply laboratory training in social, ethical, emotional, and character values, then education will find in the modern 'American System' of extra-curricular activities its greatest agents."[26] West Charlotte's 1941 yearbook featured a choral club, patrol force, drama club, camera club, tennis club, and band, along with the "Lioness Usher Club," the football team, and both boys' and girls' basketball teams. As the school grew, the offerings expanded.[27]

Blake was especially involved in the drama program, which had particular significance for African American schools. Black theater had blossomed with the Harlem Renaissance, and leading black intellectuals such as Alain Locke, Marcus Garvey, and W. E. B. Du Bois extolled theater's potential to combat stereotypes and express community aspirations. Mounting a theatrical performance required organization and cooperation, and enacting theatrical roles allowed young people to experiment with wide ranges of emotion and behavior within the safety of the stage's magic circle. Blake's alma mater, Atlanta University, had a vibrant drama program, and while at Second Ward he both directed and starred in community productions. In the mid-1930s, he worked with Shaw University president William Stuart Nelson to found the North Carolina High School Drama Association, and arranged a statewide competition held annually at Shaw. Renowned North Carolina playwright Paul Green was persuaded to donate a trophy. In the spring of 1940, West Charlotte's production of Parker Hord's *The Gypsy* won the Paul Green Cup for the school.[28]

West Charlotte's athletic programs offered yet another way for young people to expand their horizons. Jack Martin had a broad vision for his students, seeing sports less as a quest for victory or prestige than as a means to an end. He was "ahead of his time," recalled Charles McCullough. "He was well read, and he was a man who was firmly interested in young men being more than just athletes." Like many of his black coaching counterparts, Martin used sports to teach his athletes the habits of discipline, determination, and self-control they would need to navigate the challenging world beyond the school.[29] He also focused them on broader aspirations. In addition to coaching, he became a respected referee and made a point of bringing players along when he traveled to assignments at the region's colleges. "He'd always take one or two guys with him, to give you that exposure," Rudolph Torrence recalled. "If he was going to call a college game on Saturday, then we rode with him. And we got that experience and exposure of watching a college game, plus being in that college environment. And it just gave us something to look forward to."

Martin's efforts were particularly significant for young men, many of whom were hungry for role models. "Most of the kids that I grew up with were single-parent kids," Rudolph Torrence explained. In his case, the combination of his mother's early death and his father's work as a plasterer, which kept him on the road, had profound effects on family relationships. Although the elder Torrence always provided for his children, he never formed a close emotional connection with his son. As Martin spurred Torrence on to greater efforts and offered a wide range of advice about both sports and life, "he was filling the slack for the father role, for me and for most of the other guys."

Sports and other activities also offered a way to keep young men in school. The limited range of jobs available to African Americans, along with the need to help with family finances, meant that many young black men had a hard time seeing the point of completing high school. Some were also drawn to an underground economy that involved liquor, drugs, and stolen goods. "Back in that particular time there were a lot of problems with young men," Charles McCullough noted. "There were some very poor families, who didn't have jobs, who couldn't get jobs. . . . There were a lot of things going on." Like North Carolina's other black high schools, West Charlotte had a high dropout rate—what statewide administrators sometimes referred to as "student mortality." When West Charlotte opened in 1938, it enrolled 124 eighth graders. Five years later, 57 graduated—37 girls and 20 boys. While "mortality" rates dropped some after World War II, even then nearly a third of West Charlotte's students continued to leave the school between eighth and twelfth grade.[30]

As part of efforts to keep students moving in the right direction, teachers took on roles outside school walls, slipping seamlessly into the life of the community. Pop Miller explored several local churches before settling on Greenville Memorial AME Zion, the church attended by many of his industrial arts students. "When the kids would come to class you talked to them and asked them what church they belonged to," he explained. "I wanted to go to the church where my students were coming from. I wanted to meet their parents, and I did." Teachers headed community organizations and helped out with tasks that required more education than many parents had been able to obtain. "A parent would come to us, whether they knew you or not,

Basketball team, 1946, with Rudolph Torrence at center, and majorettes, 1957. *The Mirror*, 1946; *The Lion*, 1957. The West Charlotte annual was called *The Mirror* until 1949 and *The Lion* after that. Courtesy of the West Charlotte High School National Alumni Association, Inc., and the Robinson-Spangler Carolina Room.

because they didn't have anybody else to go to," explained Barbara Davis, who often wrote obituaries for students' family members. "We were counselors and principals and caretakers and janitors."

Teachers became an integral part of the community's collective approach to discipline, working together with parents to keep young people in line. "They all had eyes in the back of their heads," recalled Mable Haynes Latimer, who graduated in 1952. "They could see everything. They just didn't tolerate foolishness. And before they would reprimand you, they've already called your parents. They already knew. And that's what most kids didn't want."[31] Pop Miller's disciplinary actions became legendary. "If we were to misbehave, he would come up behind you and go 'Boom!' on your ear with that finger," laughed Charles Jones, who as a college student would help organize Charlotte's 1960 sit-ins. "It didn't hurt but it was enough to get your attention and let you know you were required to behave." Jones saw Miller's efforts as "a sign that he really cared enough about us to want to require us to behave ourselves and to be somebody. All of my teachers were extraordinary human beings who not only taught but cared about us as people."

Teachers also ventured onto ground that parents could be reluctant to tread, most notably the rocky realm of adolescent sexuality. Mary Anna Neal Bradley would never forget the afternoon when her seventh grade homeroom teacher sent all of the boys outside, instructing them to stand in front of the classroom window so she could keep an eye on them. The teacher then delivered a stern lecture to the girls, warning them that they should not risk ruining their lives for "three or four seconds of pleasure." Other teachers offered practical reminders. Every Friday, longtime English teacher and Shakespeare enthusiast Bill Lindsay would send students off with the admonition: "Men, don't forget your raincoat, because you never know when it's going to rain." Some students understood him better than others. "For years I didn't know what the man was talking about," said Harriet Love. "But actually he was telling the guys, if you're going to be sexually active, you need a condom. . . . He would say that every Friday. And for the longest no one would say anything about it. Because we didn't talk about condoms, and he didn't either. But later I learned, and I said 'Well, that's what he meant.'"

The west side's neighborhoods united behind the school and the young people it nurtured. Football games were packed with spectators, and large crowds turned out for the annual homecoming parade, led by the marching band up Beatties Ford Road. Students were constantly raising money for trips and activities, and residents did what they could to help. "People were able to give something to West Charlotte," said Harriet Love. "They were able to share things. Sometimes if there were games, maybe a person in the neighborhood would take a truckload of kids to the game. Maybe they didn't have children. Different little things. . . . And many of the neighbors probably did not go to school at all in North Carolina. They may have been from South Carolina, or whatever. And many of them didn't have twelve years of education. But they were still in favor of us having it."

This solidarity was heightened by a legendary rivalry that developed with Second Ward High School. Mecklenburg County would eventually hold six black high schools, each carrying the many hopes of the community it served. But the competition between West Charlotte and Second Ward was especially intense. The rivalry became a cornerstone of black Charlotte culture, and a key element of both schools' identities. The Queen City Classic, the annual football game that pitted the two schools' teams against each other, became one of the most anticipated events in the city, sparking a week's worth of festivities that one participant described as a "huge homecoming." Teachers and administrators at both schools used the rivalry to motivate their students in academic competitions, debate contests, athletic events, and a plethora of other arenas. "The fact that there were two predominantly black schools in the city just brought on the competitiveness," Rudolph Torrence explained. "And both schools were being told by their principals and their instructors that they were the better school."

As West Charlotte's staff built programs and nurtured students, the neighborhoods around the school expanded rapidly. While Charlotte's population growth had slowed during the Depression, it regained momentum during World War II and accelerated further in the postwar era. Charlotte's population doubled between 1940 and 1960 — reaching above 200,000. The number of black residents swelled from just over 31,000 to just over 56,000. Since residential segregation remained the norm, the influx of black families spurred further development on the west side.

Housing construction found a new source of funding in the federal government, which had begun to take a larger role in community development. While Charlotte's fiscally conservative leaders had long resisted stepping into the housing market, the growing availability of federal housing funds eventually overcame their reluctance. In 1940, Fairview Homes opened its doors as the city's first public housing complex for black residents. Up-and-coming developer C. D. Spangler then obtained support from the Federal Housing Administration (FHA) to cover an adjoining landfill with a subsidized development called Double Oaks. New rental construction was joined by additional homebuilding in communities of single-family homes such as Lincoln Heights, Oaklawn Park, McCrorey Heights, and Druid Hills.[32]

Like their counterparts across the country, North Carolina's African Americans seized on the patriotic rhetoric first of World War II, and then of the Cold War, to press for greater opportunities in numerous areas of economic and political life. "The world situation, in which democracy is being challenged by anti-democratic philosophies, demands that America live up to its promises and ideals," the *North Carolina Teachers Record* asserted in 1955. "America's greatest potential can never be realized as long as racial barriers can be used to separate and divide her citizens."[33]

Black Charlotteans could draw on a long history of efforts to confront racial inequities. During the 1920s and 1930s, local activists had prevented the execution of a black resident who had shot and killed a white policeman, blocked a move to oust the black Prince Hall Shriners from the ranks of the national Shriners, successfully challenged the exclusion of African Americans from Mecklenburg County juries, and helped to depose the city's powerful postmaster on charges of political corruption after he failed to comply with a federal requirement to hire black mail carriers.[34] Activities picked up sharply in the 1940s. In 1943 a group of Johnson C. Smith students led by student council president Reginald Hawkins conducted several pickets at the main Charlotte post office to call for greater employment of African Americans, especially returning war veterans. Throughout the 1940s, several organizations pressed the Charlotte police department to appoint more African American policemen, and to include African Americans on city planning boards.[35]

Postwar efforts were increasingly led by the local NAACP. Under the capable leadership of Kelly Alexander, son of funeral home director Zechariah Alexander, the Charlotte branch became the most influential in the state. In 1948, the branch launched a "Votes for Freedom" voter registration drive that registered more than 5,000 new black voters. It then started a campaign to integrate city recreational facilities. In keeping with national NAACP priorities, it also turned its attention to public schools.[36]

In 1948, the branch employed Martin Jenkins, a professor of education at Howard University, to prepare a report that compared Charlotte's African American schools with its white ones. The report focused primarily on the efforts that would be needed to equalize the city's black and white schools. Jenkins began by citing a Supreme Court ruling: "The admissibility of laws separating the races in the enjoyment of privileges afforded by the States rests wholly upon the equality of the privileges which the laws give to the separated groups." He then offered an interpretation. "While in a very real sense it is impossible to establish equality within a segregated framework, the State should assure at least substantial equality in so far as this is possible," he wrote. "This principle must operate in such fashion that no colored child in the State will be subject to inferior educational services at any level, from pre-school through the university, *because he is colored*."[37]

The contradiction in Jenkins's statement, that it was "impossible to establish equality within a segregated framework," but that "the State should assure at least substantial equality," reflected a broader set of uncertainties that accompanied the national NAACP efforts to address school inequalities. Goals such as improving employment opportunities for African Americans, or increasing African American participation in public planning, required integration. But when it came to improving educational opportunities for black children — especially in a relatively well-funded school district such as Charlotte's — strategies became less clear-cut. For reasons that ranged from fear of white retaliation to concerns about the welfare of black children in white-run institutions, many African Americans continued to favor greater investment in black schools over calls for integration. The NAACP, which had set its sights on ending legal segregation, chafed at these efforts. The Charlotte report's focus on "substantial equality" between black and white schools in fact caused a degree of consternation in national NAACP circles, and chief NAACP attorney Thurgood Marshall wrote Kelly Alexander to emphasize that the organization was "dedicated to the policy of insisting on the removal of segregation."[38]

The report offered a number of positive findings. At the time, Charlotte's school population was approximately two-thirds white and one-third black. North Carolina had equalized teacher pay in 1944, and teachers in Charlotte's African American schools were as well-qualified and well-paid as those in white schools. In elementary schools, class sizes were generally the same. The quality of construction appeared to be similar in black and white schools, as was the level of upkeep — Jenkins observed, for example, that the "need of paint is general in both the white and Negro schools and may be attributed to a general rather than a racial policy."[39] He was particularly impressed by the black elementary schools, writing that while some inequalities needed to be addressed, "the inequalities found at the elementary school level are not of a fundamental nature."[40]

High schools, however, were another matter. There, Jenkins found that African American students learned in larger classes, were offered fewer advanced courses, and had access to fewer library books as well as far less equipment in science, business and technical classes. Classes offered only at white high schools included: auto mechanics, sociology, advanced French, advanced chemistry, advanced art, commercial art, general office practice, solid geometry, and trigonometry. While all the white high schools had their own gymnasiums, auditoriums, and cafeterias, West Charlotte used a science classroom as a temporary cafeteria and borrowed Johnson C. Smith's facilities for events such as plays and basketball games.

The differences in educational equipment and supplies were especially dramatic. Central High had a well-equipped art studio and a separate music building; West Charlotte had neither. For business classes, West Charlotte had a set of typewriters. White high schools had not only typewriters but also mimeograph machines, adding machines, billing machines, transcribing machines, Dictaphones, and filing and bookkeeping equipment. Trade equipment at West Charlotte consisted of trowels and mortar boxes, used to teach bricklaying, and a small amount of shoe repair equipment. The white Technical High School had fully equipped machine and auto-mechanics shops, equipment for learning electrical and refrigeration repair, and a mechanical drafting room. Furnishings and equipment were valued at $74 per student at Central High, and $80 per student at Technical High. At West Charlotte, the figure was $18 per student.

Shortly after the report was completed, the NAACP called on city officials to take immediate action to end the inequalities. "[Since] Negro pupils are excluded from the superior schools established for white children," an NAACP statement emphasized, "the educational inequalities arise out of the factor of race and consequently result in depriving the Negro children of their constitutional right to an equal education."[41] Kelly Alexander and statewide NAACP chairman J. S. Bowser presented a petition calling for "steps to equalize facilities and instruction." The school board stonewalled, claiming that "everything possible is being done to provide equal opportunities for all children," and suggesting that some classes were not offered at black schools because black students were not interested in them. Bowser and Alexander did not hide their dissatisfaction. "The discussion at times grew heated," the *Observer* reported. Eventually, Alexander lost his patience, and pronounced: "Our only hope for relief is to get members of our race on the School Board."[42]

Two decades would pass before an African American was elected to the Charlotte school board. But legal efforts bore more fruit. The NAACP's legal campaign had sparked a series of Supreme Court rulings that placed greater pressure on Southern schools to provide genuinely equal facilities. In response, North Carolinians in several districts filed lawsuits that demanded "school equalization." In a handful of cases, those lawsuits demanded that schools be integrated if the needed improvements were not made. Across the state, officials saw the writing on the wall. As the *Winston-Salem Journal and Sentinel* noted in 1952, "the money will have to come from somewhere to build better schoolhouses, if we are to maintain our policy of segregation of the races in the public schools of North Carolina." In 1953, state voters passed a $50 million school construction bond, much of which went to improve black schools.[43]

In Charlotte, school improvements included a brand-new West Charlotte High School, set on a fifty-acre plot of land a mile west of the old building. The dazzling complex of low-slung brick, concrete and glass structures included academic, vocational, and science buildings, a freestanding library, and a spacious student center. It won a national award for school design, and the price tag topped a million dollars. The old West Charlotte building—which had become so overcrowded that the school had been forced to hold classes in two different shifts—became Northwest Junior High School.[44]

The new West Charlotte sat at the heart of an especially ambitious development, a 1,200-home neighborhood called University Park. The project was the brainchild of Kelly Alexander's brother Fred. Fred Alexander managed the Double Oaks apartments in addition to working in the family funeral home. He realized that many members of Charlotte's growing African American middle class were eager to purchase modern-style homes in newly built neighborhoods—and that many of them had the means to do so. Alexander convinced C. D. Spangler to plan out a neighborhood of curving streets and red-brick ranch homes, and helped secure initial funding. For his part, Spangler persuaded the Federal Housing Administration to guarantee long-term mortgages for families who bought University Park homes. The FHA, whose loan guarantees helped make the dream of home ownership a reality for millions of postwar American families, had been notoriously reluctant to back loans for African Americans or in African American neighborhoods. Its strategy of "redlining" those neighborhoods would stunt development in black communities across the country. But Spangler made a strong case for the creditworthiness of black Charlotteans. The FHA guarantees, which sharply lowered required down payments as well as monthly payments, significantly expanded black home-buying opportunities.[45]

In the fall of 1954, students and teachers in grades ten, eleven, and twelve moved to the new West Charlotte building. Mary Anna Bradley was a freshman that year, and recalled the celebratory parade from the old building to the new — complete with band, banners, and floats. "It was going to be our first year," she said. "They showed you the school and took you around. We were just in awe. Bright and shiny and clean. It was pretty. A lot of glass. It looked so modern."

Even as West Charlotte students marveled at their new quarters, however, the broader question of how to define equality remained unsettled. While North Carolina's black leaders had been reluctant to mount legal challenges to segregation, the NAACP had persuaded African Americans in several other states to step forward. One case was filed in Clarendon County, South Carolina — a county that had sent many migrants to Charlotte. Others arose in Washington, D.C.; Prince Edward County, Virginia; Wilmington, Delaware; and Topeka, Kansas. In the fall of 1953, the Supreme Court heard the combined cases under the name *Brown v. Board of Education of Topeka*. In the spring of 1954, the justices issued the decision the NAACP had been seeking. In a unanimous ruling, the Court held that schools segregated by law could not be equal. The landmark decision overturned the "separate but equal" principal established in *Plessy v. Ferguson* more than half a century before, and augured massive change in the South, as well as in the United States as a whole.[46]

The ruling topped the Charlotte newspaper headlines, overshadowing the visit of President Dwight Eisenhower, who happened to be in Charlotte the day the decision was announced. But what it meant for schools in Charlotte — and the rest of the country — was far from certain. The Supreme Court justices themselves were unsure on this point; even as they issued the landmark decision, they scheduled a new round of hearings to determine how it should be implemented. Charlotte school superintendent Elmer Garinger hastened to assure parents that the decision would mean few changes for the community, describing Charlotte schools as "community schools," with boundaries that "roughly coincide with those of residential neighborhoods populated by a single race."[47]

Young African Americans were often heartened by the news — especially in parts of the state with particularly glaring disparities between black and white schools. Julius Chambers, who would eventually move to Charlotte and become the foremost civil rights attorney of the post-*Brown* era, graduated from Montgomery County's segregated Peabody High School a few weeks after the Brown decision was announced. He was painfully aware of the limited education he had received at a school that "did not have the resources to provide a good education for any of the students who went there."

The decision gave him hope. "I heard the Court in *Brown* saying blacks were now free," he said. "This was the signal I could do anything."[48]

African American educators, who were thoroughly familiar with the struggles required to win resources for black teachers and schools, were less ebullient. They did not know what the decision would bring. But they did know that desegregation would be fought long and hard. "I remember my husband and I were in the kitchen fixing dinner when we heard on the radio news that the Supreme Court had outlawed the segregation of schools," Elizabeth Randolph remembered. "My husband said, 'Well, do you think it's going to happen next year?' And I said, 'No, indeed, it won't happen next year. It'll be a long time.'"[49]

CIVIL RIGHTS

On February 9, 1960, West Charlotte graduate Mary Anna Bradley put on her Sunday best and joined nearly two hundred of her fellow Johnson C. Smith students on the two-mile walk from the Smith campus to the center of town. Eight days earlier, four students at Greensboro's A&T University had gone into F. W. Woolworth, taken seats at the whites-only lunch counter, and politely refused to move until they were served. Inspired by that bold action, African American college students began to fill lunch counter seats across the South, demanding the rights and respect that parents, teachers, and ministers had long told them they deserved. That first day was frightening. "We didn't know what was going to happen," Bradley recalled. But the students fortified themselves with the well-mannered discipline that their mentors had worked so hard to instill, and they made an impressive sight. "We were so dignified," she continued. "I mean, dressed really nice, and just quiet. Just a nice looking group."

The sit-ins ushered in an era of hope and conflict, as African Americans across the South worked to dismantle the unequal society created by Jim Crow. In Charlotte, civil rights activists mounted efforts that targeted inequalities in political, educational, and economic institutions, using lawsuits, boycotts, negotiations, direct protests, and political campaigns. Some residents focused on persuading institutions to accept talented black individuals. Some sought to build black voting strength. Some favored behind-the-scenes negotiation. Some pursued public confrontations. Young people played key roles in many of these efforts.[1]

As challenges to Jim Crow widened, the shift altered the role West Charlotte High School played in its students' lives. For two decades, the school and the community around it had focused on developing the skills that would allow young people to make their way in the society around them, hewing to the idea that individual achievement was the most prudent and effective strategy to build productive lives and challenge the assumptions behind segregation's racial hierarchies. At home and at school, Ed Anderson explained, the message was clear: "Study, work hard, be prepared to compete in the world." But when young people began to directly confront the racial order, they stepped farther than many school leaders were willing to go. Soon after the Charlotte sit-ins began, Malachi Greene recalled, Clinton Blake took to the school announcement system to warn his students to stay away. His words were blunt: "If I catch any West Charlotte student down there in that mess, you're going to get expelled."

These conflicting views meant that during the civil rights movement, West Charlotte served primarily as a haven from the transformations taking place outside its walls. Throughout the decade, as racial conflicts expanded, West Charlotte remained a place apart, an arena where young people could grow up, test abilities and ideas, make mistakes, strengthen connections to friends and community, and enjoy the pleasures of youth. "When you were on campus, you felt safe," explained Leonard "Deacon" Jones. "You were allowed to witness what was going on from a safe place. You felt safe to discuss what was happening, you felt safe if you chose to participate, and you felt safe if you chose not to." Nearly a decade would pass before the turmoil that consumed the nation reached West Charlotte itself.

The racial and political ideas that propelled a rising generation of young people to public action grew less out of their schooling than out of experiences with family and church, with radio and television, with political events and personal encounters. The experiences and ideas of this generation marked a definite departure from those of their predecessors. When Amanda Graham was at West Charlotte in the 1940s, she and many of her friends assumed that "segregation was going to be forever. Wouldn't ever stop." Mae Orr, who had grown up listening to the stories told by former slaves, had a similar perspective. "I knew we had come out of slavery," she explained. "And I thought that was a big step. And I was going to do the best we could with what we had."[2] But the economic growth of the 1950s and 1960s, combined with slowly but steadily falling racial barriers, created a new sense of excitement and expectation, expanding young people's ambitions and heightening their dissatisfaction with the Jim Crow order. "We were the ones who were always asking questions," explained Ella Dennis. "Everybody was questioning. Not taking stuff for granted." Patsy Rice Camp felt a similar restlessness. "I wanted answers," she stated. "I could not understand injustice. I wanted change."

Rising expectations were especially evident in the University Park neighborhood that took shape around West Charlotte High. Stan Frazier, whose family was one of the first to move into the new development, grew up surrounded by a palpable sense of accomplishment. His parents had come to Charlotte from rural South Carolina, and had spent their first years in the Double Oaks apartment complex. Like many of the young couples moving into University Park, they were delighted to be leaving rental housing for a home of their own. Even as a small child, Frazier sensed the pleasure his parents and their neighbors felt in walking the newly paved streets, surrounded by meticulously maintained lawns and flower beds. The new families developed close bonds, and a group of stay-at-home mothers "watched the neighborhoods like hawks." Children experienced a powerful sense of belonging. "You felt you were part of something special," Frazier explained. "If you did something wrong, everybody knew. If you did something sports-wise, everyone knew your name. Walking in your neighborhood, you felt that you were part of something."

Outside of work, west side residents had few reasons to leave their thriving enclave. Businesses lined Oaklawn and Beatties Ford roads, ranging from Fabbes Cleaners and Campbell's Grocery to the Grand Theater and the stylish Excelsior Club, which attracted some of the top black entertainers in the country. Young people swam at the Fairview and Double Oaks pools, danced at the YMCA, enjoyed burgers at the Varsity and devoured banana splits at the Igloo Dairy Bar. These and other activities created a sense of joyful community. "It was fun," Madge Hopkins recalled of the YMCA dances. "Just being there in the crowd and the boys and girls dancing. And then there was always someone who was in the circle who could just really dance and the kids would say, 'Now, throw down.' And we would watch and everybody would gather around. And there was always some boy you had a crush on that you were just praying would ask you to dance. People would pair up and couples would walk home in groups of boys and girls."

This vitality reflected the expanding opportunities created by a robust national economy and rapid urban growth. As Charlotte's population grew, so did the number and variety of jobs. Demand grew for the doctors, nurses, and teachers that served a growing black community, as well as for the skilled service jobs that had sustained African American families for generations — work such as tailoring, bricklaying, cooking, cleaning, and gardening. Small businesses multiplied, among them beauty parlors, barbershops, and funeral homes. The first generation of West Charlotte graduates began to secure professional positions in integrated settings, including Rudolph Torrence, who joined the city police force, and Thereasea Elder, who became Mecklenburg County's first black public health nurse. Each year, West Charlotte added to a growing list of successful graduates who had established themselves in many different fields.

The economic boom and softening racial lines of the postwar era were also lifting more members of a growing African American middle class into public view. Two new mass-circulation magazines — the monthly *Ebony*, which debuted in 1945, and the weekly *Jet*, which launched in 1951 — offered stylish takes on black celebrities and their accomplishments. Charlotteans followed the exploits of pioneering African American athletes such as Joe Louis, Jackie Robinson, Althea Gibson, and Willie Mays, as well as leaders such as Air Force general Benjamin O. Davis Jr. and Congressman Adam Clayton Powell Jr. Charlotte's African Americans remained concentrated at the bottom of the economic ladder — in 1959 the city's black median income was less than half of the white median income, and the large majority of African Americans worked at low-level positions such as manual laborer or truck driver. Nearly two-thirds of black residents lived below the poverty line. Still, optimism spread. "There was a real and genuine feeling that change was in the air," Ed Anderson later wrote.[3]

African Americans also saw their profile rise in Charlotte. Charlotte's popular music scene — an arena of particular significance for young people — was transformed in 1947, when radio station WGIV adopted an "all-black" format and hired local educator "Genial Gene" Potts as its main disc jockey. Mary Anna Bradley spent summers listening to the radio with her sister, Joanna Neal Dowling, and with neighbor Barbara Funderburk, who could pick up the new dances faster than anyone. "Once we got it, we would dance all day long," Dowling recalled. "And mom would say, 'Oh you're wearing out my rug.'" Both black and white performers came to Charlotte's Coliseum, including young stars like Jackie Wilson, Frankie Lymon, and Paul Anka. Fathers who owned cars could usually be persuaded to drive groups of young women to the concerts. While seating was segregated, after the concerts ended black and white girls jostled on equal terms to get the best views of band members as they boarded their buses, and to contend for handshakes or autographs.

High school students themselves stepped onto a larger stage. The Second Ward–West Charlotte Queen City Classic football game grew into one of the city's most anticipated events, flooding the downtown area with spectators every fall. West Charlotte and Second Ward each contributed a Carrousel Princess to the city's Thanksgiving-time Carrousel Parade, and the schools' marching bands became a much-anticipated feature of the annual event. The African American bands, whose high-stepping style sparked enthusiastic reactions from both blacks and whites, became a point of particular pride for students and alumni. "When West Charlotte came through, it looked like the whole of Charlotte would follow that band," Saundra Davis recalled. "They used to tear up the parade because so many people would follow them. So they got to the place where instead of West Charlotte being in the middle or first, they would put them at the end so they wouldn't tear up their parade. Everybody followed West Charlotte."

West Charlotte's sparkling new campus and expanded course offerings nurtured excitement and ambition. "As we enter our third decade of ser-

West Charlotte band. *The Lion*, 1969. Courtesy of the Robinson-Spangler Carolina Room.

vice, the world is entering the Space Age," Clinton Blake wrote in the 1959 yearbook. "West Charlotte High School is geared to prepare her students to meet the demands of this new era."[4] Science classes explored scientific and technological marvels, including the Sputnik launch that started the space race. History classes came via television from UNC–Chapel Hill. Teachers envisioned a future of solar-powered homes, ovens that turned on by themselves, and phones where, as Mary Anna Bradley put it, "you could talk to somebody and they could see you." Students set their sights on new horizons. "By the time we got to high school, we *knew* that education was serious for a black child," said Patsy Camp. Employers were beginning to look for qualified black candidates, "and we could not give them an excuse for not finding a person who was black who was prepared." "It was instilled in us that anything was possible," Madge Hopkins echoed. "We could do anything we wanted to."

For many of the west side's younger residents, Jim Crow could seem more an inconvenience than an obstacle. Like their counterparts across the country, Charlotte's African American parents did their best to shield their children from the indignities of official segregation, and rarely spent much time discussing racial inequalities. Ambitious African Americans often found white allies for their endeavors. Malachi Greene's father had been encouraged to move to Charlotte by a white employer who valued his skills, and who helped him purchase the family's first Charlotte home. When Mary Anna Bradley and Joanna Dowling were in college, their father's employer arranged to give him extra hours to help pay their expenses. When the mother of one of Mae Orr's companions developed tuberculosis, jeopardizing the young woman's college education, Orr advised her friend to ask the family whose home she cleaned to help her with tuition, and they did.

Charlotte's size also meant that overt racial oppression was easier to avoid than in smaller communities — especially on the west side. Future West Charlotte teacher Spencer Singleton, who grew up in downtown Third Ward, found racism a daily irritation. "I didn't really see Charlotte as a friendly city for blacks," he said. "For me anyway. Everyday life, everyday encounters with Caucasians was a problem." Young people on the west side were more insulated. In 1960, Malachi Greene became the first black Charlottean to enroll at the University of North Carolina. He soon found that his black classmates, all of whom came from rural areas, were far better prepared than he to deal with the harassment they encountered. "I was a Charlotte boy in a small town putting up with crap," Greene recalled. "Charlotte was a big town where we pretty much lived a normal life. And I get up there and it was an entirely new experience." Ed Anderson's mother had lost a cousin to racial violence in the family's Georgia hometown, and whenever her sons went back to visit she issued "extra-cautionary instructions," including a stern warning about giving whites a wide, deferential berth on the town's streets and sidewalks. "We had to move over on the sidewalks and let white people go by," Anderson explained. "She didn't give us those instructions here in Charlotte, although she taught us to be polite, walk on the right side. But we had to make *sure* to move out of white people's way in Washington, Georgia."

Still, the shadow of white supremacy hovered over many activities. Young people were aware of the racial challenges their parents faced, although they often dwelt more on their parents' ability to overcome racial obstacles than on the obstacles themselves. Stan Frazier's father, a veteran of World War II, got his first Charlotte job as a custodian at a machine shop, and was determined to move up to a machinist's position. "I recall—I think I was in the third grade—he brought home a micrometer," Frazier said. "It had centimeters and millimeters on it. And he asked me what did I know about it? And he said he had to learn that instrument if he was going to get that machinist's job." After Frazier's father mastered the micrometer, and became the company's first African American machinist, he endured plenty of racial harassment: coworkers sabotaged his machine, changed its settings, and sometimes soiled it with excrement. But he stuck with the job and became one of the top performers in the firm. "That's something I really admired about him, being really steadfast and persevering," Frazier said.

Occasionally, young people experienced the thrill of seeing their parents take private stands for racial respect. Gerald Johnson, who would eventually run Charlotte's black newspaper, vividly remembered the day when his father answered the phone, and found a white insurance agent on the line. "He said, 'Bill' — my father's first name was Bill — 'Bill you are behind in your payments and you need to catch up.' And my father said, 'Bob, I can tell you what the problem is.' And he said, 'I'm Mr. Williams and don't call me Bob.' And my father said, 'Well I'm Mr. Johnson' and slammed the phone down. And I'm at the table watching him do that and when he walked away with the smile on his face the guy called back. And when he called back, he said, 'Mr. Johnson,' and my dad said, 'OK then Mr. Williams,' and they started up again, but the guy gave my father the respect that he demanded and that just sent a terribly strong message to me at the time as a kid. Even though times were hard and we were living in a segregated environment, that just gave me so much confidence and encouragement that I could make it in the world. It was just an outstanding incident in my growing up."[5]

As members of a new generation grew older and ventured further, however, their rising expectations increasingly clashed with the inequalities that suffused life in a segregated world. They became more aware of the "white" and "colored" signs that barred them from facilities such as lunch counters and department-store dressing rooms, and relegated them to separate and decidedly unequal restrooms and waiting areas. Closer to home, they were less willing to tolerate inequities such as the second-hand textbooks that remained the norm at African American schools.

Many West Charlotte students encountered these inequalities most directly on their bus rides home from school. Charlotte schools did not provide bus service for black or white students until 1960, when the city and county systems merged to create Charlotte-Mecklenburg Schools. Before that, city students who lived far from their schools often took city buses home. Charlotte's hub-and-spoke street system meant that most students, white as well as black, rode from school to the central intersection of Trade and Tryon streets, known as the Square. They then waited to board outbound buses that served their various neighborhoods. Not only was bus seating segregated,

African American students who ducked into nearby stores were constantly reminded that bathrooms and water fountains were both separate and unequal, that African Americans could buy hot dogs and peanuts but could not sit down to enjoy them. "If we wanted something to eat, now we could buy something," Mary Anna Bradley said. "But you could not sit down and eat it. You had to take it out. And you had to go to the back to get it. It used to bother me. I really didn't talk about it, but it would bother me."

Students who had graduated and gone on to college felt the discrimination even more keenly. "If you were black, young, in college — downtown Charlotte was the place that folks gathered to socialize, to check on each other, to see who had gone away to Spelman or Winston-Salem Teacher's College or A&T," Charles Jones explained. "And if you were courting a young lady and wanted to be your best, you of course put on your Sunday go-to-meeting clothes, so you look good, a little sweet water, comb your hair. . . . But if you wanted to get something to eat, you couldn't eat it there. You had to take it out if you were black. . . . So here you were trying to be your best, but inherent in the whole process was the fact that, if you were black, get back."

Awareness of the darker sides of white supremacy also grew in the wake of the *Brown* decision, as the ruling sparked a new and disturbing wave of racial violence around the South. In September of 1955, the latest issue of *Jet* arrived in Charlotte with searing photographs of the mutilated corpse of 14-year-old Emmett Till, who had been brutally lynched in Mississippi after being accused of insulting a white woman. In 1956, after African Americans began a boycott of segregated buses in Montgomery, Alabama, bombs went off at black churches, businesses, and homes, including the house of the boycott's charismatic young spokesman, Rev. Martin Luther King Jr. Then, in the fall of 1957, reactions to Charlotte's first, tentative attempts at school desegregation made it clear that the prospect of integration could also produce a frightening level of anger among white Charlotteans.

North Carolina's white leaders, like their counterparts across the South, had done everything they could to maintain the racial status quo. On the surface, they had taken a moderate stance. Right after the *Brown* decision, North Carolina governor Luther Hodges announced that the state would follow the Supreme Court's orders, winning praise for his reasonable words. Then, however, the state's white leaders turned to a stonewalling approach that would become known as "freedom of choice." Instead of assigning black students to historically white schools, they required black families who wanted their children to attend those schools to request transfers. The strategy rested on the calculation that separate — and perhaps even unequal — schools could pass legal muster if they resulted from parent choice rather than legal compulsion.[6]

North Carolina's plan involved a carefully devised set of rules that sharply limited African Americans' ability to choose white schools. Placing responsibility for desegregation on individual black families meant that families who filed transfer applications risked the retaliation commonly employed against African Americans who challenged the racial status quo. Even when families decided to run those risks, they faced a daunting array of bureaucratic hurdles. Legislation passed in 1955 conferred responsibility for student assignment on individual school districts and gave districts the power to enact "reasonable rules and regulations" that would "provide for the orderly and efficient administration of . . . public schools, the effective instruction of the pupils therein enrolled and the health, safety, and general welfare of such pupils." The vagueness of these criteria made it easy for district officials to reject the vast majority of transfer applications without ever citing race.[7]

Not until three years after the *Brown* decision, following intensive lobbying by the state NAACP, were a handful of black North Carolinians actually assigned to historically white schools around the state. Among those students were five Charlotteans. Girvaud Roberts was assigned to Piedmont Junior High, her brother Gus to Central High, William Hamlin and Delois Huntley to Alexander Graham Junior High, and Dorothy Counts to Harding High.[8] Counts, who had just finished ninth grade at Northwest Junior High, was the only west side student in the group. The Charlotte school board only granted transfers to black students who lived closer to white schools than to black ones — a strategy that excluded most of Charlotte's west side residents. But Dorothy Counts lived next to Johnson C. Smith, where her father taught philosophy, and the Countses' home sat marginally closer to all-white Harding High than to West Charlotte.[9]

The desegregation effort suffered its first casualty well before school began. Soon after the assignments were announced, William Hamlin's father started to receive threats at work. The family's home phone began to ring with late-night warnings. Hamlin's father took immediate precautions. He sent the children to stay with their grandparents in South Carolina. He then spent nights sitting by the family's front window, watching unfamiliar cars drive slowly down the street. Eventually, William Hamlin explained, he "decided that it really was not worth the threats that he had received and the danger it may place his children in." The family moved to the west side and enrolled William in Northwest instead.

On September 4, 1957, the four remaining pioneers set off for school. The day went relatively smoothly for Huntley and the Roberts siblings. But Dorothy Counts was greeted by a mob of hostile white teenagers. "I've never seen such anger," recalled Reginald Hawkins, who escorted Counts to and from Harding. "Now I'm a war veteran, twice. I've never seen such anger on the face of people as I saw when I carried Dorothy in and out of that school." Dramatic pictures of the calm young woman surrounded by angry whites circulated around the world. For the next several days, Counts endured threats and taunts whenever she entered or left the school. School officials did little to stop the harassment, even after a rock shattered the back window of the family car one afternoon. After a week, Counts's family withdrew her from Harding and sent her to live with relatives in Philadelphia.[10]

West Charlotte students, many of whom knew Counts personally, saw in her experience an unforgettable example of the racial animosity that lurked beneath the progressive surface of their up-and-coming town. Joanna Dowling, who was a year older than Counts, had given little thought to the meaning of segregation. But the violence changed her thinking. "That's when it frightened me," she related. "When I saw the reaction of the whites. . . . That's when I realized the seriousness of segregation and how evil it could be." Malachi Greene, who had been Counts's classmate at Northwest, had not realized that she had been chosen to integrate Harding. But as soon as he and his friends learned of the harassment, they were furious. "I didn't think about much of anything except that I hated the fact that Dorothy was getting her butt kicked, because Dorothy was a *good* friend," he said. "She was a good friend of mine, of ours, all of us." In their fury, Greene and some of his West Charlotte classmates talked about going over to Harding to confront Counts's tormentors. In the end, however, "smarter people prevailed."

The Charlotte unrest was soon eclipsed by the far greater turmoil that greeted the nine black students that arrived at Central High School in Little Rock, Arkansas, on September 28. The angry demonstrations that consumed Little Rock dominated national news for weeks and forced President Dwight Eisenhower to deploy National Guard troops to the city. The furor that had greeted Dorothy Counts, in contrast, passed relatively quickly, leaving many Charlotteans relieved that their community had avoided Little Rock's fate. Delois Huntley and the Roberts siblings remained at their schools for the rest of the year, and Gus Roberts became the first African American to graduate from one of Charlotte's historically white high schools. But change continued at a snail's pace. While the NAACP continued to encourage black Charlotte families to apply for transfers to white schools, only two or three

Images of the hostility that greeted Dorothy Counts at Harding High School in 1957 circulated around the world. Photograph by Don Sturkey. Courtesy of the *Charlotte Observer.*

were approved each year.[11] Around the region, efforts to press for further gains bore little fruit. In Charlotte and across the South, frustration built.

Then, in 1960, the four Greensboro students sat down at Woolworth's lunch counter. The floodgates opened. Sitting calmly at a segregated lunch counter gave young people a way to protest segregation while upholding the standards of conduct and dignity their parents and teachers had instilled. Charles Jones, who had finished college and was enrolled in seminary at Johnson C. Smith, heard a radio report about the Greensboro sit-in as he was driving back to Charlotte from Washington, D.C. "Yes!" he recalled saying to himself. "Here's the handle!" The Smith student council met the next evening. Jones found a ready ally in B. B. DeLaine, whose father, J. A. DeLaine, had led the movement that produced the Clarendon County desegregation case. Students who wanted to sit in at Charlotte lunch counters, the council announced, should meet at the school clock tower the next day. They expected a handful of participants. More than 200 showed up, including Mary Anna Bradley and Barbara Funderburk. Similar meetings occurred across the South. The region's lunch counters soon filled with calm, well-dressed black college students, politely asking to be served.

Owners of Charlotte's downtown establishments at first stood firm, hoping the students would grow weary of the protest. As the weeks passed, however, the endeavor grew more elaborate. A fleet of vans, cars, and even funeral-home vehicles transported Smith students to the city center, where they set up picket lines, plotted strategies to reach lunch counter stools before employees could remove the seats, and even planned daring ruses, most notably the day when an especially light-skinned couple — Betty Lundy and Thomas Wright — gained admission to the all-white dining room at Ivey's department store. A number of whites joined the demonstrations. The efforts, and an associated boycott, had significant effects on downtown business. Eventually, Mary Anna Bradley recalled, the area "was like a ghost town." In July, five months after the initial action, business owners gave in. As police held back shouting hecklers, black students were ushered into stores, and allowed to sit and eat.

Charles Jones shared the moment with his father, a minister who had spent his career in rural southern communities, and who had taught his son to pick his battles as a matter of survival. "Dad and I went to Kress," Jones noted, "and Daddy ordered a tuna fish, I think, or a hot dog — I imagine it was a hot dog — coffee, Coke. . . . I looked at my father, he looked at me and said, 'You've learned one of the lessons. This is a time to stand and I'm proud of you.' And his generation passed on to me, not only the approval and acceptance, but that praise, and we sat quietly and ate and the lunch counter slowly opened up from that point." Jones would go on to play a key role in the Student Nonviolent Coordinating Committee (SNCC), which fought for civil rights around the South.[12]

Once the sit-in victory was won, young people pressed on, confident that history was on their side. "Wednesday afternoon, November 14, Paulette Hawkins and I, Margaret Trapps, were refused service in the Silver Grill lunch bar of the Charlottetown Mall for the age-old reason that we were Negroes," Margaret Trapps reported in the West Charlotte's school newspaper in 1962. "Any establishment that renders its services so discriminatively is obviously under immature, trivial, backward illusion."[13] While West Charlotte's staff rarely discussed civil rights activities openly, politically active students knew they had support. "In most instances, it's not a direct discussion point," explained Kelly Alexander Jr., the son of NAACP leader Kelly Alexander. "It's subtle cues. Nothing really overt. Simple things like comments, off-the-cuff comments they might make, or the degree to which you might get a break based on things that they may know that you have done away from the campus."

In many ways, Charlotte offered fertile ground for civil rights activities. Across the South, segregation's white supporters generally fell into two camps — those for whom racial separation formed a fundamental cornerstone of white identity, and those for whom it was a means to a larger end, such as control of state or city politics. While those who held the first position were ready to sacrifice almost anything to preserve "racial integrity," others were more willing to make strategic concessions in situations where defending segregation threatened to undermine their broader goals. Charlotte's leaders generally fell into the latter category—city affairs were handled by a tight-knit group of business leaders who were dedicated to promoting their city as an orderly, progressive community that fostered economic success. Most of them had little desire to change their city's racial order, and they worried about the disruptions that racial change might cause. But they were keenly aware of the danger that racial strife posed to the reputation of their up-and-coming city, and they feared that too much intransigence on racial matters would lead the federal government to take control of the city's racial affairs. Since African Americans made up just over a quarter of Charlotte's population, there was no threat they would "take over." When pressed, leaders preferred to meet civil rights demands with compromise rather than confrontation.[14]

This approach was evident in May of 1961, when buses carrying the Freedom Riders, sponsored by the Congress of Racial Equality (CORE), arrived at Charlotte's central bus station. The Riders were testing a Supreme Court decision which held that local segregation laws could not be enforced in institutions linked to interstate transportation. During the Charlotte stop, Field Secretary Joe Perkins staged an impromptu "shoe-in" by sitting in a whites-only shoeshine chair and refusing to move. He was promptly arrested and charged with trespassing. The rest of the Riders continued on to Rock Hill, S.C., where they were met at the bus station by a group of local whites and suffered a violent beating that sparked national headlines. The morning after the incident, Perkins appeared before a Charlotte judge. To his great surprise, the judge invoked the Supreme Court ruling, dismissed the charges and sent him on his way.[15]

Reginald Hawkins was particularly skilled at using leaders' concern about public image to press for change. In the spring of 1963, while an outraged nation watched officials in Birmingham, Alabama, meet civil rights demonstrators with fire hoses and police dogs, Hawkins determined it was time to raise the pressure. Like activists in Birmingham, Charlotte organizers had been negotiating with city leaders over persisting segregation in hotels and restaurants. On May 20, widely celebrated as the anniversary of the day that Mecklenburg residents called for independence from Great Britain, Hawkins led a group of Johnson C. Smith students on a march from campus to the county courthouse. Rather than risk a Birmingham-style confrontation, members of Charlotte's Chamber of Commerce launched a hasty series of behind-the-scenes negotiations. Within days, they announced that the owners of Charlotte's hotels and restaurants had agreed to serve all patrons equally. They underscored their commitment to the change by arranging for interracial groups that included prominent civic leaders to share lunch at key local establishments.[16]

A few days after the announcement, Martin Luther King Jr. came to Charlotte to address a joint graduation ceremony for Charlotte-Mecklenburg's six black high schools: West Charlotte, Second Ward, York Road, J. H. Gunn, Sterling, and Torrence-Lytle. A few weeks earlier, in jail in Alabama, King had written the widely circulated "Letter from Birmingham Jail," in which he sharply chastised national religious and political leaders for their refusal to pursue racial justice. His words in Charlotte held more hope. He praised county leaders for their good sense, lauded young people for their activism, and urged everyone to press ahead. His words made a lasting impression on many of the graduates, including West Charlotte's Isaiah Tidwell. "He spoke about the winds of change that were beginning to blow in this country, and how doors that had been closed to our parents would be open to us," Tidwell later recalled. "I'll never forget it."[17]

Efforts on political and legal fronts brought further gains. Decades of voter registration drives helped black voters place Fred Alexander on the Charlotte City Council in 1965, making him Charlotte's first elected black official in the twentieth century. Change came in more symbolic realms as well. In 1965 the NAACP's Legal Defense Fund sent Julius Chambers to Charlotte to set up a law office and pursue civil rights cases. One of the first cases he filed was a lawsuit against the Shrine Bowl, a prestigious North Carolina–South Carolina all-star high school football game whose organizers had long refused to include black players. A judge ordered the Shrine Bowl integrated, and in the fall of 1966 West Charlotte's Titus Ivory became one of two African Americans to suit up for the North Carolina team.[18]

The struggle was never easy, and deep-seated opposition frequently swirled beneath the surface. Charlotte's most dramatic violence took place in the fall of 1965, soon after the Shrine Bowl suit was filed. Early on the morning of November 22, west siders awoke to the sound of squealing tires and loud explosions, as bombers targeted the homes of Fred Alexander, Kelly Alexander, Reginald Hawkins, and Julius Chambers. But civic leaders acted quickly to mute the attacks' effects. While the bombers were never identified, the act drew immediate and widespread condemnation. A rally called to denounce the violence gathered an integrated crowd of 2,500 participants.

Driver education class, 1966. Kelly Alexander Jr., holding the door, was jolted out of bed in the fall of 1965, when a bomb exploded outside his bedroom. *The Lion,* 1966. Courtesy of Ella D. Dennis.

Kelly Alexander Jr. had been thrown from his bed when the sticks of dynamite placed outside his bedroom wall exploded, shattering the window and sending glass flying just above his head.[19] Years later, however, the memory of the sudden explosion was balanced by his appreciation of the community response, of "the rapidity with which the broader community circled the wagons against that kind of violence."

Both Kelly Alexander Jr. and Reginald Hawkins Jr. were students at West Charlotte, and the two Alexander homes sat across the street from the school's entrance. The morning of the bombing, West Charlotte students gathered on the school's front lawn to contemplate the damage and talk about what it might mean. Once they learned that no one had been hurt, however, their fears started to fade. "I just knew that we had to look out for each other," Ella Dennis explained. "That was just my thinking at that time. I don't even know if I thought it would come to West Charlotte. Because Kelly's father, all these people were civil rights people, and out in the forefront. We just thought it was aimed at them. . . . I think that's pretty much where we were with that—I was anyway."

Like the bombs, the turmoil of the era had limited effects on West Charlotte itself. Students might challenge authority outside school walls, but on the campus Clinton Blake and his staff continued to reign supreme, and life went on much as it had in previous decades. There were some changes— Charles McCullough returned to his alma mater in 1960 and took the reins of the basketball team from Jack Martin. Clinton Blake would retire in 1966, nearly three decades after he opened the school. But Joseph "Daddy" Towns still taught history and photography; Barbara Davis headed up the newspaper and yearbook; Pop Miller roamed the halls; and Bill Lindsay continued to teach Shakespeare and dispense relationship advice.

"It was just sort of a magical feeling," recalled Gerald Johnson. "You just loved being at the school. . . . I had friends who didn't care about going to class, didn't care about studying or doing homework, but they loved being in the school environment in terms of having friends, participating in sporting activities." While there were definite divisions among students, often based on economic status, the school had a place for everyone. The most serious students took classes that prepared them for college, Johnson noted, while others were tracked into industrial courses, where "the teachers just reached out to them and helped them in any way they could, even if they didn't want to get the education that they wanted to give them."[20] Patsy Camp voiced similar sentiments. "Everybody was appreciated, from the football field, the basketball court, to the history, the English, to the home economics to the shop," she said. "Whatever you did you had to be good at it."

School and community still worked together to keep students in line, sometimes to dramatic effect. Deacon Jones encountered that formidable combination one Friday evening when he and a group of fellow students decided to sneak into a West Charlotte football game without paying. Jones was the last over the fence, and as soon as he hit the ground, he knew he was in trouble. "There were these two shiny shoes standing there," he explained. "Officer Torrence." Rudolph Torrence had patrolled his alma mater's field for years, and he gave gate-crashers little mercy. Back over the fence Jones went, tearing his shirt and landing hard. Angry, he lashed out: "I told him 'One of these days, you big tall sucker, I'm going to get you.'" Torrence did not flinch. In the intricate web of west side society, he knew exactly where Jones fit. "I'm going to tell Deola what you said," he replied. The mention of his mother's name made Jones even angrier. "How do you know my mother?" he fumed. "What is it with you people up here? Everybody knows my family!"

Torrence stood firm. "I'm going to tell your mama what you said, boy." Like countless West Charlotte students before him, Jones found a second punishment awaiting him at home. But the lesson sank in. "I realized—anything that's free in life, that you try to get, there's always a price to pay," he said. "Those kinds of engagements, those kinds of lessons, those are the things that change your life."

As in previous generations, students focused most of their attention on school affairs, classes, clubs, dances, and sports events. In the spring of 1966, just a few months after University Park residents had been awakened by the explosions that rocked the Alexander homes, they were roused once again by a more joyful noise—the ringing of West Charlotte's school bell in honor of a state championship. The basketball team had upset the renowned "Pony Express" from Durham's Hillside High to capture the state title, and when the bus carrying the team's jubilant supporters got back to campus, Ella Dennis noted, "we were lit up, ready to let the neighborhood know that we had won."

Proud of their school, West Charlotte students talked less about attending white schools than about competing with them. "Our dialogue was basically centered around the fact that we were just as good as any other students in Charlotte-Mecklenburg," noted William Hamlin, who harbored no regrets about his family's decision to pull him out of the 1957 desegregation effort. "There was always an itching that we wanted the opportunity to meet our counterparts, whether it be in academics, or sports, or whatever, head to head, to see who was best. There was a lot of talk about 'Boy, I sure would like to see us sing at a competition that involved them. I sure would like to see them debate with us. I sure would like to see them compete with us athletically.' That was basically the dialogue. We just wanted the opportunity to show that we were as good as we knew we were."

In terms of competition, one of the early highlights of integration came in the spring of 1967, when the black and white state athletic associations merged and West Charlotte met Myers Park High School on the basketball court for the first time. It was a storied matchup. West Charlotte was the reigning champion of the black North Carolina Athletic Conference. Myers Park had finished second in the white North Carolina High School Athletic Association state tournament. The night the two teams met, fans from both schools packed the Myers Park gym, and latecomers had to linger outside, waiting for news. The teams put on a great show, staying within a few points of each other all night. "They had an outstanding veteran team and we had an outstanding veteran team, " Charles McCullough recalled. When the final buzzer rang, West Charlotte had triumphed, 72–70.[21]

The next year, 1968, was one of the most turbulent in the nation's history. Growing protests against the Vietnam War forced President Lyndon Johnson to abandon his reelection plans. On April 4, Martin Luther King Jr. was shot in Memphis — an event that sparked despair and anger throughout black America. King had been scheduled to be in Charlotte to campaign for Reginald Hawkins, who was running for governor, but had cancelled at the last minute to grapple with a Memphis sanitation workers' strike. Barely two months later, Robert Kennedy was assassinated while running for the Democratic presidential nomination. Chaos erupted at the subsequent Democratic Party convention, as Chicago policemen attacked anti-war demonstrators.

Throughout it all, West Charlotte remained a refuge. That September, Stan Frazier arrived on campus to the same warm embrace that had greeted generations of his predecessors. "I felt like I was in heaven," he recalled. "The teachers, from the first day of class, they talked about success. They talked about not letting you fail. Even if they had to knock you upside your head you would not fail at that school. . . . I felt predestined to be successful."

Change, however, lay just around the corner. While officials across the South continued to resist school integration, the NAACP persisted in its legal campaign, gaining ground one step at a time. One of the most important of those cases began to unfold in Charlotte, under the guidance of Julius Chambers, who was on his way to becoming the most respected civil rights lawyer of his generation. Chambers had decided to pursue a legal career after his father, who owned a garage, could not find a lawyer willing to bring suit against a white customer who had failed to pay a substantial bill. The financial setback had dealt a blow to Chambers's education, forcing him to enroll in the county's inadequate black public high school instead of the private academy his older siblings had attended. But he had more than made up for lost time. He came to Charlotte with a stellar record: he had served as president of the student body at North Carolina College, and as the first African American editor-in-chief of the *North Carolina Law Review* at the University of North Carolina. His first job out of law school was at the NAACP Legal Defense Fund's New York office, where he began to handle the desegregation cases that had become the organization's major focus.[22]

The NAACP had identified North Carolina as a particularly promising arena for civil rights litigation. Chambers's talent and drive led the Legal Defense Fund to send him to the state as one of its first local litigators, charged with selecting and filing the cases needed to make sweeping federal legis-

Science students, 1965, and tailoring students, 1964. *The Lion*, 1964, 1965.
Courtesy of the Robinson-Spangler Carolina Room.

lation into on-the-ground reality. He did not disappoint. As soon as he arrived in Charlotte, he began to file lawsuits related to housing, employment, and education.[23] Practicing the integration that he preached, he gathered an interracial group of lawyers that included Adam Stein from Washington, D.C., and the stylish, fiery James E. Ferguson II, who had helped organize Asheville's sit-ins before moving on to North Carolina College and then Columbia Law School.[24]

Soon after Chambers set up shop, a group of parents and NAACP leaders approached him about challenging Charlotte-Mecklenburg's assignment policies. A decade after *Brown*, Charlotte schools remained substantially segregated: the district had 57 all-white schools, 31 all-black schools, 15 predominantly white schools with a handful of black students, and 6 schools that were somewhat more balanced. A number of black families agreed to join the suit, among them Johnson C. Smith professor Darius Swann and his wife, Vera. Swann's job with Johnson C. Smith gave the family a degree of protection against white retaliation, and the Swanns agreed to be the lead plaintiffs in a case that entered legal history as *Swann v. Board of Education*.[25]

The Swanns had a deep belief in the importance of an integrated world. They had met while students at Johnson C. Smith, and after they married they traveled together to India to serve as missionaries. One day, Darius happened to see a newspaper with a photograph of Dorothy Counts braving the Harding High School mob. The Swanns knew the Counts family well—Darius and Herman Counts were from the same part of Virginia, and Darius had studied philosophy with Herman at Johnson C. Smith. Determined to join the fight for freedom, the Swanns decided to return to the United States. Darius took a position at Johnson C. Smith's seminary, and the family settled near the school. The Swanns then sought to enroll their son James at nearby Seversville Elementary. Located in the white community of Seversville, which sat just south of Biddleville, Seversville Elementary served 297 white and 26 black students. On the first day of school, however, the Swanns were politely informed that their neighborhood was assigned to all-black Billingsville Elementary, which sat much farther away. They immediately requested a reassignment. The request pointed out that Seversville was closer to their home, but saved its most impassioned rhetoric for the broader issue of integration.[26]

"We believe that an integrated school will best prepare young people for responsibility in an integrated society," they wrote. "Having lived practically all of his life in India, James has never known the meaning of racial segregation. We have been happy to watch him grow and develop with an unaffected openness to people of all races and backgrounds, and we feel it our duty as parents to insure that this healthy development continue." When their request was turned down, they contacted Julius Chambers.[27]

The *Swann* case was initially dismissed. A federal judge would only order a remedy for a situation that had been caused by wrongful government action. Charlotte-Mecklenburg Schools was shifting from a race-based assignment plan to one that was more geographically based, and the school board successfully argued that persisting school segregation stemmed from housing patterns that had been created by individual families' choices about where to live. But change was coming. NAACP lawyers, aided by ever-tougher federal regulations, had been laying the legal groundwork for a more aggressive approach to school desegregation. A series of decisions, which culminated in a 1968 Virginia case known as *Green v. Board of Education of New Kent*

County, shifted the legal requirements school systems had to meet. Under the new formulation, school districts were not simply required to eliminate dual-school systems. Rather they were charged with the "affirmative duty" to ensure that schools were actually desegregated. As soon as the Supreme Court ruled in *Green*, Julius Chambers announced that he would reopen his North Carolina desegregation cases. In March of 1969, Chambers came before federal judge James B. McMillan to reargue *Swann*.[28]

Chambers cast his argument broadly. Charlotte's still-segregated schools, he argued, were a direct result of the housing discrimination that had separated the city into black and white sectors, and concentrated low-cost housing on the west side of town. The school board's actions in the years following the *Brown* decision had reinforced these patterns—not only had the board continued to assign students to single-race schools, it built new schools in neighborhoods that were either exclusively white or exclusively black. Since schools were a major factor in a family's choice of neighborhood, placing still-segregated schools in still-segregated neighborhoods encouraged families to make choices that perpetuated segregation.[29]

These arrangements, Chambers contended, continued to harm black children. He laid out evidence of the striking gaps in performance between the system's black and white students. His evidence also showed that African American students who attended majority-white schools performed far better than those who remained in all-black schools. As a result, he argued, the only way to ensure that all children received equal opportunities was to fully integrate every school in the system.

McMillan was taken aback by the scope of Chambers's ambition. No lawyer had ever called for that degree of change. The *Green* case, which required the New Kent County schools to fully desegregate, involved a school district with two schools and 1,300 students, in which desegregation posed few logistical challenges. Desegregating Charlotte-Mecklenburg Schools, which educated 83,000 students, would be a staggering task. But Chambers made his case well, and McMillan listened carefully. In late April, the judge issued an opinion that called for Charlotte-Mecklenburg to eliminate all racially identifiable schools.[30]

The order sent shock waves across Mecklenburg County. Apart from Chambers, few residents had imagined that such drastic change—which would touch every school and every community in the county—would ever come to pass. But, McMillan stated, that was what the law required. Only complete desegregation of every school in the county would suffice to overcome the inequalities created by a long history of separate and unequal education.

For African American families, the order sparked multiple reactions. McMillan's decision was in many ways a victory, a strong statement in favor of educational equality. But families also felt uneasy. While black families were used to long bus rides — black students had frequently been bused past white schools to attend African American ones — many parents and teachers worried about their children's experience at predominantly white schools. "I never felt that our kids would get the same thing in the white situation as they would get from us," explained Barbara Davis. "That was just my basic feeling. . . . I was leery of being consumed. And that's what I was afraid of. I didn't want our people to be consumed by the white people."[31]

The situation was complicated by political realities. Although the number of black voters was expanding, black political power remained limited. The single black member of the school board, Coleman Kerry, had been appointed to fill a vacancy in 1968. A black candidate would not win a school board election until 1972.[32] The lack of black political power meant that a legal victory for equality was implemented in a decidedly unequal way. Across the South, school boards dealt with integration orders by closing down historically black schools.[33] Charlotte was no exception. In July of 1969 the school board announced that they would close seven black schools, many of which had served African American communities for decades. Fairview Elementary, Alexander Street Elementary, and Isabella Wyche Elementary were among the schools destined for closure. Atop the list — the greatest shock of all — sat Second Ward High School.[34]

Second Ward, one of black Charlotte's oldest and most beloved institutions, had fallen victim to the board's concern that white families would refuse to attend historically black schools, as well as to the city's patterns of wealth and power. Second Ward's center-city location made it a logical candidate for integration. While the building showed its five decades of age, the board had already approved plans for a new, up-to-date facility, to be called Metropolitan High School. "They were just going to make it this great school," recalled Spencer Singleton, who graduated from Second Ward in 1968. "They had a 3-D scale model of this Metropolitan High School right in the hallway when you entered the building. We had a huge hallway there. And they had it sitting on the table." But the neighborhoods from which Second Ward/Metropolitan would have most logically drawn white students were home to some of the city's wealthiest and most powerful residents, including the majority of school board members. On July 22, the board approved a plan that closed Second Ward, shelved the plans for Metropolitan High, and scattered Second Ward's students among several other schools.[35]

The announcement that Second Ward would close sparked widespread outrage. African American residents packed the next school board meeting, among them a group of young men who wore the black berets that had become a trademark of the Black Panther Party. AME Zion minister George Leake announced that a protest petition sponsored by the newly formed Black Solidarity Committee had gathered 19,000 signatures. "Righteous indignation and anger were the immediate reaction" to the closings, Leake informed the board, along with "violent moods and words." His fury filled the room. "You force our back against the wall and you ask us once again to have good faith," he stated. "Every time we have faith, you treat us like a bunch of dogs."[36] But the school board stood fast. In a decision that he would later say that he regretted, McMillan allowed the closings to go forward.

Soon after the decision, the building where generations of black Charlotteans had spent their high school years was unceremoniously bulldozed. Former students flocked to the site to gather up the fragments. "I can remember when they started tearing the building down," graduate Rufus Spears recalled. "There were a lot of students, former students who came back just to get one brick to save as a memento."[37] One by one, five of the six historically black high schools whose graduates had listened to the hopeful words of Martin Luther King had been closed or downgraded. In 1966, in an initial round of reconfiguration, J. H. Gunn, Torrence-Lytle, and Sterling had been closed, and York Road had been turned into a junior high. With Second Ward gone, West Charlotte became the only historically black high school left.[38]

In September of 1969, several hundred former Second Ward students arrived at West Charlotte. It was a wrenching transformation. African Americans across the city had mourned the loss of Second Ward—"It was like losing a member of your family," Rudolph Torrence recalled.[39] But the two groups of former rivals simply did not get along. The Second Ward students were deeply angry about the sudden closing of their school and unhappy about being on the campus of their longtime rival. "All during the year, there was uneasiness," recalled Gerson Stroud, the former principal of York Road High School, who had taken over at West Charlotte in 1968. "All during the year . . . West Charlotte students for West Charlotte students. Second Ward for Second Ward."

West Charlotte students cheer at one of the last pep rallies held before busing permanently transformed the school. *The Lion*, 1969. Courtesy of the Robinson-Spangler Carolina Room.

Discomfort mounted in the spring of 1970, when Julius Chambers came to West Charlotte to explain what lay ahead. The 1969–70 desegregation plan had been only a beginning, Chambers explained. The next year, 1970–71, every school in Charlotte-Mecklenburg would be fully desegregated. Because approximately 70 percent of Charlotte-Mecklenburg students were white, every school would have a white majority. Most of West Charlotte's students would be assigned to historically white schools.

By that time, West Charlotte students had been hearing about school desegregation for years, watching change move closer and closer. Still, they found it hard to believe what Chambers was saying. "There was an anger that they would ever think about doing something to West Charlotte," Stan Frazier recalled. But mainly, the students were dumbfounded: "We couldn't grasp what was happening."

Proof arrived via the U.S. mail. "Before the year ended, several kids got letters saying they would be going to different schools," Frazier continued. "I mean kids were going everywhere." An era of West Charlotte history had come to an end.

BUSING

In the fall of 1970, Charlotte-Mecklenburg Schools launched the most far-reaching school desegregation program ever attempted. The previous year, when geography played the major role in school assignment, only a quarter of the system's 80,000 students rode a bus to school. In the fall of 1970, every school was required to mirror the system's racial makeup — 70 percent white and 30 percent black. More than half the students — 43,000 — rode buses that year, many to schools far from their neighborhoods. The move required 600 buses and dozens of new bus drivers. School systems across the state had sent surplus vehicles to Charlotte to help handle the extra routes the plan required, and working out the complicated logistics delayed the start of school for two full weeks.[1]

That first day dawned tense and uncertain across the district. "Many of the whites who came were absolutely scared out of their minds," longtime West Charlotte teacher Mertye Rice later recalled. "They had heard so much about what black kids do — black people steal, black people rape, all these myths."[2] African American students prepared for potential conflict. Rosalie Meeks, who graduated from West Charlotte in 1945, recalled telling her children that they should not start fights, but "when somebody hits you, and hits you first, then you hit them." A suburban-based, predominantly white group called the Concerned Parents Association had called for a wholesale boycott of the schools. Several schools received telephoned bomb threats, and their students were let out early.[3]

Despite the threats, the first few days went relatively smoothly. "I think for the most part we were all just trying to feel each other out," explained Agnes Alexander, who was bused from Druid Hills to historically white Eastway Junior High. "Not any of us had ever been around white people in a setting like that. We were more touchy feely — just trying to figure out what the other group of people were all about — and I'm sure they were doing the same thing for us." Still, the atmosphere remained uneasy. "Everything was just so unsure," Alexander noted. "You didn't know what to expect."

The uneasiness proved warranted. While many Mecklenburg County residents did their best to bridge racial divides and make the judge's orders work, the upheaval ushered in a period of unrest across the county, sparking threats, fights, marches, and boycotts. The school board fought McMillan's orders at every turn. West Charlotte became a focus of particular conflict, and the prolonged struggles over which white students would be assigned to the school raised fears that it, too, might be forced to close its doors. It would take four long years for Mecklenburg County's residents to come to terms with McMillan's ruling and reshape their school system to serve a de-segregating world.

The first rounds of busing plans, which closed black schools and bused most black children to white neighborhoods, had especially disruptive effects on African American communities. Rather than unfolding in isolation, busing became one of several converging forces that undercut black neighborhoods and institutions, tearing at the social fabric that Charlotte's African Americans had built up during a century of effort.

African Americans who pushed for school desegregation had combined idealism with hard-nosed practicality. Darius and Vera Swann had wanted their son to "grow and develop with an unaffected openness to people of all races and backgrounds." Julius Chambers focused on resources, calculating that Mecklenburg leaders would only support all schools equally if all schools educated both black and white children. "I don't think that those who are now in power would provide the facilities and services that would be necessary in order to accomplish equal educational programs," he told the U.S. Senate in the spring of 1971. "As I view it, the only way that we can obtain quality education for all children, black and white, is to accomplish racial mixing of students in the various schools."[4] West Charlotte graduate Saundra Davis, whose elementary school daughter was bused across town under the plan, concurred. "I didn't want my children to have to be bused out of the neighborhood," she said. "I really didn't. But if that meant my children getting a better education, yes. Let them be bused. Somebody had to do it. The ice had to be broken somewhere. For the simple reason, the white schools had always had the better things."

The breaking of that ice, however, came at a high price. Desegregation meant the end of the all-black institutions that generations of educators had shaped to fit the needs of their students and communities. When schools and teaching staffs were integrated, the staffs that black principals had spent years assembling were scattered across the district. The number of black teachers also began to fall. The school board's decision to close black schools cut significantly into the district's black teaching corps. New positions were filled primarily by whites. For the 1968–69 school year, the Durham-based *Carolina Times* reported, Charlotte-Mecklenburg hired 722 new teachers, only seventeen of whom were black. In 1966, before the first round of school closings, black teachers made up 44 percent of Charlotte-Mecklenburg's teachers. By 1969, they were down to 22 percent.[5]

West Charlotte, the only black high school left open, was especially hard hit. "The year when busing actually commenced," principal Gerson Stroud painstakingly explained, "all of the black faculty at West Charlotte was transferred, with the exception of nineteen. Now mind you, I don't remember exact figures. But we probably had 130, 140 teachers. And to be reduced to nineteen. And then you see we were transferring all of the experienced teachers. We had to replace all of the black teachers, and the white teachers had to be in the majority." District leaders refused to transfer experienced white teachers to West Charlotte. Rather, they gave Stroud first choice of the system's newly hired teachers, many of whom were straight out of college.[6]

For many of Charlotte's African Americans, the disruptions caused by the desegregation plan became yet another stage in a larger process of dislocation, which had been set in motion by a combination of federal policies and local decisions that reshaped cities across the country. Between 1960 and the early 1970s, Charlotte political leaders used federal "urban renewal" funds to bulldoze black neighborhoods in First Ward, Second Ward, Third Ward, and Greenville, displacing nearly 10,000 residents along with hundreds of small businesses, churches, and other institutions. Three major highways— I-85, I-77, and NC-16—were routed through the west side, displacing more residents and creating formidable barriers between the communities that remained. What had once been a small-scale, closely knit series of African American neighborhoods that stretched from the center city out across the west side gave way to more scattered settlements separated by broad expanses of concrete.[7] "It didn't take them long," Kenneth Simmons noted about the destruction of Greenville. "Those little houses were all made of wood and those bulldozers, once they got everybody out, they could knock them down seemed like in a day."[8]

Residents displaced by these projects did not travel far. While Charlotte was expanding rapidly, with dozens of new housing developments springing up at its southern and eastern edges, most of the displaced families could not afford the new neighborhoods—and lending discrimination meant that even those who could often found it difficult to obtain mortgages. Most settled in the aging housing stock just north and west of the city center, areas where new development had been stifled by zoning and loan policies that discouraged investment in older neighborhoods, especially those occupied by African Americans. Some families ended up in public housing projects, most of which had been built on the west side as well. Others moved to nearby, historically white neighborhoods, where the way was cleared by the entrepre-

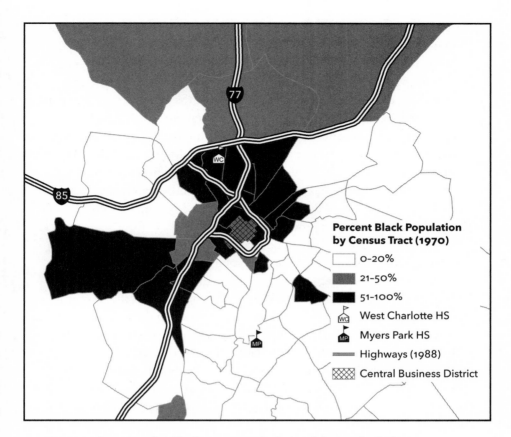

Percent Black Population by Census Tract (1970)

☐ 0–20%

▨ 21–50%

■ 51–100%

West Charlotte HS

Myers Park HS

═══ Highways (1988)

▨▨ Central Business District

By 1970, urban renewal and highway projects had evicted thousands of African Americans from Charlotte's center city and surrounded west side neighborhoods with major roads. The dark census tracts reflect the spread of displaced African Americans to neighborhoods just outside the center city, as well as to the west and northwest. The two dark tracts to the southeast mark the historically black communities of Cherry and Grier Heights. Map by Miriam E. Martin.

neurial zeal of realtors who saw profits in converting white-owned homes into rental housing for African Americans. In the fall of 1965, for example, the white community of Seversville, just down the hill from Biddleville, was inundated by a "flood of real estate men," some of whom warned homeowners that "you're going to have to sell because colored people are taking over."[9] These multiple developments accelerated an ongoing white exodus to newly built suburban communities, making Charlotte a more segregated city in 1970 than it had been in 1940.[10]

The departure of white residents from central-city neighborhoods meant that most of the displaced black families who moved to those neigh-borhoods continued to live in all-black communities. But they were not the same communities. The process of displacement and the scramble for afford-able housing shredded much of the supportive social fabric that had sus-tained those families during the Jim Crow years, the patterns of settlement and relationship-building that had created communities in which residents knew their neighbors and watched out for each other's children as a mat-ter of course. The result was a profound sense of dislocation. "The church I attended—leveled," Ed Anderson recalled. "The elementary school I at-tended—leveled. My home—erased. . . . All of our little community was just wiped out and we were scattered everywhere. We lost contact with a lot of people." That fabric would prove difficult to reweave.[11]

While the neighborhoods around West Charlotte High remained intact, residents were keenly aware of the depth of loss that urban renewal caused, as well as the limited alternatives available to displaced residents. The 1969 school board vote to close Second Ward and six other black schools only in-tensified the sense that city officials had little interest in the welfare of Afri-can Americans. The vote "was a big shock," explained Angela Wood Fritz, a West Charlotte High student whose father was an administrator at Second Ward. "There was a lot of 'Uh-oh. I see what they're going to do to us. They're going to close down all of our schools and make us move.' . . . It was just all of a sudden. Bam: 'This is how it's going to be. Deal with it.' There was a lot of anger."

That anger showed in a sharpening of tone on racial issues, one that re-flected growing national frustrations about the intransigence of white su-premacy and the weakening of African American institutions. Several civil rights organizations, including SNCC and CORE, shifted their focus from fighting segregation to promoting black self-determination. CORE took an especially strong stand against busing. In a brief filed with the Supreme Court in the *Swann* case, CORE leaders called for the preservation of black schools. "Integration, as it is designed, places the Black child in the posi-tion of implied inferiority," the brief stated. "Not only is he asked to give up much of his culture and identity, but with the dispersal of Blacks he loses many of the communal ties which have traditionally been the cornerstone of the Black community."[12]

Charlotte residents felt similar frustrations. "We, the black teachers of Lincoln Heights School, have viewed with much concern the reaction of the School Board to the recent decision of the District Court requiring deseg-regation of students and staff personnel in the various schools of the system," a group of Lincoln Heights teachers wrote to the board in 1969. "We have watched the efforts of integration, always meaning that blacks were to assimilate and, in fact, be absorbed by white institutions, white programs, white cultures. . . . You now tell us that we are still inferior and have no contribution to make to the school system, that your integration still means only that blacks are to move to white schools, that there must be some special training for black teachers, that you will accommodate and assimilate us into your white society. To this we say we are tired and resent your insult that you still presume our inferiority, that you still will presume that we are incapable of performing equally as well as whites."[13]

The August rally sparked by the closing of Second Ward and other black schools took a similar tone. More than 1,000 demonstrators, flanked by Black Panthers carrying walkie-talkies, marched from the city center to the Second Ward grounds. Signs read "Justice is Gone" and "Justice is dead in this stinking All-American City." Emotions ran high, and several demonstrators fainted from the heat. In his speech on the Second Ward steps, youthful march coordinator Benjamin Chavis called for blacks and whites to work together to meet the challenges of the new situation. He also made a threat: "If the school board continues to apply this racist policy, we are going to have to solve it by action means."[14]

Heightened black outrage, however, brought few results. The school board majority was more worried about the Concerned Parents Association, whose antibusing candidates had captured all three open school board seats in the May 1970 election. The closed schools remained closed. The desegregation plan that went into effect in the fall of 1970 relied heavily on "one-way" busing—sending African American children out of their neighborhoods to historically white schools. Given the court order, busing a higher proportion of black children was inevitable. But the school board had made the situation worse by closing black schools, and by limiting the number of white students assigned to those few that remained.

On the ground, even good-faith efforts to promote equal schooling unfolded in a decidedly unequal arena. African Americans made up less than a third of the system's staff and students, and held little power on the school board or over the day-to-day details of school management. While many teachers, parents, and administrators tried to treat students equally, the effects of white supremacy still ran strong, a tangle of stereotypes and presumptions that ranged from out-and-out fear of African Americans to the fundamental assumption that black schools, teachers and students were simply not as good as white ones. Skewed discipline numbers reflected this bias: 6,500 students were suspended across the system that school year—double the previous year's total—and nearly 90 percent of the suspended students were African American.[15]

Bill McMillan, a Second Ward graduate who would become West Charlotte's principal in 1978, spent the year visiting schools plagued by racial difficulties at every level. "Kindergarten teachers afraid of kindergarten children," he noted. "Teacher white, children black, teacher afraid of students. Throughout the entire school system we had some of those." Then there were schools where "black children felt very fearful," because they felt out of place, sensed the unease of white teachers and administrators, and had no black administrators that they could turn to for advice or support.

"I'm pretty certain without reservation that there were some people who were trying their darndest to make that environment as wholesome for all children as I was," McMillan explained. "I would say, on the other hand, that there probably were some who maybe were trying, but didn't know how and were making a mess of things." Before integration, Pop Miller estimated, "there was maybe a year's difference between blacks and whites." In the shakeups that followed, however, "things went the other way," and some black students began to fall further behind. "Students were lost," recalled Barbara Funderburk, who had become a teacher and who was assigned to Myers Park High in the fall of 1970. "They were just misplaced."

Communities around some newly desegregated schools presented challenges as well. "How can I say this?" asked Eunice Pharr, who taught at rural West Mecklenburg High, where a number of West Charlotte students were reassigned. "They really didn't want the blacks in that area. . . . If some black child just happened to walk down the road after school they would call the police. There was a junior high school right down the street, Wilson Junior High. So if you had a brother or sister to walk down to that school to get a younger sibling they would call the police." Not only were black students treated unequally, Pharr said, whenever there was a disturbance, "when the fighting would begin, they would call—I used to cry—they would call the county police. At that time we had the county police and the city police. The county police was made up of all white. So when they came they came with an attitude. They would grab those black children and put them in handcuffs and put them in a long prison bus."

Black teachers sent to historically white schools faced their own struggles. Many were astonished to see the resources white schools enjoyed. "I tell some people it was like dying and going to heaven," Barbara Funderburk said about her first days at Myers Park. "Teachers had their own cafeteria. Had telephones in their departments. It was just an entirely different world." But like black students, many felt profoundly out of place. Madge Hopkins, who had also become a teacher, was moved from Second Ward to East Mecklenburg High. "I equate East Mecklenburg, my first experience there, to the ice box," she explained. "We didn't have air conditioning at Second Ward but there was air conditioning at East Mecklenburg and that room was icy cold. I was a teacher interacting with students. They sat, I taught, they left. It was cold. I was the only black person in the room."

One of the most difficult aspects of the experience, she continued, was the sense that administrators distrusted her abilities. "There's nothing like being isolated and not being trusted," she explained. "Especially not to teach English to white children. They didn't trust me to do that. You take their skills class, you may do one or two regular classes, you never do AP, you're not trusted to do this. And that might not have been what they felt but that's what I felt." She stayed only two years. "The first year I hated it," she said. "The second year got a little better but I had gotten married and I, like all of my friends that had been sent to white schools to integrate, we were going with, 'let's see how quick you can get pregnant,' because there was no maternity leave, there was resignation at an early point of your pregnancy. I was so happy to get out of there."

The situation at West Charlotte changed dramatically as well. As the system's only historically black high school, West Charlotte continued to be run by African American administrators who believed in black teachers and supported black students. But the sudden influx of new white teachers turned some classrooms into tense and disconcerting spaces. "You had a lot of teachers who weren't comfortable being there," recalled Stan Frazier, who was a senior that year. "You started getting that feeling when you would go in the classroom and they would say odd things." At the time, he explained, black leather jackets had come into fashion, and many students wore them. "I had a teacher who made mention she didn't want 'Black Panthers' in her classroom," he continued. "And as young kids, we were looking at each other saying 'what the heck is she talking about?' We had no clue. But she had made up her mind that we were Black Panthers because we had black leather jackets." Gerson Stroud soon learned that a white teacher who would not eat lunch in the cafeteria was a teacher who wanted out. "This was a true indication of their feelings," he explained. "And after a year, there would be requests for transfers."

Yearbook editors used a collage of headlines to convey the turmoil students felt during the first full year of busing. *The Lion*, 1971. Courtesy of the Robinson-Spangler Carolina Room.

Desegregation also posed a challenge to West Charlotte's cultural traditions. For decades, the school had embodied the pride and ambition of the surrounding community, not only in the diplomas bestowed each year but in cultural displays such as the dynamic verve of the marching band. The loss of Second Ward and other historically black high schools made West Charlotte the county's last representative of those high school traditions. But the sudden shift to a majority-white student body called their future into question. The issue broke into view during the fall's first pep rally. As the *Boston Globe* later described it, "black youngsters who were holdovers from last year began singing and dancing to their old school music and waving the fist of black power." The action prompted angry phone calls from white parents, and a group of white students soon presented Stroud with a petition requesting that the next pep rally include the playing of "Dixie."[16] A few months later, two West Charlotte students voiced their feelings about the shift. "The whites want to just come over here and take over our school," one black student told a local reporter. "It's not just theirs anymore: it's ours too," a white student responded.[17]

The multifaceted strains led to fights. "On any given day one could break out," Frazier explained. "There was an uneasiness among people. It could be simple as someone saying something. . . . If teachers said things that were wrong, and students didn't like it, suddenly it would get in the wind that something would jump off in the seventh period, or sixth period." The specific reasons behind most of these clashes remained obscure. "A lot of things, you didn't know why," Frazier continued. "It was an eerie feeling on some of those things because you didn't know and you didn't get close to a lot of people because the closeness just wasn't there anymore. . . . It was just a foggy year for all of us." West Charlotte's white students, uprooted from their own communities, felt even more disoriented. Years after Frazier graduated and became a teacher, he ran into a white classmate from that year, who described it as "the worst experience of her life."

Those tensions took a toll on education at the school and across the district. "I think it was just a matter of stamina and endurance," recalled West Charlotte English teacher Patsy Sutherland. "And just rolling with the punches there for a while. . . . I really don't want to say that education took a back seat to the social and political issues. But there were moments when I think that you had to deal with those issues before you really then could focus on the education." Those students who moved forward often did so by drawing on family support and previous experience. "A lot of learning didn't take place," Stan Frazier noted. "If we hadn't had that capacity built in us, a lot of us probably wouldn't have gone to college."

Throughout the fall of 1970, anger and uncertainty suffused the community. Although the Concerned Parents Association boycott had limited effect, the group continued to hold rallies and pack school board meetings to call for an end to busing. Bomb threats at schools became routine. Attendance at sports events dropped. "I think that there was a general fear in the community that 'we don't want to be in an environment that's going to put the races together in masses and may cause something,'" William Hamlin surmised. The school board had appealed McMillan's decision to the Supreme Court, and a number of residents and board members still held out hope that the court would reverse McMillan's decision. But although the case was argued in October, no decision was expected before spring.[18]

Conflicts sharpened that winter, especially at high schools. On February 8, 1971, Charlotte papers carried the news of dramatic developments in Wilmington, N.C., where a black student boycott over inequalities at desegregated schools had sparked several days of unrest that included shootings, firebombs, and two deaths.[19] A week later, more than a hundred black students at South Mecklenburg High School walked off school grounds. Many boycotted classes again the next day. While the walkout followed a fight between black and white students, it quickly became clear that the black students were primarily concerned with their school experience as a whole. Shortly after the walkout, the students presented the school board with a list of concerns that underscored the challenges black students were facing at predominantly white schools across the county. First and foremost, they called for equal discipline of black and white students. They requested more black administrators, particularly a black counselor and a black principal or assistant principal. They also addressed cultural issues, asking for courses in black culture and for a schoolwide commemoration of the birth and death of Martin Luther King Jr.[20]

A few days later, West Charlotte's African American students called a meeting to express support for the South Mecklenburg students. As the black students were meeting in the auditorium, a group of white students gathered in the cafeteria, following complaints that a white student had been attacked by a black student. Then trouble started. "A boy came down the hall and said there was a fight in the cafeteria," one black student told a reporter. "I got up and went there. They were swinging so I just joined in."[21] A white student told a similar story. "I heard there was going to be a big rumble and all the blacks were in the auditorium and the whites were in the cafeteria," he recounted. "I saw a bunch of blacks go into the cafeteria and all of them and the whites just jumped into it at one time and chairs were flying. A couple of people got chairs up beside the head, and it looked like they were using sticks and belts." Estimates had as many as 200 students participating in the fight. The police arrived in force, although the fighting had subsided by the time they reached the campus. Two white students were briefly hospitalized with minor injuries.[22]

Black and white students clashed at two other schools that Friday, and at several others the following Monday. The incidents rattled both students and parents. Nearly 650 students stayed home from West Charlotte on the Monday after the fights, and a group of white West Charlotte students picketed the school system offices, calling for greater "protection." District officials temporarily closed Myers Park and West Mecklenburg, assigned administrators to patrol several schools, and invited parents to join them in monitoring the situation.[23] School board chair William Poe suggested that "outsiders" might be headed for the city to cause trouble with a "concerted effort" of "hits" at the system's high schools. A meeting of 300 West Charlotte parents dissolved into a shouting match that included accusations that black "troublemakers" were treated too lightly and charges that teachers did not discipline white students because they feared for their jobs. When students attempted to take the mike, they were prevented.[24]

It would probably have made sense to let the students speak. Subsequent events indicated that many students were determined to find ways to navigate racial tensions. The next few weeks saw black and white students working together at a number of schools, organizing schoolwide meetings and what they called "friendship rally love-ins." The week after the big fight, a series of West Charlotte student "rap sessions" about racial tensions swelled into "a singing cheering collection of black and white teenagers," who embraced each other as they sang school songs. "You could just tell it was the beginning of a good feeling," one student explained. The *Charlotte Observer* reported that the effort also sought to return control of the school back to the staff and students. "Students stress that the main idea behind the rally was to show parents and plainclothes police who have patrolled the school for days that they could handle their problems," the paper reported.[25]

Throughout the rest of the school year, fights and boycotts would continue to periodically disrupt classes at a number of schools. But the majority of students worked to find a way forward. In the 1971 yearbook, West Charlotte students gamely summed up the most difficult year the school had ever experienced. "It is the dawn of a new era, and we, the sobered survivors of the turbulent sixties, are determined that the mistakes of that decade shall not reoccur," the introduction ran. "We have witnessed assassination, racial and political riots, and campus disruption; war, hate and a general lack of understanding have caused us to look twice at our values and our society. . . . Realizing that to change things for the better, everyone must do something, we, the staff of the W.C. *Lion*, would like to make a suggestion: COME TOGETHER. Where there is hate, why not put in a little love? Where there is war, peace; where there is misunderstanding, let us find tolerance. At first glance, that may seem simple enough, but it is really a tremendous task. It means giving of oneself, sharing with others, investigating the problems of our society . . . and finding workable solutions."[26]

A year of experience had given West Charlotte students a clear understanding of the depth of effort that would be required to move their city from the era of Jim Crow to a genuinely integrated world. The need to embark on those efforts gained urgency that April, when the Supreme Court threw its full support behind the *Swann* ruling. The landmark, unanimous decision termed James McMillan's demands "reasonable, feasible, and workable." Still, it would take political leaders considerably longer than students to come to terms with those requirements. Three more years of conflict and instability would pass before a group of citizens took matters into their own hands and found a way to bring the broader community together.

Crafting a full-scale busing plan was an ambitious and uncertain undertaking, one that involved far more than simply moving students from one school to another. It required, as one probusing group noted, "a radical rethinking of what our schools are all about and what we expect of them."[27] In white as well as black communities, schools had functioned as extensions of the particular communities they served, seeking to shape young people according to values and expectations shared by the families who lived near the school. Busing, in contrast, sought to use schools to break down divisions among communities, with the goal of building a more integrated and more equitable society. While McMillan's orders focused on righting racial wrongs, class was involved as well. The end of legal segregation had not meant the end of economic privilege, and many families with the means to choose their neighborhoods fought fiercely to keep their children in those protected enclaves.

Soon after McMillan's initial verdict, a group of suburban parents had worked with lawyer Robert Potter to draw up a petition that called on the school board to "impress upon the court the undesirable disruption to the

The first integrated staff of the West Charlotte *Lion. The Lion*, 1971.
Courtesy of the Robinson-Spangler Carolina Room.

living pattern of all citizens that would result in from requiring any student on a daily basis to be bused or otherwise transported to a school several miles from his home."[28] They continued to stress that theme in public meetings. "I am not opposed to integration in any way," a suburban father announced at one such event. "But I was 'affluent' enough to buy a home near the school where I wanted my children to go. And I pay taxes to pay for it. They can bring in anybody they like to that school, but I don't want my children taken away from there."[29]

As that comment made clear, open racial resistance of the kind that greeted Dorothy Counts at Harding High rarely surfaced in public debates over the busing plans. Rather, most opponents of McMillan's order sought to shift the discussion from the ground of racial justice to that of individual rights — arguing that the push for racial integration should not override individual choices about which neighborhoods to live in and thus which schools children would attend. This approach allowed for some one-way busing of black children to white schools and neighborhoods, but opposed two-way busing, which would also send white children into black schools and neighborhoods. It was warmly supported by President Richard Nixon, who had made opposition to "forced busing" a key component of his 1968 presidential campaign, and who continued to argue against it from the White House.[30]

The political and economic power wielded by well-off whites, along with concerns that they would turn to the county's growing array of private schools, made school board members reluctant to bus children out of those neighborhoods. Those concerns had shaped the 1970–71 plan, which relied heavily on one-way busing of black children to historically white schools. When McMillan demanded reductions in one-way busing, the board focused the bulk of two-way busing on working-class white neighborhoods north and west of town. Under those plans, some black children were scheduled to be bused away from home for all twelve years of their schooling and white children from the north and west were bused for as many as eight years. White children in some southeastern neighborhoods, including the old-wealth communities of Eastover and Myers Park, were hardly bused at all.[31]

The blatant racial and class inequality of this strategy kept city politics in turmoil and the school system in court. It was difficult to leave the system — the 1960 consolidation of city and county schools meant that in Charlotte, unlike in Atlanta, Richmond, or Boston, families who wanted to escape busing had to move not simply to the suburbs, but out of the county altogether. Instead, white families seeking to avoid the plan did their best to move to southeastern neighborhoods — a process that further reduced the number of whites living on the west side. The shifting population increased the assignment churn, forcing the school system to scramble to maintain the required racial balance at all the system's schools.[32]

Building community tensions over changing assignments, as well as over the stark inequities in busing requirements, continued to spill over into the schools. Throughout the period, fights and other disturbances periodically disrupted instruction, further heightening anxieties and discontent. Students and teachers sat tight. "Black kids stayed with black kids and white kids stayed with the white kids. That was pretty much it," explained Agnes Alexander, who arrived at West Charlotte in the fall of 1971. "Anything you had to do when you got to choose your group — you always chose the people that you were the most comfortable with, which would be the black people."

Maintaining racial balance at West Charlotte posed a particularly thorny problem. Black students whose families had strong West Charlotte ties often found ways to attend the school, even when they lived in areas assigned to other schools. "I just happened to move in with my aunt," future West Charlotte basketball coach Gosnell White recalled of his own family's efforts to ensure that he attended his father's alma mater. White families who wanted to keep their children at more familiar schools, or who worried about sending them into African American neighborhoods, engaged in similar maneuvers. Many white families assigned to West Charlotte chafed at the assignment, not only because they were reluctant to send children to a formerly black school in an African American neighborhood, but also because the white neighborhoods that sat closest to the school were precisely those southeastern neighborhoods that the school board stubbornly refused to bus. In the fall of 1971, more than half of the white students assigned to West Charlotte failed to show up.[33]

The result was constant shifts in the neighborhoods and students assigned to the school, making stability especially elusive. "Every year there was a different assignment of students," Gerson Stroud explained. "And you had to change everything. It was just like starting over every year." Students vented their frustrations in the spring of 1974. "Can West Charlotte survive?" they asked. "For four years we have gone through proposals, plans, and pupil assignments. . . . How long can students be dealt like cards?"[34]

One of the school board's responses to the challenge of getting white students to attend West Charlotte involved assigning fewer students to the school. In 1971–72 and 1972–73, the school operated at two-thirds of capacity. In the spring of 1973, the school board proposed to reduce the school's population to less than 1,000 students, a move that would have sharply reduced course offerings as well as the school's ability to effectively compete with larger high schools in sports and academic events. Assignment expert John Finger privately suggested that the best way to solve the problem would be to close West Charlotte. McMillan, however, rejected the idea, and issued a forceful order that highlighted the board's attack on the school.

"West Charlotte, so far as the evidence shows, has competent teachers and staff, and many students have undergone a very satisfactory educational experience there," the judge wrote. "This has been against considerable odds, because the evidence strongly suggests that West Charlotte is still thought of by some of the [school board members] as a 'black' school and therefore its $3 million plant ought to be closed for conventional high school use as soon as the court will allow it." He continued, "From the beginning of the desegregation program the student population of West Charlotte has been maintained in an atmosphere of 'brinkmanship'; the school each summer is 'projected' to have a proposed black population; somehow, many of the whites 'projected' to be assigned do not arrive or are allowed to transfer and the school population hovers throughout the year at or close to the 50 percent mark and in Mecklenburg County at this stage of desegregation this produces an unstable and impermanent atmosphere."[35]

The board heeded McMillan's warning and modified the plan, assigning a group of randomly chosen students from southeastern neighborhoods to West Charlotte. In February of 1974, however, members suddenly changed direction. A group of parents and school administrators had been working to create an "open school" that would allow students to pursue individual educational interests, with an emphasis on collaboration, inquiry, and hands-on activities. The open program, which would become Charlotte-Mecklenburg's first "magnet" offering, was designed to run from elementary through high school. Despite questions about how much demand the program would generate, the school board tentatively approved a plan to turn West Charlotte into an "open" high school that would enroll only open-school students.[36]

That move heightened fears that West Charlotte's days were numbered, and west side residents took immediate action. Within a few days, they had met with key officials, gathered 3,000 petition signatures, and organized a march from Beatties Ford Road to the next board meeting. Amid the strains and uncertainty of the desegregation struggle, the action stood out as exhilarating. "The black community rallied like I had never seen it before," Stan Frazier noted. "They did petitions, they talked. . . . Churches got together and talked about it publicly. It was one of the few times I saw the black community just really get together and say 'enough is enough. You did this to Second Ward. You will not close this school.'" Young and old joined in. "It was my first civil rights protest," recalled Latrelle Peeler McAllister, a West Charlotte sophomore who lived directly across from the school. "We have pictures of us marching up Beatties Ford Road. It was the whole community that gathered around, and the House of Prayer's church band came. We all gathered to rally around our neighborhood school."[37]

Five years earlier, equally dramatic protests had not saved Second Ward.

West Charlotte's supporters march to save their school, 1974. Courtesy of the
Robinson-Spangler Carolina Room and the *Charlotte Observer*.

But times had changed. At the start of the school board meeting, superintendent Rolland Jones announced that he was withdrawing the open school
proposal because the outpouring of community opposition would render it
unworkable. His frustration, and that of the board members, was obvious.
At the end of what the *Observer* described as "a rambling speech of educational philosophies," Jones labeled the concern that West Charlotte might be
closed as "paranoia" and gave the gathered crowd a lecture. "The paranoia
and racism of the black members of our school family are no more defensible
than the racism and paranoia of the white members of our school family," he
said, claiming that African Americans were overly focused on past wrongs
and that "at some point we need to forgive and forget all the old grudges."
A "dumbfounded" board then voted 5–3 to scrap the open school idea. Although McMillan's deadline for filing the next year's assignment plan was
only days away, members could not agree on an alternative.[38]

In the end, the task of coming to terms with McMillan's ruling would
fall to a different group of residents. The pressure of McMillan's order, which
gained added weight from the Supreme Court affirmation, had begun to
forge a new coalition among black and white residents in the neighborhoods

most affected by the busing plans. As school board members argued, these parents were creating new connections at their newly integrated schools. They were also discussing their dissatisfaction with the glaring inequalities in the assignment plans—the school board's reluctance to bus white children out of wealthy southeastern neighborhoods continued to intensify the amount of busing required of African American communities and of less-affluent white communities in the north and west. By the fall of 1973, these common concerns had prompted the formation of an organization named the Community Advisory Group (CAG), which brought together community leaders that ranged from longtime civil rights leader Kelly Alexander and steel company executive Jim Postell to young mother Maggie Ray.[39]

The women who organized the group started the first meeting with a potluck supper, reckoning that "southerners were always more civil over dinner."[40] Participants came from all parts of the county and from many points on the political spectrum. The first meeting seemed promising, and a group of the participants began to come together weekly, looking for common ground. As they got to know each other, it became easier to pursue the process that West Charlotte students had recommended back in 1971: "giving of oneself, sharing with others, investigating the problems of our society . . . and finding workable solutions." Despite their disagreements, Maggie Ray later noted, participants "all had the good of their children at heart, and we held on to that, and that kept us together." There was also a strong practical incentive: "Everybody was sick of having to change schools every year."[41] The CAG presented its first outline for a new assignment plan in February of 1974, at the same meeting when the school board gave tentative approval to the West Charlotte open school proposal. After the open school idea fell apart, the CAG intensified its efforts.

By then, growing numbers of area residents were determined to reach a solution. Chamber of Commerce leaders, who realized that racial strife and civic uncertainty were once again undercutting Charlotte's image as a progressive, forward-looking community, had begun to play a larger role in school affairs. In 1972 they had backed a group of probusing candidates that included entrepreneur C. D. Spangler Jr., who had helped his father build the University Park neighborhood back in the 1950s, and banker Phillip O. Berry, who became the first African American ever elected to the school board. These leaders openly encouraged the CAG's efforts.

In July of 1974, when the group presented the school board with its final plan, West Charlotte sat at the center. In a dramatic demonstration that southeastern families would do their part, the plan assigned several of the city's most prestigious white enclaves to the school. Even those residents most staunchly opposed to busing agreed the plan was fair. McMillan gave his approval, and the school board, with two dissenting votes, accepted it. After a carefully arranged series of meetings, so did most residents. When the buses rolled that fall, almost all of the white students assigned to West Charlotte arrived at its doors. Warnings that wealthy white families would flee the system in droves proved unfounded. A year later, McMillan would declare the effort a success and close the *Swann* case.[42]

The new plan brought yet another major change to West Charlotte — the school's first white principal. At the same time that the school board approved the plan, it replaced Gerson Stroud with Sam Haywood, the highly regarded leader of Independence High School. The *Observer* did not mince words when discussing Haywood's selection, calling it "aimed at least partially toward making the school more acceptable to white students."[43]

The board decided that West Charlotte would house a scaled-back version of the "open school" and allotted 300 seats for the program. In an immediate confirmation of Julius Chambers's calculation that only full desegregation would "accomplish equal educational programs," plans were made to upgrade the school's facilities. Within a year, West Charlotte boasted a new, paved parking lot for student cars, two new tennis courts, and a thoroughly refurbished interior. Classrooms, the yearbook reported, "were painted in varying shades of pastels, and any traces of 'institutional green' were obliterated from the interiors. . . . The library was considerably brightened by orange and green paint; soon after school began, carpet was installed adding to the comfort of the studious."[44]

"It took integration to get the parking lots paved," observed Gosnell White, who had graduated in 1973. "Those were gravel parking lots out there for all those years, and we had asked and asked for paved parking lots. Right in front of the gym, and where the students park now was rocks. And right there where the teachers park was rocks. And then I come back when I'm in college, we're one of the model schools and everything's paved, the office is immaculate. And I'm like, 'Well, what a difference a day makes.'"

The most striking demonstration of West Charlotte's transformation, however, took place just as the new plan went into effect. On September 2, 1974, Charlotte students headed back to school with minimal disruption. Several days later, students in Boston boarded buses to start that city's first year of full-scale, court-ordered busing. The violence that resulted dwarfed anything Charlotte had seen. Television cameras captured angry white residents pelting buses of black students with bricks, rocks, and racial slurs.

West Charlotte students welcome Boston students to the school.
Photograph by Elmer Horton, courtesy of the *Charlotte Observer*.

Banks of police officers on horseback and in riot gear recalled some of the most dramatic images of the southern civil rights struggles. A photo of a white teenager stabbing a black activist with a pole that carried an American flag spread around the world.[45]

The turmoil in Boston gave one of West Charlotte's new students an idea: to invite a group of Boston students to visit West Charlotte and see integration in action. The Bostonians accepted the offer, and in November 1974 five students from South Boston High spent a few days in Charlotte. The irony of a group of Northerners coming South to learn lessons in race relations was lost on no one, and a crush of reporters followed the students everywhere they went. Dealing with the attention was a challenge, Sam Haywood recalled, and the coverage sparked considerable hostility — "I think every KKK member in the South wrote me a personal letter calling me a nigger-lover and threatening me." But he was proud of his students. "We received publicity around the world," he noted. "I was proud that those kids were here and proud that our kids were doing it. . . . You know if adults had got out of the way, kids could solve most of the problems."[46]

For Charlotteans, that visit would solidify into an indelible memory, marking the city's dramatic transformation into a national model for effective integration. For African Americans, the central role played by West Charlotte brought additional satisfaction. Under segregation, West Charlotte had been a shining symbol of the ambition and determination of the city's African Americans. During the early, uncertain years of busing, when school board members refused to assign their neighbors to the school, and many white families resisted sending their children to the west side, supporters had worried that they might lose their beloved school altogether. The Boston visit inaugurated a new period, one in which West Charlotte High would become Charlotte's desegregation flagship, lauded around the nation as an example of a successfully integrated school in a successfully integrated city. "To me the most significant factor was the fact that they didn't think it could be done over here," said Gosnell White. "And here we became the model school. I remember the group from Boston coming here to see how we had done it—how we integrated our school in a black community, and people got along so well."

*BUILDING AN
INTEGRATED
SCHOOL*

"On a spring afternoon at West Charlotte High School, a trio of teenage girls — two black, one white — chatter aimlessly in the parking lot," the front page of the *Wall Street Journal* informed its readers in May of 1991. "Inside the building, a multiracial horticulture club decorates a foyer. The student executive committee, a warm picture of integrated young America, convenes in a nearby classroom. Te' Ali Coley, a black committee member of pro football proportions, delivers the party line: 'If you're racist when you come here, you have to change your ideas or put them under cover.'"[1]

By 1991, it came as no surprise that a front-page story on school desegregation would feature West Charlotte High. From the mid-1970s through the early 1990s, Charlotte-Mecklenburg Schools was the most desegregated major school system in the nation, and West Charlotte was its undisputed flagship. The school drew from a diverse array of neighborhoods that included black and white students from multiple economic backgrounds. Its English as a Second Language program, begun in 1980, enrolled students from three dozen different countries, including many refugees from the recently ended Vietnam War. The well-regarded "open education" program attracted families from across the county. This diversity of students came to share a powerful sense of identity based not on neighborhood or upbringing, but on a commitment to the school and what it stood for: what it meant to be a proud West Charlotte Lion.

"It was such a melting pot of Charlotte," recalled Latrelle McAllister. "We had people from all socioeconomic levels. We had students with all types of interests and orientations. We had some of the brightest students in the city and we had some of those students who had been identified as, actually, failing. We were all together in some form or fashion." As a result, she said, "there really wasn't a tolerance for anything other than working together." In 1985, yearbook editors described West Charlotte as a jigsaw puzzle, with school pride as the glue that brought pieces together. "A piece here. Another one there. Each student was an individual, a single piece of the giant puzzle that was West Charlotte," they wrote. "Each student felt free to be himself. When the time came, however, to show support for their school or help the community, students came together and made the pieces fit."[2] New students felt that spirit as soon as they walked onto school grounds. "Everybody got along," explained Mary Helms. "We all were there supporting each other. Ready to have fun together. You kind of pump your chest out a little bit. 'I'm a Lion.'"

Building an Integrated School

The efforts of West Charlotte's staff and students became part of a range of activities that sought to build on the movements of the 1960s, dismantling old hierarchies and assumptions and experimenting with new forms of interaction, organization, and expression. It was a time freighted with possibility. "When you think about it, most of us that grew up in the seventies were rebels anyway," explained Latrelle McAllister. "White students as well as black students were really at a time in the culture where doing something different was okay with them. That was the norm. The norm was to do something different. We grew up in the time of the streakers." That youthful energy spilled over into the classroom. "The great thing about teaching literature at West Charlotte was that you could teach ideas to these students," said Brian Tarr, who joined the English department in 1976. "They loved ideas. They loved new ideas. They loved perspectives different than their own."

Fashioning new institutions out of the wreckage of old ones required significant effort. At West Charlotte, students, staff, parents, and alumni all faced challenges—most notably building new kinds of relationships with new groups of people. Since no one had a roadmap, everyone had to pitch in. Their accomplishments showed the extent to which it was possible to realize the twin aims of the *Swann* lawsuit—equalizing resources and cementing ties among people from vastly different backgrounds. They showcased the dynamic energy created by such collaborative endeavors. They also underscored the extensive work required to build and maintain a genuinely integrated school in the midst of political, economic, and cultural change.

Building an integrated West Charlotte started with the staff—especially the efforts of the school's veteran black teachers. "That faculty was just so generous in their preparation for us," explained Patsy Sutherland, one of the many young, white teachers who started their careers at the school. "We had lots of meetings, lots of introduction to what the faculty expected, what the community was like." As Sutherland and her companions struggled through the challenges that all novice teachers faced, their senior colleagues were always ready to help. "There were so many really kind people who just daily would come to us. 'Are you doing OK?' 'Things OK?' 'Is there anything we can do for you?'" she recalled. "Just very helpful."

The veterans also inspired enormous respect. Becoming West Charlotte's principal, Sam Haywood said, was "probably the best thing that ever happened to me," because of what he learned from his staff. "They had some of the most outstanding black teachers at that school," he explained. "I would put them up against college professors. Strong teachers and strong people.

Good men, good women who really were role models for these kids."[3] It took Haywood some time to grasp the many responsibilities that came with being the first white principal at a historically black school. "I made some really big mistakes," he noted. But he was willing to listen, to recognize his own shortcomings, and to grow. He paid particular attention to counselor Marge Belton and to Mertye Rice, whom he would later describe as "probably the greatest teacher I have ever known in North Carolina." He and Rice cemented a lasting friendship. "I would say if anybody helped me to grow up it was probably Mertye Rice," he continued. "It's just kind of good to be close to people like that."[4]

Rice, who had been teaching at West Charlotte since 1954, epitomized the teaching excellence of the segregated era. "She taught you from the time you walked in the classroom until the time you left," recalled Kenneth Simmons. "You knew what to expect because her expectations were clear. You knew how to prepare, arrange yourselves, get ready. You knew how she was going to operate." She could stop a student with a glance. "She had a way of looking at you," Simmons continued. "She talked with her eyes. . . . And she was only that tall, and weighed 90 pounds, and could not have hurt a fly. But you felt it." She also knew how to show she cared: "You wanted her to be proud of you. If you did well, then she just laid it on. The love. I don't mean hugs and kisses, but there was another kind of approval."[5]

Rice was fiercely proud of West Charlotte's segregation-era accomplishments. When Sam Haywood became principal, he thought the school would be more "welcoming to all kids" if he removed the reminders of its African American history: the trophies and memorabilia that filled the lobby, as well as the photograph of Clinton Blake that hung outside the principal's office. As soon as Rice saw what he had done, she came to tell him he was wrong. "Mr. Haywood, I think you need to know that you need to put the picture back on the wall," he recalled her saying.[6]

At the same time, she was thoroughly committed to desegregation, believing it was "right by every measure of fairness and justice."[7] She embraced West Charlotte's new students and teachers, working with her classes and with the student government to make the school into a place where everyone could feel at home. "Students were students, and all of them were precious, and they could sense immediately that she felt that way," explained longtime colleague Elizabeth Randolph.[8] "She had a great way of getting people to do right and think beyond their old ways of doing things," noted Maggie Ray, who started teaching science at West Charlotte soon after the desegregation plan she helped to craft went into effect.

Mertye Rice and Sam Haywood in 1979, the year Rice was named Charlotte-Mecklenburg's Teacher of the Year. *The Lion*, 1982. Courtesy of the Robinson-Spangler Carolina Room.

The effective mix of young white teachers with older, more experienced African Americans made for a strong, supportive faculty culture. Eunice Pharr arrived at West Charlotte in the early 1970s, after her difficult stint at West Mecklenburg High. She found the school a joyful place. "Immediately, immediately, the atmosphere was different from any place that I had ever been," she explained. "The faculty bonded. We just worked with each other and we bonded. . . . I was so excited every morning when I got up to go. Some people said 'How can you come in every morning smiling and happy?' I said, 'I mean why couldn't you be coming over here?'" Sam Haywood felt a similar warmth. "It's just a place that I love," he explained.[9] Many teachers stayed fifteen years or more.

West Charlotte's parents, black and white, played key roles as well. Parents supported the integrated school for many reasons and in many ways. When Mary Helms's family moved from Florida to Charlotte, her mother deliberately chose a neighborhood that fed into West Charlotte. Her mother liked the school's academic reputation, Helms explained, but also recognized the limitations of the predominantly white private schools Helms and her siblings had previously attended: "She felt that after that cookie-cutter, vanilla experience in the private school, that we needed to branch out and really see what the real world is like." Amantha Barbee's father, who had taught biology at West Charlotte during segregation, always pressed her to broaden her horizons. "My father had a saying, and I carry it with me till today," she explained. "He said 'Amantha, there are many types of music in life. And you need to make sure that you can dance to everything that's being played.'" West Charlotte parents "were truly thinking outside the box," Barbee continued. "We're blessed that our parents were strong enough to see the importance of not just an academic education, but an education in life."

For African American parents, support for West Charlotte was undergirded by a sense of the school's symbolic significance. As Charlotte's only remaining historically black high school, West Charlotte embodied the abilities and achievements of the city's African Americans. Even as parents and alumni embraced the new white students, they saw the school's continuing success as a living link to the past, an affirmation that community accomplishments had lasting value. "It belongs to us," said Harriet Love, who sent both of her children to the alma mater she loved so well. "It belongs to the community. It belongs to the west side if they want to call it the west side. It's *West* Charlotte."

For many white parents, the crosstown bus rides their children took exemplified their commitment to public schools. Mary Lou Babb, who sent three children from Eastover to West Charlotte, recalled a meeting at Christ Episcopal Church that took place soon after Eastover parents learned that the 1974 desegregation plan had assigned their children to the school. "There were a lot of people that were angry. All of us were angry to begin with, I suppose, because we didn't know what to expect," Babb explained. But the families also understood that their participation was critical to the success of the busing plan, and thus to the school system as a whole. Although many could have paid for private school, most decided to put their children on the bus. "Practically everybody had grown up in the public school system and they didn't want to abandon it," Babb said.

The influx of some of the city's wealthiest families had notable effects, underscoring Julius Chambers's argument that schools would only be equal if they all enrolled parents with political clout. Well-off parents pitched in on all the nuts-and-bolts activities they were accustomed to supporting: raising funds, helping out in classrooms, volunteering for school events. They also brought their influence to bear in other ways. One year, for example, English teacher Betty Seizinger was assigned a trailer classroom with a portable air conditioner. She soon began feeling ill. "I had headaches all day," she explained. "My eyes were stinging, my throat was kind of hurting. I would have to come home and just kind of crash and take a bath. And I thought 'Gee, I wonder if this is bad air?'" She requested an inspection, but got no action. Finally, she decided to broach the issue with her varsity debate team, which included several students from prominent families. "I am having real trouble here," she recalled saying. "And while you all are at your parents' dinner table . . . I want you to tell them that Mrs. Seizinger, if she dies, is going to sue big time — now don't laugh. And that something has to be done." The response was immediate. "The next morning before my class started, it was taken care of."

Parents' efforts included careful oversight of West Charlotte's leadership. When Bill McMillan was named principal in 1978, one of his first invitations was to another meeting at Christ Episcopal. "My area superintendent had called some people together because they wanted to meet me," he said. "I think it was all because 'Who is this fellow? Is he the person who ought to be leading our children?' We had a good number of parents there that day and some who were not even parents but were members of that church. All of them asked me questions. I talked to them about what I was expecting. We talked about goals and I talked about the environment — I talked about what I expected out of teachers, what I expected out of students and the kind of organization I wanted to be a part of."

West Charlotte's multiple constituencies, as well as its high profile in the desegregation plan, kept the school at the top of district priorities. Jay Robinson, who became superintendent in 1977, proved especially adept at managing the system's racial complexities, and he was keenly aware that black support for the busing plan depended in part on the continuing success of the beloved and highly symbolic school.[10] District leaders also knew that prominent white families would only send their children to West Charlotte if it offered a top-quality education at every level. That awareness gave West Charlotte principals a good deal of clout. Whenever McMillan thought West Charlotte needed something, whether a larger library, a stronger drama program, more science equipment, or a swimming pool, he generally met with a favorable reaction: "If you could give good evidence that West Charlotte needed it, West Charlotte got it."

These efforts created a vibrant, nurturing environment for students. The school was a whirlwind of activity. Some endeavors had deep roots in the school's history, such as the service-oriented Key Club, the NAACP, and the famed marching band. Others were new, among them the ski club and the soccer team. Students from the open program, who took both standard and open classes, added a distinctive spark. The program's innovative curriculum, which began in elementary school, attracted a lively, multiracial group of families and produced students who were always looking for new ideas and new forms of expression. West Charlotte students attended football games, looked forward to homecoming, and headed downtown to watch the band delight the crowds at the Thanksgiving parade. They joined the Rubik's Cube craze, played video games with names like *Pac-Man*, *Space Invaders*, and *Donkey Kong*, and marveled at the advent of cable television, which offered temptations like ESPN and MTV. "We were allowed to be teenagers," Latrelle McAllister noted.

As teenagers, they pushed boundaries where they could, especially in desegregation's early years. When McMillan became principal, he quickly determined that while black and white students got on just fine, the school was lagging academically. "The mix, I think, was wonderful," he explained. "Students got along well, black and white, they even cut up together. They cut up so much together when I had to suspend some I had to suspend both blacks and whites." But getting along did not always include going to class together—or going at all. Students often left the campus for lunch, and sometimes did not return. They did not worry about being late to class: "When the bell rang you had 500 still laying around outside." In addition, a number of the open school students "felt that being an open school meant that if I wanted to lie under a tree and commune with nature, that's all right."

McMillan went to work. He required students to stay on campus during lunch. He set up phone brigades to inform parents if their children missed class. He exhorted students at every turn. "They had a slogan back then: 'We're Number One and Don't You Forget It,'" he explained. "I wanted them to live up to that, so I repeated that slogan every day on the intercom. . . . You tell them enough, you treat them that way, they act that way."

West Charlotte regained ground athletically as well. Charles McCullough and his basketball teams had struggled through the years of student churn, forcing him to fall back on the advice of his old mentor, who knew all about doing more with less. "We had Jack Martin and he knew how to handle those kind of things," McCullough explained. "You control what you can control, and find a way. . . . We were in shape. We ran and ran and ran and ran and ran. And we competed. We were in the game most of the way. And if you stay in the game, every once in a while you're going to surprise somebody." When the student body stabilized, those methods once again began to pile up victories. McCullough guided his team to an unbeaten season and a state championship in 1986, and then to back-to-back state championships in 1991 and 1992.

The school also rebuilt its performing arts programs. McMillan was able to lure band director Marvin Davenport from Johnson C. Smith and to hire Frank Williams, "the best choral music person this city had ever had." Director and playwright Charles LaBorde was hired to build a top-flight drama department. "They truly were looking for strong programs across the board that would attract everyone," LaBorde said. "We set out to create the best program there was in town and without a doubt it was."[11]

Whether in English or biology, theater or basketball, teachers made it clear that success came through discipline and hard work. "We were teaching them about discipline and pride in what you're doing," LaBorde noted of his award-winning dramatic productions.[12] Students responded. "We were going to work twice as hard to be the best," Mary Helms recalled. "We put our hearts and souls into everything we did." By the time that future Charlotte mayor Anthony Foxx arrived as a sophomore in the fall of 1986, that multifaceted pride had become an institution, passed down from one generation of students to another. "The special feeling of pride and community and unity that I think we built was integrated almost from the very beginning," recalled Foxx, who grew up in his grandparents' home in the nearby Dalebrook neighborhood. "I remember having an assembly with the sophomore class and the seniors would tell us: 'Look, this is what we do at West Charlotte, we do well in school, we do well on the field, we do this that and the other and that's what you guys are going to have to do.' It was all very matter of fact, but that's what we began to believe. You felt a sense of obligation to continue that."

West Charlotte sophomores cheer at a pep rally. *The Lion*, 1985.
Courtesy of the Robinson-Spangler Carolina Room.

Faculty members passed their culture on as well. "They more or less in a subtle way gave you an orientation as to what West Charlotte was all about," explained Barbara Ledford, who became principal in 1989. "And each of us — when you came new, myself included — was familiarized through very informal ways, but very direct ways, as to say this is the way we do it at West Charlotte. This is the way that we treat people at West Charlotte." When English teacher Robert Yost arrived at the school and started a chess team, he was inspired by his colleagues' accomplishments. "As I became acquainted with the history of West Charlotte, it really kind of gave me a sense of pride to do something that had never been done here before," he said. "So even though we had reputations in different areas, now we were building a reputation for chess." He and the football coach began to egg each other on: "Who's going to win the first state championship?"

Part of their success, staff and students regularly reminded themselves, came because they had learned how to work together. Nearly every yearbook opened with a celebration of the school's diversity, casting it as West Charlotte's greatest strength. In 1984, for example, editors lauded the way that students "from virtually every economic, cultural and ethnic background ... respected each other's differences and learned from them as well. The strong bonds that were created made for a closer-knit student body and thus provided for an atmosphere of excellence. The unity and excellence that West Charlotte projected set the pace for other schools to try to match."[13]

Building an Integrated School

Rather than plunging into a melting pot, however, the many different students at West Charlotte created intricate cultural designs. Although
Charlotte-Mecklenburg schools were desegregated, most students continued to live in neighborhoods divided by race and class.[14] These variations,
combined with the racial and class divides that continued to shape American
popular culture, produced a clearly identifiable set of social clusters. Seating patterns during lunchtime often reflected racial and class differences, as
did the makeup of some sports teams and after-school activities. Yearbook
editors gave the distinctions a humorous spin in 1982, when they chronicled
"several basic groups, each with their own distinctive customs."[15]

One set, "with the alligator as a mascot, gossiped and bopped their way
from September till June. Bass Weejuns treading hallowed ground, khakis,
and pink-and-green were universal symbols of this group," editors wrote,
noting that such students also favored "beach music, the Kinks and the Drift-
ers." Another group "displayed the rebel cause on their shirts and blasted out
fiery music. 'Did you know AC/DC is comin' to Charlotte?' shouted a heavily
southern-accented voice as Molly Hatchet blared out of the speakers of his
pickup truck." A third "rode the soul train," and "turned a plain brick wall in
the lobby into 'the' wall in a matter of seconds. It became a standard meeting place for students to 'jam their boxes' at maximum level. . . . Pointed-toe
shoes, huge radios and a variety of hats made some in this group a unique
aspect of the school."

Still, as West Charlotte students explored the questions of identity that
formed such a significant component of adolescent life, the combination of
diversity and openness allowed them to step into a wide variety of roles, create a broad range of relationships, and take in multiple experiences from dif-
fering perspectives. Because the school drew on so many different communities, students felt a degree of freedom when they arrived—they were not
locked into the roles they had held in junior high school. The population's
diversity expanded their options. "We had such a socioeconomic diversity;
we had poor white children and middle-class white children and rich white
children, and we had poor black children and middle-class black children
and quite a few debutantes, so we had well-to-do black families involved,"
explained Maggie Ray. "And then we had the ESL group, which were at that
time just newly escaped from horrible violence. These refugees were there,
and we had our hippie group there, which was nicely racially mixed; the dra-
matists and the people who could read tarot cards and all that stuff. . . . Anybody you wanted to be you could be, and you could try it out."

Students devised strategies for encouraging each other to step outside

West Charlotte's 1982 yearbook described social groups that included "free-spirited non-preps" (above) and those who "rode the soul train" (opposite). *The Lion*, 1982. Courtesy of the Robinson-Spangler Carolina Room.

of boundaries, employing humor as well as serious discussion. The student council, for example, introduced new students to the school through a playful skit. "The white students in the student government would be on the beach playing and sun tanning and having their shades on," Ray explained. "Then they would close the curtain and then open the curtain, and there'd be all the black students as if it were the same people with this wonderful tan, thirty minutes later. So that sort of set the tone for the whole year, that we have different skin colors and we can laugh about this."

As the skit suggested, students made a concerted effort not to automatically define themselves or others by race or other characteristics. Differences became something to learn from, not to exploit or resent. "We all knew everything about each other. And that included economically," explained Amantha Barbee. "But that just didn't matter. . . . We knew who was driv-

Building an Integrated School

ing the Mercedes to school, but who cares?" Classmate Tammy Hill echoed that sentiment. "I grew up very poor," she said. "Very, very poor. My mom had a third-grade education. But it didn't bother me being poor because nobody picked on me. My sister and I, we joke to this day and time, we grew up so poor, and we really didn't realize we were that poor. At that school we blended in with everybody. We didn't feel like outcasts. I loved it."

While some students stuck with their own neighborhoods or ethnic groups; others branched out. "If I was interested in the arts, for instance, then there were folks that were interested in theater and dance and music. They were more likely to form a clique or a group. More so than a black-white type thing," said Tim Gibbs. "Everyone came from different backgrounds, but once you got to West Charlotte it was like everyone was on equal ground," echoed Emille Pharr-Smith. "At some schools you feel like you have to put up a front in order to fit in," student body president Jamie Boyer told a reporter in 1988. "Here, you feel like somebody for what you really are."[16]

Teachers were as diverse as their students. Maggie Ray, who taught in the open program, had a relaxed style that included sitting cross-legged on her desktop. English teacher Thelma Funderburk, in contrast, stressed discipline and order. "I had Maggie Ray, who was this free spirit, and I had Ms. Funderburk, who was the strictest teacher I think I had in high school," explained future city councilman David Howard, who arrived at the school in 1983 for his senior year. "You came in before the bell rang, you sat down, you had to have your pad out, your pencil to the left. . . . You did not speak in her class without raising your hand. I mean just very, very, very strict rules. And I loved her class. So it was a range of people that made sure that everybody there was going to be a success."

Staff created an intricate web of relationships with their diverse group of students. Latrelle McAllister felt a vivid connection with the past when her father, who had graduated from the school three decades earlier, took her to see counselor Marjorie Belton. "I was a very shy teenager," she recalled. "I had my father walk me to school the first day. He took my hand and placed it in Ms. Belton's hand. That was a very historic moment, but the symbolism went further than that. She took his gesture of entrusting me to her very seriously." Elliott Hipp, who came to West Charlotte from Myers Park that same year, felt Belton's warmth as well. The shock of venturing outside of his protective community was so great that at first he doubted he would last the year. Belton helped him through. "She was my best friend, she had taken me under her wing, she trusted me, she supported me," he explained. "I felt like she was paying attention to nobody in the entire school but me. And I'm sure that everybody else in the sophomore class felt exactly the same way, because that's the kind of person she was."

Students and teachers created a multiplicity of cross-racial relationships. Amantha Barbee took her first history class with Carol Poole, one of the young white teachers who had come to the school in the 1970s. "I was the worst history student on the planet," Barbee explained. "And she called me in at the end of the semester and she said, 'You know what. I know your parents. And I know they would kill you if I wrote your real grade on this report card. But I need you to make a commitment to me, outside of this paperwork, that you're going to work with me. And we're going to get you where you need to be.'" The two women began to meet one-on-one, and the lessons Poole planned went well beyond the standard history curriculum. "She said:

Building an Integrated School

'You are a college-bound black woman who knows nothing about your own history, because we don't teach it. So I am going to teach it to you.' That's the kind of teacher this young, white woman was."

Deacon Jones watched his daughter develop relationships that reminded him of his own high school days. "I saw teachers—I don't really know if I'd call them teachers," he explained. "Life friends. I saw my daughter develop relationships that changed her life. And I saw her change for the positive for having gone to West Charlotte. I saw people reach out and touch her in ways she needed that her mother and I couldn't reach. And they were there. Caring, supportive, no different than they did for me. Different people, different faces. But no difference. And there was this pride, even with my daughter, about the school song. We were a part of a special family. It caused her to open up and want to learn."

When *Charlotte Observer* reporters examined the city's high schools in 1988, they cited the diversity of West Charlotte's student body as one of the school's main sources of success. The series introduced the issue of class into the desegregation plan, highlighting the struggles of schools that met the plan's racial requirements, but that enrolled particularly large numbers of disadvantaged students. West Charlotte stood out as an exception. While the school had the fourth-highest percentage of low-income students in the system, it offered the widest range of high school courses, and had little trouble retaining top-flight teachers. The multiple successes of the diverse group of students—whether in science, drama, athletics, or other areas—lifted everyone. Despite West Charlotte's relatively high poverty numbers, for example, it had the system's second-lowest dropout rate. "There is an atmosphere of achievement that becomes quite contagious," commented principal Lewis Lane.[17]

As Mertye Rice and Marge Belton had known, part of the strength of West Charlotte's new culture came from pride in the school's African American history. For black students from longtime West Charlotte families, that history served as a source of pleasure and support. Harriet Love's son John Love Jr. had grown up surrounded by reminders of the school and its accomplishments. When he arrived at West Charlotte, learning from teachers who had taught his parents fostered joy and pride. "We knew that we were a part of a legacy that we actually wanted to be a part of, and it was very exciting," he explained. "There was pride about being African American and going to the school. . . . The vibe of West Charlotte is really about pride, and it's about a real sense of pride. It's about a sense of belonging, a real sense of belonging. It's about a real sense of ownership in something in your community."

English as a Second Language students, 1986. *The Lion*, 1986.
Courtesy of the Robinson-Spangler Carolina Room.

Black families from other places also felt that connection. Asheville's
Stephens Lee High School had been a rival of West Charlotte in the days
of segregation. When Stephens Lee graduates James and Barbara Ferguson
enrolled their children at West Charlotte, their experience underscored that
shared history. "There was an atmosphere, an ambiance that made African
American students feel at home," James Ferguson observed. "It made them
feel a part of history. . . . It was some sense of unspoken pride that black students didn't feel like they had to be uprooted and taken away from home

Building an Integrated School

and put in a white school in order to have a school that they could take some real pride in."

The history of West Charlotte's African American era was carefully kept alive by the West Charlotte National Alumni Association. The Association formed in 1981, a time when the television series *Roots* had inspired widespread interest in black history, and when many of the school's early graduates were starting to retire and look for new activities. "The devotion, love, respect and appreciation for the nucleus which shaped their lives drove many to a desire of supporting and continuing to illuminate the excellence of West Charlotte High School," an Association history noted.[18] Alumni Association members adopted the motto "Reviewing the Past, Living the Present, Reflecting the Future," and became a familiar presence at the school. They established a Clinton L. Blake scholarship, awarded every year to "a worthy and needy West Charlotte High School graduating senior" who "represents Principal Blake's legacy of academic excellence."[19] They mentored students, volunteered at school events, donated to fundraisers, and funded a local public television documentary, *The Mighty Lions*, that chronicled the school's history.

White students developed their own appreciation of the school's past. Carrie Abramson recalled the pleasure she felt sitting at homecoming games surrounded by fans who had graduated decades before. "There was such a swell of support at homecoming from all of the community around, and so many people—and it was much more of an African American event," Abramson said. "The community was really there, and the community was definitely more African American than it was white." Still, she continued, she felt entirely at home. "It was a sense of pride in the school," she explained. "Everybody shared that and everybody smiled at each other and everybody was excited and we all cheered together and we all said the same cheers. They knew all the same cheers we knew." The experience deepened her appreciation of the school's significance. "I was proud of the fact that people still came to the football games," she continued. "I was proud of the fact that people still came and still supported the school and the team and were so involved in what went on there."

At a time when the dynamic cultural energy that sprang from the civil rights movement had infused American popular culture with new rhythms, images, and forms of expression, white students also reveled in the distinctively black style of West Charlotte's cheerleaders and band, which emphasized connections between performers and spectators. "That was the core of the culture," said Elliot Hipp. "It was go to football games, sing and dance with the band, yell and scream with the cheers. One of the dances was the Bump, and we were all standing in the stands doing the Bump, and it was really cool. It was the heart of the school. . . . It was something they never would have done at Myers Park and it was ours for our school." Anna Spangler Nelson concurred. "They were the jivingest cheerleaders in the country," she said. "They were loose, they were fun. They were great dancers. And truly their passion showed through. . . . A lot of dipping and bending and kind of grooving — I know those words are outdated, but at the time that was kind of the thing. And we just had great pride in all of that."[20]

Brian Tarr's son Jeremy fell in love with the West Charlotte band at an early age. "The West Charlotte marching band was the best thing in the world, the drum line," he explained. "To go and to hear the bass drum in your heart just beating. It was so loud. There was this energy, and everybody was so excited. I always wanted to be around that, and I always wanted to be a part of it, because I had this dream of being in the marching band when I got old enough. That's why I started playing saxophone in fifth grade because I wanted to be in the West Charlotte band." When Tarr reached high school, band director Marvin Davenport became a cherished mentor, musically and otherwise. "I learned life lessons from Mr. Davenport," he explained. "He was a total role model. I could talk with him about things and he would talk with me about whatever I wanted to talk about."

Still, experiences at the school also highlighted the challenges of overcoming centuries of white supremacy. Most of Charlotte's white residents had never ventured onto the west side, and had grown up surrounded by a culture that portrayed African Americans as inferior to whites. As a result, the red brick homes and well-kept streets that surrounded West Charlotte were an impressive and sometimes surprising sight to the school's white families. "They had a great facility and it was in a nice area," said Mary Lou Babb. "Most of us had never been over there, but it was a very nice area." Saundra Davis, who lived just a few blocks from the school, saw bringing white Charlotteans to West Charlotte as an essential part of breaking down racial stereotypes. Many of Charlotte's white residents thought the school was "rowdy and down class" because they "just had the wrong concept about black people on the whole," she surmised. "I think that's the whole thing in a nutshell. They had one concept of black people. Everybody is not the same, and they had to come to realize that."

More than a decade later, Jade Harris ran into similar assumptions when she was hired to teach history and government in the open program. She

Members of the sophomore council ride through west side streets in West Charlotte's homecoming parade. *The Lion*, 1989. Courtesy of the Robinson-Spangler Carolina Room.

loved her open-school classes. "Just the creativity," she explained. "It was very project-based and the kids could just be free to think. Cooperative learning could really be cooperative learning." But she also felt she had to prove herself. It had been several years since West Charlotte had hired a black history teacher, "and here I just show up. And that was a bit of a challenge. Because you still had some parents: 'I don't mind my child being at West Charlotte. But I don't know that I want my child to have a black teacher while at West Charlotte.' So I did meet that. . . . I guess they just had to get used to having a person of color, a brown face, in front of you teaching U.S. history, teaching government and law."

As Harris's experiences suggested, racial stereotypes continued to run strong in the broader community. For all of West Charlotte students' accomplishments, the school's African American history, combined with its location in an urban black neighborhood, meant it walked a fine line in terms of public perception. As in the busing plan's early days, keeping the required percentage of non-black students at the school required ongoing efforts by school system administrators. Charles LaBorde's wife worked at the central office, and often fielded calls from parents wanting to transfer students who had been assigned to the school, telling her that "they have fights up there all the time and you know what it's like, it's not safe." [21] The ESL program that added so much to the school's sense of diversity had in fact been placed at West Charlotte in part to ease those pressures — the desegregation plan required balancing the ratios of black and nonblack students at every school, and ESL students conveniently counted as nonblack.

Some of these challenges surfaced in March of 1980, when the *Charlotte Observer* published a front-page article titled "Waning Image Threatens School That Made Desegregation Work." The article noted that West Charlotte was 49 percent black, the highest percentage in the system, and that a number of white families had expressed concerns both about that ratio and about the number of prominent positions — principal, football coach, basketball coach, band director — held by African Americans. "Simply stated, some white parents are alarmed by the climbing percentage of blacks," the article continued. "They say West Charlotte is regaining a reputation as a 'black' high school and becoming a place where whites feel like outsiders." Students at some of the junior highs that fed the school talked about "West Chocolate" and "Hershey High" and circulated stories about unruly students and inferior teachers.[22]

West Charlotte's students and staff responded forcefully, defending their school and demanding that superintendent Jay Robinson publicly condemn the article. Inside school walls, students and teachers banded together. "We used to laugh," explained Bill McMillan. "I would say, 'They're on the outside and they want what you have, and that's the only reason they're doing this — because they want what you have. We're number one and don't you forget it.'" Brian Tarr, who lived near a number of the families who avoided the school, took a philosophical perspective. "You realize that the people who don't want diversity are the ones who are missing out," he explained. "Life is so much more rich because of diversity. And, you know, we finally got to the point at West Charlotte where at least I would say: 'Well, those white folks who don't want to come to West Charlotte, that's their problem. It's not our problem. They're the ones who are missing out.'"

Even West Charlotte's strong school spirit did not make balancing the school's many groups and interests a simple task. In oral history interviews, students and staff talked warmly of unity and connections but also stressed the challenges they faced. Brian Tarr, who found working at the school so invigorating, described his experience as both a great joy and an ongoing struggle. "It's hard work, getting along with people who are different," he said. "It's no different I guess than any other relationship. It's just real hard

Building an Integrated School

work. One's feelings are going to be hurt. One will make mistakes and feel terribly guilty. There'll be successes too. But it's just hard work. . . . Just because you want to do it doesn't mean it's going to be easy."[23]

"Oftentimes it was a bit of a battle," explained John Love Jr. "And it was about standing up for what your culture is, or what it is that you believe, or your way of doing things, or you and your friends' way of doing things, without apology." He pointed to a senior class debate over graduation invitations, in which a white student summed up her position by saying: "Well I just think we should go with something more traditional." His reply invoked a broader picture. "My response was: 'In whose tradition?'" he explained. "Because it was that whole thing about the assumption that this white Anglo Saxon Protestant aesthetic is the tradition for all. And so we were sort of on it enough and savvy enough to say: 'No no no no no. There are other traditions, what are you talking about?'"

One of Bill McMillan's greatest challenges was getting more African Americans into higher-level classes — an endeavor that required working both with the teachers who served as gatekeepers and with students and families. When McMillan arrived at the school, black students filled the ranks of the band and the high-profile sports teams, and took prominent roles in student government and other activities. But he thought too many were setting their academic sights too low, and that teachers were not always pushing them to aim higher. While better-off black students flocked to higher-level classes, many others clustered on the lower rungs. In 1980–81, for example, only 15 percent of the school's black eleventh graders were enrolled in one of the top two English levels, as opposed to 34 percent of white students.[24]

McMillan saw the divide as a clear reflection of the city's segregated past. Assumptions about white supremacy remained embedded in the system, he noted, and some teachers had to be persuaded to take a chance on black students whose abilities were not immediately obvious. Some black students also lacked confidence. "Segregation was a success in that it made a lot of people feel inferior and not want to strive or not want to seek the higher levels of success," he said. He understood that phenomenon well — although he had been a well-regarded student and teacher in Charlotte's segregated schools, he had not been sure that he could measure up to whites until he entered graduate school. "I went to UNC Charlotte and discovered that whites were not the most knowledgeable people," he explained. "Whites didn't necessarily have all the answers; blacks had them also." He pushed students toward the same realization: "I wanted my students to have that, to get in and maybe find out that you can succeed." He held numerous meetings with students, with their families, and with teachers, urging the students to take on more challenging classes and pressing teachers to work with them.

Making sure that activities involved a broad range of participants could also require deliberate efforts on the part of staff and students. "I remember being on the sophomore class council," Carrie Abramson explained. "Having discussions around planning events, and planning parties, and things like that for the class. . . . I remember in that context there being a lot of discussions around how can we get people to interact, and how can we sort of break down some of those barriers." Those discussions could be uneasy. "It wasn't always comfortable, for me anyway, to acknowledge the fact that there was tension there — admitting that you didn't all know each other and that there was separation," she continued. "So I wasn't always comfortable with that. But it was a reality. I think it was something people understood was true, and we did try very hard to create opportunities for people to get to know each other and to remove some of those barriers."

While Robert Yost's chess club drew a diverse group from the start, Betty Seizinger found she needed to make extra efforts to recruit African American students to the debate club. "I would just have two or three and the team kept getting bigger and bigger and I said, 'Why aren't I getting black students to come in? What is going on here?'" she explained. Eventually, she "realized that I had to approach the most respected black English teachers who taught tenth and eleventh grade and encourage students to take debate. And in fact I asked for time to have some of my students come in and explain what was going on in debate and how it really wasn't that hard and after Mrs. Seizinger made you learn how to do debate you could do all of these other forensic events." The efforts paid off. "After two more years I had forty percent blacks," she noted. Once the students began to work together, they developed close connections. "I had many many of the students become very good friends through debate," she continued. "So I know that it can work, but I also know that if you don't go out there and do it yourself it is not going to happen."

Some gaps did not close. After school, most students headed back to segregated neighborhoods. Some activities proved more difficult to integrate than others, and some students found the process easier than others. While Jeremy Tarr enjoyed his time in the marching band, for example, he never lost his sense of being an outsider. "I always felt white in the band," he explained. Cultural boundaries also shifted in conjunction with national developments. In the late 1980s, for example, a rising generation of African American urban youth became increasingly restless with the unfinished business of the civil rights movement, especially the challenges faced by impoverished inner-city communities. Young people's responses to urban decline emerged onto the national scene through the forcefully inventive rhythms and rhymes of rap music, which had become the top-selling genre of American popular music by the late 1980s. While many of West Charlotte's black students embraced the new style, along with its assertive messages, white students took to it less readily.

In November of 1989, student reporter Taryn Gordon wrote an article about the dearth of white students at school dances. In the 1970s, she reported, dances drew both blacks and whites. By 1989, however, the vast majority of attendees were black, and deliberate efforts to attract more white students had seen little success. Gordon touched on a range of potential factors, including white students' preference for parties at private homes, concerns about safety at the nighttime events, and the prevalence of rap music. There were also hints of deeper divides. Some white students, she reported, "do not feel that they are welcomed at dances," and she quoted an anonymous junior as explaining "I'm white and that about sums it up." Some black students spoke with equal bluntness. "They don't want to be around black people," opined senior Eric Moses. "White people are scared of a bunch of black people together," stated Angela Gantt. "They're intimidated."[25]

The 1991 *Wall Street Journal* article that had lauded the school's racial harmony also included a story that captured racial distance. One day, Maggie Ray told the reporter, a young woman came to school wearing a T-shirt emblazoned with a statement that had become popular among black college students: "It's a black thing. You wouldn't understand." Ray, who had worked so hard to create the desegregation plan that brought black and white students together, was taken aback. "I told her, 'You're alienating me,'" she recalled saying. "'I'm your friend.'" A discussion of race and civil rights ensued, but the sense of distance remained. When the reporter talked to the student about the incident, she responded: "I felt bad about offending her — but I wasn't sorry for wearing the shirt."[26]

Still, difficulties and divides, when confronted rather than ignored, were learning experiences in themselves. Many students cited the experience of grappling with differences as one of the most important lessons they learned at the school. "Although there was an acknowledgment probably, at least in my mind, that there were different communities, or different cliques or different groups within the high school, there was an acknowledgment that everyone needed to be included," Carrie Abramson explained. "And that everyone's viewpoint was as important as anyone else's. And that it was really important to have representation from different voices. As well as just listening to different voices. That was important and that was expected. And it wasn't acceptable not to."

"I think I gained a more realistic sense of how the world works outside of my own community that I grew up in," said John Love Jr. "I think I gained a sense and skills about how to deal with a variety of different people that are coming to a situation with a variety of different issues, agendas, needs, wants, desires, that whole thing. I learned the importance of remaining true to self, and remaining true to my ideals and ways of doing things and things that I knew or felt were right. Questioning but not totally dismantling every minute my moral compass, if you will. And being brave and challenging the things that need to be challenged or need to be thought about. All of that kind of stuff. The lessons were pretty huge."

In the spring of 1982, Mertye Rice penned an article that commemorated the work done by that year's graduates—the first class to go through twelve full years of desegregation. "Boys and girls, primarily black and white, but other ethnic and racial groups as well, went to school together, learned together, played together, fought together, cried together, and out of it all evolved a spirit of togetherness unknown in this community before," she wrote. "While all of the furor swirled about them, the boys and girls of the class of 1982 were slowly, cautiously groping their way toward some accommodation." That effort, she continued, had been tremendously worthwhile. "It is my conviction that the class of '82 is not just different but better. While the remnants of discord persist and will continue to do so, I suspect, for some time, this group of youngsters should constantly remind all of us what can be accomplished with courage, patience and determination. . . . They dared hope and dream and they made it work."[27]

Similar stories unfolded across Mecklenburg County, as desegregated schools became a way of life. No corner of the county remained untouched; multiracial groups of parents, teachers, and students worked together at school after school. Often these groups included West Charlotte veterans— Elizabeth Randolph organized and helped implement the district's kindergarten program, and Pop Miller spent nine years as a successful and beloved principal at East Mecklenburg High, where he trained future West Charlotte principal Barbara Ledford. By the end of the 1970s, the results of these efforts had begun to show in academic as well as social arenas. Student performance

Building an Integrated School

on national tests rose across the board, with impressive gains among both blacks and whites. Performance gaps between the two groups narrowed. Across the county, those who had labored to make desegregation work felt deeply proud of the accomplishment.[28]

Arthur Griffin Jr., a Second Ward graduate and longtime educational activist who was elected to the school board in 1988, summed up his perspective on the change in terms of athletic competition. "Growing up at Second Ward, we'd say, 'Let's go beat the white boy's ass,'" he explained. "We'd say, 'Why won't they let us go play Myers Park?' Not for sheer competitiveness, but there was a sense of anger and hostility. We wanted to play white schools so we could beat them up and bloody them. Not to just play them, athletically." By the time his children were in school, however, his views had changed dramatically. He recalled sitting with a friend at a football game between West Charlotte and South Mecklenburg High, where his children attended. "And West Charlotte kids were on one side, my kids were on the South Meck side. And we were saying, Man, isn't this something? All these white people over there on West Charlotte's side, yelling for West Charlotte to beat. You had these black folk over here on the South Mecklenburg side, yelling for South Mecklenburg to beat West Charlotte. Isn't it something? And we almost cried, just saying, look how far we have come, with respect to the races getting along. Not to fight them, not to cut them. . . . We've learned to live a lot better."

The public realm began to change as well. The cross-racial grassroots coalition that had pressed for fairness in the busing plan scored a second major victory in 1977 when residents voted to replace at-large city council elections with a mix of district and at-large seats. District elections made it easier for African Americans to win seats on the council, where they were able to ensure that the city's boards and advisory committees were racially mixed. Although school board elections remained at-large until 1995, effective political organization increased the number of African Americans elected to the board. The newly diversified city council passed legislation requiring that public housing be scattered through the city, rather than concentrated in a few neighborhoods. A new generation of police officers, among them Deacon Jones, began to implement "community-involved" policing, in which police focused not simply on fighting crime, but on working closely with community members to aid in neighborhood development. Sam Smith, one of the west side's white business leaders and a key player in the campaign for district elections, summed up the new philosophy: "You can't have a community unless it works for everybody."[29]

These political efforts reached a high point in 1983, when city council-man Harvey Gantt ran for mayor. Back in the 1960s, the native of Charleston, South Carolina, had been the first black student at Clemson University, where he studied architecture and urban planning. He had established a successful practice in Charlotte, and he joined the city council in 1974. In a community where only one quarter of voters were black, Gantt scored a decisive win. Longtime community leader W. T. Harris linked that victory directly to school desegregation. "I would say to you that prior to school integration, we couldn't have done that, regardless of how good he was," he explained to a researcher soon after the election. "We have grown tremendously."[30]

These racial advancements became a prominent component of Charlotte's identity as a progressive, forward-looking southern city. The sense of possibility, along with a business-friendly climate, made Mecklenburg County an especially attractive magnet for businesses looking to relocate in the emerging region that had become known as the "Sunbelt." Between 1970 and 1990, more than a thousand new firms moved to the county, and the population swelled by more than 150,000 residents. Civic leaders routinely cited school desegregation as a key to that success. "I believe public school desegregation was the single most important step we've taken in this century to help our children," leading banker Hugh McColl would famously write. "Almost immediately after we integrated our schools, the southern economy took off like a wildfire in the wind. I believe integration made the difference. Integration—and the diversity it began to nourish—became a source of economic, cultural and community strength."[31]

Charlotte still had plenty of obstacles to overcome. Many residents, especially African Americans, continued to inhabit multiple worlds, some of which were less welcoming than others. As a young black man growing up on West Boulevard, David Howard was keenly aware of his movements between the city's different spaces. "We spent the weekends in our own world," he explained. "In our own world we were fine. But when you went downtown, you were careful. When you went to Eastland Mall, you were careful. You wanted to make sure that you didn't wind up in scenarios that you couldn't get out of." While Howard managed to avoid conflict or arrest, friends of his "went looking for those issues and got in trouble. Not everybody made it out."

In this sometimes-hostile environment, attending a successfully integrated school such as West Charlotte offered a powerful vision of what the larger world could become. "We got exposed to things beyond us." Howard said. "We were able to dream. . . . We all grew up in a system where we were

Building an Integrated School

exposed to each other and we were challenged. Where we were equals. We were told, 'Not only are you equal, but we value you so much that we made sure you got exposed.'" For Amantha Barbee, being at the school also fostered a broader sense of community responsibility. "We knew consciously or unconsciously that we had to be good citizens of Charlotte," she said. "It was a community—and I don't mean by zip code. It was a community of hearts."

"Basically what you had was a little community of people who shared many of the same beliefs and philosophies and ideas," said Barbara Ledford. "And it was just special. After we had been featured on the front of the *Wall Street Journal*, I went by and laughed with the newspaper staff students and talked about it. They said, 'Do you really think that we were as good as they said we were?' meaning humanity-wise and whatnot. And I had to think for a minute because the article had really been very, very complimentary. And I said, 'No, we are probably not that good, but you all are a lot farther down the road than anybody else I have ever seen.' And I think that I can say that in all honesty. Humanity-wise, they were farther down the road than anybody else I have ever seen."

PULLING APART

It was 1984, and President Ronald Reagan had come to town, riding high. Four years earlier, Reagan had seized the presidency with a call to shrink the federal government's influence over American society and promote a competitive, individualized approach to social and economic affairs. It was a message that played well in business-focused Charlotte. Reagan's speech started smoothly, with praise for small government and American ingenuity that sparked warm applause. Then he hit a snag. "Forced busing," he proclaimed, "takes innocent children out of the neighborhood school and makes them pawns in a social experiment that nobody wants." The crowd went cold. "You Were Wrong, Mr. President," *Charlotte Observer* editors responded the next day. "If you had talked to some of the good Republicans here you would have found that many of them are very proud of their public schools and would fight anyone—even you—who tried to destroy what this community has accomplished."[1]

West Charlotte students seized on the opportunity to affirm the value of their school. Yearbook editors featured Reagan's quote in that year's annual, adding their own sharp critique: "They said it wouldn't work. They said it isn't working. Busing opponents, however, need only take a quick survey of West Charlotte Senior High School to see that busing has worked. Each day, students came north from as far as Lake Norman, south from Pineville, east from Hickory Grove, and west from Coulwood. These different cultures and backgrounds came together by participating on athletic teams, in classroom activities, in club projects and in school functions." In the end, they concluded, "Students, parents, faculty and administration didn't just make the best of an 'experiment' but took advantage of the situation . . . academically, athletically and socially."[2]

This public rebuke of a popular president became a celebrated moment in Charlotte's history, an assertion of the city's pride in its racial achievements. But powerful new obstacles lay ahead. The political retrenchment called the "Reagan revolution" was transforming the terms of political debate, government action, and individual decisions. In the busing struggles of the early 1970s, antibusing advocates had argued for a "color-blind" system of school assignment that championed the choices made by individuals. In Charlotte, that argument ran up against a legal system focused on righting racial wrongs, and a group of civic leaders determined to preserve their city's racially progressive reputation. But the approach had continued to gain momentum around the country, part of a conservative response to the federal government's expanding role in civil rights and other areas. Reagan's ascendance gave it new strength. In the decade following his stop in Charlotte,

Even as opponents of busing gained strength around the nation, West Charlotte students continued to celebrate their diverse school and its achievements, which included the 1992 state basketball championship. *The Lion*, 1992. Courtesy of the Robinson-Spangler Carolina Room.

clashes over race and schooling would once again intensify, prompting significant shifts in student assignment, a major new lawsuit, and a painful upheaval at West Charlotte itself.

Ronald Reagan came to Charlotte at a time when residents were already wrestling with the stubborn persistence of racial inequality. The end of legal segregation had indeed opened up a plethora of new opportunities for the city's African American residents. But even the most successful still contended with a thicket of longstanding habits, preferences, and prejudices that rendered the concept of color blindness far more ideal than reality. Gerald Johnson had returned to Charlotte in the 1970s, bringing a new family and an expertise in computer systems. He moved into the integrating neighborhood of Hidden Valley, and got along well with his multiracial group of neighbors. Still, he found that plenty of divisions remained. Despite federal regulations, his first workplace had separate bathrooms for blacks and whites. Years later, when he took a job at one of the city's leading banks, he learned that race played an integral role in the institution's cutthroat employee politics. While the bank's leaders championed a racially mixed staff, the jockeying for position that went on at lower levels proved less progressive. "It was just a lot of in-fighting," he explained. "It's a dog-eat-dog world and as a consequence, racism plays a very heavy role in that scenario."[3] Johnson eventually left the bank to run the *Charlotte Post*, the black newspaper that his father had purchased in the 1970s.

William Hamlin encountered his own challenges when his children entered West Charlotte. Hamlin had initially expected racial disparities to fade away. "I was a part of this belief that if we could all integrate that there was just going to be a natural exchange of knowledge and resources and that sort of thing," he explained. The reality he encountered proved less ideal. "Our society is very witty," he continued. "And as new demands come upon us for changing we find new ways to entrench ourselves in the old." Hamlin sent all four of his children through West Charlotte during the 1980s and 90s, and led the PTA for several years. He was delighted with the school's welcoming spirit and with the academic opportunities it offered—far more than had been available to him in the 1960s. But he also felt that the school staff at times favored white students at the expense of blacks. When his children graduated from West Charlotte, he decided to send them to historically black colleges. "You increase your learning opportunity when you don't have to deal with other peripheral items such as racism," he explained.

By the late 1980s, the overall experiences of African American students in Charlotte's desegregated schools had become a source of heated public discussion. In the late 1970s and early 1980s, the situation had looked promising, as rising test scores and narrowing gaps between black and white performance raised hopes that racial disparities would eventually be eliminated.[4] Then progress slowed. While many African American students, particularly those from better-off families, thrived in desegregated environments, it became clear that others were struggling. A 1987 study, for example, revealed that more blacks than whites were classed as having learning disabilities, fewer were designated "gifted," and fewer were enrolled in advanced classes.[5] The practice of "tracking," designed to group students by ability, routinely resulted in high-level classes populated largely by white students and low-level classes filled with African Americans. "Some of us had reached a certain comfort level when the schools were successfully integrated," parent and community activist Judy Potter told a reporter investigating the situation. "We thought that would be enough. It isn't."[6]

Along with questions about disparate racial treatment in integrated schools came a growing awareness of a different set of inequalities, linked to shifts in job markets, political priorities and — most visibly — housing patterns. Housing and mortgage discrimination had officially been banned by the Fair Housing Act of 1968, which also included a charge to "affirmatively further" fair housing in order to create "integrated and balanced living patterns." But strong opposition from developers and politicians across the nation meant that few such affirmative efforts were made, and older patterns of development persisted.[7] As Mecklenburg developers sought to take advantage of the county's rapid population growth, they focused on building new subdivisions marketed to middle- and upper-class homeowners, generally located on former farmland at the edges of town. City planners, particularly under Harvey Gantt, pushed for plans that would distribute the costs and benefits of growth more evenly, and the city's scattered-site public-housing policies produced a few affordable homes in more affluent areas. But Charlotte's long-held preference for market-driven development, combined with a significant drop in federal public-housing funds, meant that those efforts had limited effects on the growing spatial and economic divide between the prosperous suburbs and the struggling inner city.[8]

Division by income also meant division by race. In the 1960s and early 1970s, federal antipoverty programs, falling racial barriers, and a booming economy had helped Charlotte's African Americans climb out of poverty at a rapid rate. While nearly two-thirds of black Charlotteans fell below the official poverty line in 1959, only one-third remained there ten years later. Whites saw a similar drop, from 15 to 7 percent. But by the late 1970s, government cutbacks and hard economic times were slowing that rise, well before African Americans were able to build the network of connections that helped funnel young people to well-paying jobs, and well before the end of the conscious and unconscious discrimination that centuries of white supremacy had embedded in southern and American culture.[9]

In Charlotte and across the country, working-class black men faced the greatest obstacles. While black women made significant inroads in the jobs created by an expanding service economy, the entry-level industrial jobs that had generally been filled by men working their way up the economic ladder proved increasingly difficult to find.[10] African American men were also affected by a fundamental shift in law enforcement, one that led to far harsher punishments for minor crimes, particularly those related to the drug trade. Ronald Reagan's intensified "War on Drugs," which focused on urban neighborhoods, created a new set of mandatory sentencing requirements that fueled a massive expansion of state and federal prison populations, with disproportionate effects on African American men. The long-term effects of imprisonment, especially on post-release employment opportunities, compounded the effort's negative effects. Youthful decisions came to have life-long consequences, sharply limiting future opportunities and playing havoc with family dynamics.[11]

Nationally, the stagnant economy of the late 1970s gave way to renewed economic growth in the 1980s. But a fundamental restructuring of the national economy, combined with limited spending on social programs, meant that the majority of new opportunities came higher up the economic ladder. Although Charlotte prospered in those years, thanks in part to its desegregated schools, and although well-educated African Americans made significant economic and political strides, lower-income black families saw limited benefits — Charlotte's African Americans in fact made less economic progress overall than their counterparts in some other North Carolina cities.[12] These persisting income gaps, and the long-term effects of decades of housing and mortgage discrimination, meant that even as the suburbs expanded, most black families remained in the older homes and apartments that ringed the center city. In 1993 west side neighborhoods contained nearly half of Charlotte-Mecklenburg's African American students. In contrast, only 15 percent of white students lived within four miles of the center city.[13]

Even with the busing plan in place, those divisions began to show up in the schools. The *Observer* series that highlighted community concerns about treatment of individual black students also underscored the growing differences among the system's schools. "Despite a school system pledge of 'Equity and Excellence,' despite a state Constitution mandating 'uniform' schools, some public schools offer a better education than others," the reporters concluded, citing income as the major factor. "Charlotte-Mecklenburg's best schools are packed with students from poor, middle-class and well-to-do families," one article noted. "The worst are dominated by students drawn from neighborhoods in the bottom half of the economic scale."[14]

The shift was a telling one. Under segregation, African American schools had systematically received unequal resources. That was no longer the case. But as Julius Chambers had predicted when he was litigating the *Swann* case, other forms of disparity could easily creep into a system in which some schools' families had greater power and resources than others'. Well-off, well-educated parents worked hard to expand the opportunities at their children's schools and to attract top teachers. They purchased classroom materials. They devoted significant resources to preparing their children for school and to addressing any academic challenges. They spent time and money on enrichment and extracurricular activities such as science fairs, field trips, and debate teams. And they ensured that the school system did not overlook their schools' interests.

Jay Robinson, who had stepped down as superintendent in 1986, offered a blunt explanation for the system's disparities: "At a school where parents are less vocal and not in a position to be strong advocates, there is a tendency not to look after their needs as you might." All the families attending higher-poverty schools, both black and white, noticed the differences. "Schools in this community were desegregated because the black schools did not offer the same educational advantages as the white ones," stated white Harding parent Sue Henry. "Now my children are facing the same problems that black children have faced for generations."[15]

The *Observer* series highlighted three high schools—Harding, Garinger, and West Mecklenburg—that had fallen significantly behind the rest of the district in terms of course offerings, teacher experience, and student achievement. All three schools drew large numbers of low-income students from west side neighborhoods. All three found it difficult to recruit and retain the area's top teachers, and all three offered fewer high-level classes than more prosperous schools. Two of Harding's principals had been sent to the school after sparking parent complaints at the better-off schools of Myers Park and South Mecklenburg. Superintendent Peter Relic attributed the differences in part to the widening gap between rich and poor—spatially as well as economically. "America looks like the America of 30 years ago, more than the America of 15 years ago," he told the *Observer*. "And schools today are an

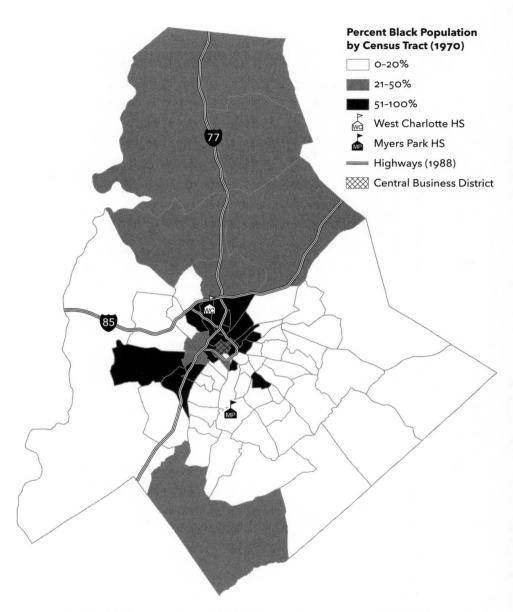

Percent Black Population by Census Tract (1970)

☐ 0–20%

▨ 21–50%

■ 51–100%

⚑ West Charlotte HS

⚑ Myers Park HS

═══ Highways (1988)

▨▨ Central Business District

As Charlotte's population grew, racial and economic separation increased. Lower-income African Americans clustered in older, lower-cost neighborhoods close to town, while better-off white families filled the suburbs. Those patterns would intensify in the twenty-first century, as the construction of I-485 paved the way for further suburban development, and growing numbers of working-class immigrants settled in inner-ring neighborhoods. Maps by Miriam E. Martin.

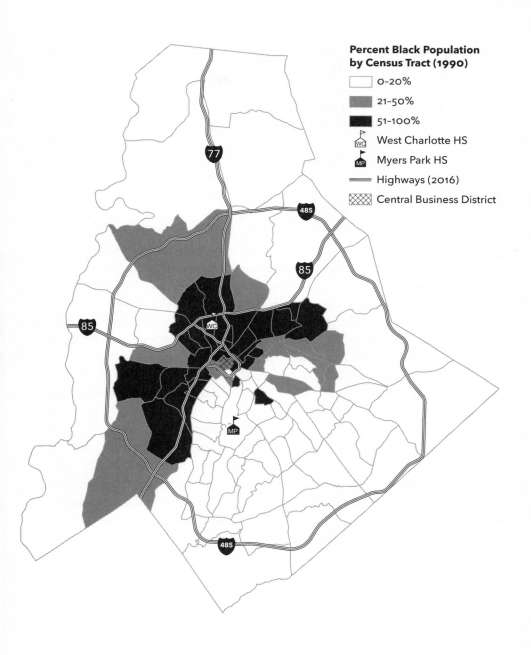

**Percent Black Population
by Census Tract (1990)**

☐	0–20%
▨	21–50%
■	51–100%
⚑ WC	West Charlotte HS
⚑ MP	Myers Park HS
══	Highways (2016)
▨	Central Business District

accurate reflection of society." In reflecting society, the schools also reflected racial divides. Since "more blacks than whites are poor," the *Observer* writers noted, "generally schools with the highest black populations still offer the weakest educational opportunities."[16]

Nationally, however, these persisting inequalities received limited attention. Rather, concerns focused on American education as a whole. In 1983 a Reagan-appointed committee published a report that bore the alarming title *A Nation at Risk*, and warned that "the educational foundations of our society are presently being eroded by a rising tide of mediocrity that threatens our very future as a Nation and a people." It called attention to a number of concerns about the nation's schools, including the relatively low scores of American students on international exams, dropping scores on other standardized tests and complaints about inadequate educational preparation from college administrators, business executives, and military officers. Tellingly, it suggested that some of these shortcomings might spring from efforts to reach beyond academic instruction in order to "provide solutions to personal, social, and political problems that the home and other institutions either will not or cannot resolve."[17]

In the conservative, business-focused climate that marked the Reagan era, the report inspired a set of recommendations that centered on making schools more "efficient" and "productive," and that championed consumer choice. Student scores on standardized tests gained new prominence as the preferred way to target weaknesses and measure progress. In keeping with the era's portrayals of public institutions as bloated and inefficient, advocates of this business-oriented strategy promised that more efficient measurement and greater pressure placed on schools, teachers, and students would improve performance without requiring additional public investment. While desegregation remained a goal in many communities, school districts began to place more emphasis on voluntary desegregation plans. Increasingly, they relied on specialized "magnet" schools designed to attract diverse groups of families by offering innovative programs such as language immersion or Montessori instruction.

This new approach to schooling found particular favor in Charlotte's burgeoning suburbs, where the ideas of efficiency and choice resonated with residents' own lives. Few of the city's new families had much experience with large, unified districts such as Charlotte-Mecklenburg. Outside the South, as members of an expanding middle class had headed to postwar suburbs, most of these communities had established separate school districts, and the quality of a community's schools had become a major factor in housing choice, housing prices, and community reputation. Desegregation orders did little to change this pattern—the Supreme Court had blocked cross-district busing plans in the Detroit-based case *Milliken v. Bradley*, a decision made just three years after *Swann*.[18] For families used to choosing neighborhoods based on their assigned schools, Charlotte's busing program was a shock. Not only did busing send children out of their neighborhoods, school assignments regularly shifted in response to the area's rapid growth. The growing distance between inner city and outer suburbs meant that the length of bus rides grew as well.

McMillan's initial order had sought to avoid this fate, by charging Charlotte-Mecklenburg Schools to avoid building schools in parts of town that lacked racial diversity. Such an approach, desegregation supporters reasoned, would discourage the development of areas that served a single race, and eventually reduce the need to bus for desegregation. But as new subdivisions rose, so did the political pressure to build schools in those areas. Starting in the mid-1980s, Charlotte-Mecklenburg began to do just that. Once new schools were built in suburban communities, suburban growth accelerated.[19] Although school officials called for countywide policies that would "encourage the maintenance of integrated neighborhoods" and "encourage affordable housing units to be included in newly designed suburban communities to enable integration of new schools," other civic leaders championed "free choice and economics," and little significant action took place.[20]

As suburbs grew, their residents began to press for change. Their arguments often echoed the reasoning found in *A Nation at Risk*, contending that a focus on maintaining racial balance had diverted attention from "the basic purposes of schooling." As one suburban mother told the *Observer* in 1988, "Charlotte has been a model for shifting children from one end of the county to the other and not a model for educational excellence by any means." Attention to these sentiments grew as the suburbs expanded their political clout. Suburban votes helped Republican Sue Myrick to a surprise upset of Harvey Gantt in the 1987 mayoral election, and in 1988 helped elect the first antibusing school board candidate in more than a decade.[21]

The national shift in education priorities also influenced longtime Charlotte leaders. In the 1970s, when southerners were working to refashion their communities in the aftermath of the civil rights movement, Charlotte's widely celebrated success with school desegregation had given it an enviable reputation as an efficient, forward-looking city. Now, however, student performance had replaced racial harmony as a key indicator of school system and community success. Anxious to address the dissatisfaction of suburban residents and to preserve Charlotte-Mecklenburg's reputation as one of the nation's top school districts, Charlotte's corporate leaders pressed for an approach more popular in the suburbs and more closely tailored to the emerging national priorities. Their influence was evident in the school board election of 1988, which produced two new corporate-backed board members who were determined to retool the system. One of those new members, banker Joe Martin, called for "a new consensus" on desegregation "that will be as good for the '90s as the 1970 plan was for the '70s."[22]

Efforts to form such a consensus began with the choice of a new superintendent. In 1991, with considerable fanfare, the board hired John Murphy, a charismatic administrator with strong ties to the growing national corps of business-focused educational leaders. The headline on an admiring article in the *Wall Street Journal*—"Forceful Educator Gets Teachers and Children to Be More Productive"—summed up his philosophy and personality.[23] In addition to promising better overall performance, his no-holds-barred approach pledged to equalize opportunities for African American students by devoting additional resources to majority-black schools. Murphy had pursued this approach in his previous position in St. George's County, Maryland, with apparently impressive results.[24]

Murphy wasted little time. He proposed a new set of academic standards and mandated closer attention to student progress, particularly as demonstrated on the statewide End of Grade and End of Course tests that North Carolina had begun to implement. Murphy and his staff crafted a set of benchmark goals for every Charlotte-Mecklenburg school, based on the tests. Principals and teachers were held accountable for meeting those goals, with financial bonuses offered to staff at schools that met their goals and reassignment or dismissal awaiting those who fell short. He also began to create targeted programs for students who were struggling. One of the more highly touted endeavors, titled "Project Success," identified students who faced particularly daunting academic challenges, and assigned designated teams of teachers to teach them core subjects in small groups.[25]

Murphy also proposed major changes to the Charlotte-Mecklenburg assignment plan, seeking to drive desegregation with choice-focused magnet schools. "I firmly believe that morale of students and parents will improve substantially in an educational setting that provides them the opportunity to select schools of their choice," he said when he unveiled the plan. "Our community served as a model to the nation in the desegregation of schools through forced busing. We now are in a position to demonstrate a model leading toward voluntary desegregation."[26] That plan, presented to the school board in the spring of 1992, scrapped many components of the previous version and placed magnet programs at several schools in center-city neighborhoods. To ensure that magnets would be integrated, the plan specified that the magnets would mirror the district enrollment — 40 percent black and 60 percent nonblack. Schools in suburban neighborhoods would be integrated by busing black students out of the center city.

The approach drew broad support in suburban communities and from business leaders. Suburban parents were delighted with their new options: they could choose to send their children to specialized magnets or to schools in their own neighborhoods. African Americans, in contrast, were divided. Some focused on the prospect of greater resources for struggling students, and on the academic boost they thought that magnet programs would bring to schools in black communities. Others, however, worried that a plan in which desegregation depended on parent choice rather than school board assignment would inevitably move toward resegregation. Center-city parents regarded magnets with considerable skepticism. Since 60 percent of the seats in center-city magnets were reserved for white students, they worried that black students would be squeezed out of their neighborhood schools and forced into longer and more frequent bus rides than they already experienced — meaning that some families would have fewer choices than others. Parents assigned to schools near proposed magnets worried that the magnets would draw committed parents away from neighborhood schools.[27]

Still, many residents, both black and white, were impressed by Murphy's impassioned description of his belief in black students' abilities, and by the promise of academic improvement embodied in his broader vision. In the end, following several compromises, the school board passed the magnet plan unanimously. Three years later, Charlotte-Mecklenburg principals lauded Murphy's efforts to raise performance. "Standards of excellence in all areas have changed the culture of the school community," leaders of the county principals' organization wrote. "This demand for excellence initially made people uneasy because it required the acknowledgment of inadequacies and required willingness to change. A new vision required us to respond to the needs of students as never before. We needed to change. And change we did."[28]

John Murphy would not stay long in Charlotte. His abrasive personality and expansive ego quickly wore out his welcome, and he departed at the end of 1995. But the focus on choice and accountability, which reflected a powerful set of national trends, would remain long after he left. In 1994, Congress passed legislation that required states to set content and performance standards, to regularly measure student performance, and to identify schools that were not meeting the standards. In 1996 North Carolina instituted a new set of annual statewide tests and began work on a statewide ranking system. In Charlotte, magnet programs continued to expand. By 1997, thirty-eight Charlotte-Mecklenburg schools — almost a third of the total number — had magnet programs.[29]

West Charlotte students had watched the gradual retreat from full desegregation with concern. By 1995, yearbook editors were troubled enough to tag a photo of the annual fall carnival with the alarming headline: "ENDANGERED." The caption laid out their worries: "Gathered together at the fall carnival, students from various grades, races and cultures enjoy themselves while watching a pie-in-the-face activity. Unfortunately, moments like this may soon be few because of the changing demographics that threaten to end the school's diverse population." The students foresaw dire consequences to such a change. "With an unbalanced ethnic makeup, the school would weaken," they wrote. "No longer could students learn about each other."[30]

The percentage of African American students at West Charlotte had climbed gradually upward since John Murphy's tenure, rising from 46 percent in the fall of 1992 to 55 percent in the fall of 1996. Shifting assignment patterns raised the number of black students from low-income neighborhoods. The school also faced new competition from its old rival, Myers Park High. In 1992, Myers Park became the first high school in North Carolina to institute the prestigious International Baccalaureate (IB) program, a magnet offering that boosted the school's appeal and made it easier for families uneasy with West Charlotte to enroll in Myers Park instead. But West Charlotte's scattered group of feeder areas, combined with the attractions of the open program, helped insulate it from the demographic challenges faced by neighbors such as Garinger or Harding. It still stood as a beacon of desegregated achievement, a school that students across the county aspired to attend.

Growing up in Hampshire Hills, an integrated community just north of the center city, William Hughes Jr. could count both family and neighborhood connections to the school. His father had grown up in Oaklawn Park, just across Beatties Ford Road from West Charlotte, and the younger Hughes spent his childhood going to West Charlotte football games and listening to his father and uncles tell stories about their experiences. Since his corner of Hampshire Hills was assigned to West Charlotte, most of Hughes's "neighborhood idols" attended the school as well. "At that point in time,

Pulling Apart

Uncertainty about student assignment led West Charlotte yearbook editors to caption this picture of the annual Fall Carnival "ENDANGERED." *The Lion*, 1995. Courtesy of the Robinson-Spangler Carolina Room.

everybody wanted to go," he explained. Jeff Black and Justin Perry, two middle-class black students enrolled in the open program, had no family ties to West Charlotte. Still, they and their classmates could not wait to become West Charlotte Lions. "West Charlotte was looked upon by all the other high schools, by everybody, as the hippest school you can go to," explained Black, who arrived as a freshman in the fall of 1996. "The band and everybody just seemed to have so much school spirit. They were at the top of everything. I just was really, really excited to come." Justin Perry, also a freshman that year, felt similar enthusiasm. "Now we get to be a part of the legacy, make our mark," he said. "There was a definite pride, and you definitely had your chest up a little bit. I'm a Lion."

What Jeff Black, Justin Perry, and their classmates did not know was that trouble was brewing at the school. In the spring of 1997, a high-profile conflict over the treatment of West Charlotte's African American students would shake West Charlotte to its core, raising new doubts about desegregation and its legacy. The dispute highlighted the persistence of racial and economic inequalities, even at one of the city's most successfully desegregated schools. It spoke to the profound unease that the city's more successful African Americans felt about the communities they had left behind. It also underscored the persisting volatility of race.

The first rumblings had begun in 1995, when newly appointed principal Will Crawford began to raise questions about the phenomenon that was coming to be known as in-school segregation, voicing his concerns about the racial divides he saw between the schools' advanced and lower-level classes, as well as the significant gaps in standardized test performance between white and African American students.[31] Kenneth Simmons, who replaced Crawford as principal in 1996, developed similar concerns. His efforts to address them sparked an explosion.

Simmons was the first West Charlotte graduate to ascend to the school's top post. In two decades with the school system he had compiled a stellar record, especially with struggling students. He had also gained a strong sense of the district's divides, starting with his first job at suburban Carmel Junior High. The experience "opened my eyes to a new world," he explained. Not only did the school have far greater resources than the schools he had attended, its better-off students arrived with multiple advantages. "I saw children there whose needs had been taken care of, " he said. "Their needs had been taken care of: emotionally, physically. Parents would come and take them to the orthodontist—I'd never heard of that."[32]

As Simmons wrestled with the academic divide between his white students, most of whom lived near the school, and his black students, most of whom came from one of the poorest parts of the west side, he broadened his understanding of what schooling should accomplish. "My Carmel children, all they needed was what I had to give them as a teacher," he said. "I didn't have to give them anything else. They had it. My African American children

Pulling Apart

needed something else. They needed lots of other stuff as well that schools weren't doing."[33] When Simmons arrived at West Charlotte, he saw similar disparities, but limited efforts to address them. "The gap was huge," he later said. "There were a very few blacks in the advanced classes, but the larger numbers of blacks were at the bottom." Especially important, in his opinion, "the better teachers were tracked with the academically better students."[34]

Simmons was particularly troubled by the performance of young black men—a concern that had been building in black communities around the nation. Throughout the 1980s, black males had the highest high school drop-out rate in the nation, as well as the highest unemployment rate. College en-rollment rates were dropping. Gun violence, often fueled by an intensifying inner-city drug trade, claimed a growing number of young men's lives. Char-lotte was no exception. In 1989 newspaper columns filled with accounts of the corrosive effects of the crack cocaine trade on low-income communities that included Fairview Homes and Double Oaks. In 1991, 80 of Charlotte's 108 homicide victims were black men, most killed by other black men.[35] West Charlotte lost two black students in two years—Alex Orange, who was shot and killed at a party in 1989, and Darius LaMont, who was gunned down out-side his house in 1990. Developments such as these sparked a nationwide dis-cussion of the "crisis" facing African American men. Young men like William Hughes and Justin Perry grew used to hearing the cautionary admonition: "Don't be a statistic."[36]

As was the custom in their thriving, philanthropically oriented city, Charlotte residents launched multiple efforts to address these challenges. West Charlotte students pitched right in. When Alex Orange was shot, for example, his grieving classmates came together to create an organization they called Students Against Violence Everywhere (SAVE). In the ensu-ing years, members taught conflict resolution at middle schools and visited elementary schools to warn children of the dangers of guns. After helping to form chapters at most of Mecklenburg County's high schools, they ex-panded the organization across the country and around the world, receiving national and international recognition.[37]

For their part, African American leaders often linked their concerns about young men to the loss of the close-knit community and family ties that had played such significant roles in nurturing black youth during seg-regation. "Our community and family structures are not as strong as they used to be," Rev. Clifford Barnette of nearby Rock Hill told a reporter inves-tigating the subject. "Today it seems like everybody's on their own. Often-

Members of West Charlotte's SAVE organization, formed after the shooting death of
Alex Orange. *The Lion*, 1995. Courtesy of the Robinson-Spangler Carolina Room.

times neighbors don't even know their neighbors."[38] Saundra Davis struck
a similar note. "You can't hardly speak to a child in a high tone now because
the parents say, 'No, no, no,'" she explained. "It's not the same any more. . . .
It's sad. You have to really know whose child to say something to and whose
child not to say anything to." In a forum on black youth, James Ferguson invoked a time when "the family extended even beyond the walls of the house.
. . . Everybody felt some responsibility for everybody else. Even for mothers
who were single parents at that time, they got assistance from the males in
the neighborhood. So everybody had a role model."[39]

This line of analysis involved a reassessment of the role that desegregated schools were playing in the lives of their black students. As well as identifying areas where black students still faced discrimination, such assessments recommended measures designed to reproduce some of the supportive structures of the segregated system. While segregated schools "were inferior physically," Ferguson noted, "they were places where you could come together, where people cared about you and tried to do something for you. . . . We've got to get that back with a very determined effort."

A list of proposals created by black parents and teachers in 1989 stressed the importance of nurturing black students' sense of themselves and their possibilities, echoing the concerns that black students had voiced in desegregation's early years. In addition to calling on school system officials to identify "at risk" students earlier, parents recommended that they hire more black teachers, especially black men, seek out textbooks with more black role models, and make more efforts to promote black history and accomplishments.[40]

The dearth of black teachers was a national problem — even as the percentage of black students in public schools was growing nationwide, the percentage of black teachers was declining.[41] This disjunction showed clearly in Charlotte's high schools, where approximately 41 percent of students were black, compared to 20 percent of their teachers. The difference at West Charlotte was particularly striking. In the early years of desegregation, West Charlotte had benefited from the deeply talented pool of teachers from the segregated era. But as those teachers retired, they proved difficult to replace. When Simmons arrived, although more than half the school's students were black, more than 90 percent of the teaching staff was white.[42]

Simmons had greatly admired John Murphy's efforts to raise standards and expectations for students who lagged behind. He also looked back to his own experience in segregated schools, where teachers sought to instill self-discipline and racial self-awareness even as they imparted academic skills. In elementary school, he recalled, one of his teachers called children to the front of her room to promote middle-class standards of dress and appearance. "I thought this was mean at first, perhaps it was cruel, and today they probably would fire her — but she would have the class to critique us on fingernails, shoes if they had mud on them, our fingernails had to be clean," he said. "We had to be well groomed when we were going to school." In middle school, one of his shop teachers "would lecture us men, maybe every two weeks he would pull us out of the shop into a classroom environment. He would always tell us about the plight of the black man. Telling us where

Kenneth Simmons, the first West Charlotte graduate to become the school's principal.
Photograph by Patrick Schneider, courtesy of the *Charlotte Observer*.

we had to go and from whence we'd come." While the West Charlotte of the 1990s boasted many talented teachers, Simmons did not see that same kind of forceful intervention in students' lives, "a real need to nurture children and make them want to receive what they had to give them." Instead, "What I saw was an attitude of: 'It's here—if you receive it, you will get it. If you don't you don't.'"[43]

Simmons did not hide his determination to hire more African American teachers and to focus more attention on African American students. He adopted a variety of strategies. In the fall of 1996, he brought in a dozen new black teachers. Following a district-wide push to get more black students in advanced classes, he changed admissions requirements for those classes, removing teachers' gatekeeping role and allowing any student who expressed an interest in advanced work to take them. He shuffled teacher assignments. In February, after a schoolwide exam showed black males scoring well below other students, he called struggling students together for an assembly in which he and several other community leaders laid out the challenges and opportunities the young men faced, and exhorted them to work harder and set their sights higher.

These efforts, however, quickly sparked controversy. Some teachers appreciated the changes. "Until Mr. Simmons came, I didn't have an opportu-

Pulling Apart

nity to teach advanced classes," Jade Harris told a reporter.[44] But many were less satisfied, especially those who thought Simmons's decisions focused too closely on race. When the period for teacher transfers rolled around, they voted with their feet. The *Charlotte Observer* reported the exodus with a dramatic front-page story. "Third of Staff Wants out of West Charlotte," the headline read. The article explained that forty-four teachers had applied to transfer to other schools — by far the highest number of transfer requests in the system. The departures, it continued, had been sparked by clashes with Simmons. Departing teachers called Simmons distant and autocratic, saying that after his appointment teachers "lost their voice in school decisions." Simmons countered that some teachers resisted his efforts to do a better job of educating African American students.[45]

The dispute quickly escalated. West Charlotte parents packed school board and community meetings, while Simmons's critics and supporters traded comments in the press. Race soon became a major focus. Some critics accused Simmons of favoring black teachers and students for purely racial reasons. Others charged that he was attempting to lower West Charlotte's academic standards, thus jeopardizing students' futures. "No one who is leaving is happy," one longtime teacher told the *Observer*. We're not doing this to be spiteful. We're not doing this . . . for anything but our own sanity."[46] Another flatly stated: "I'm white, but hell, I can't change that."[47]

Simmons also had defenders, among them teachers, students and especially West Charlotte's African American families, who saw him as standing up for their children. The day after the news of the teacher transfers broke, 600 people came to a meeting at Salem Baptist Church to discuss the issue. Word circulated that politically powerful white parents were working behind the scenes to remove Simmons. A large contingent of supporters drew up a letter to superintendent Eric Smith, who had replaced John Murphy. Teachers, parents, students, and graduates addressed the school board in support of the embattled principal. "We are ready to take a stand on this," announced NAACP president Conrad Pridgen. "We want the message to be clear. . . . We want Kenneth Simmons."[48]

For West Charlotte students, who were used to celebrating their school's unity, the sudden eruption of racial issues was both surprising and disconcerting. "It really was a shock to everyone that I talked to," Jeff Black recalled. "In my opinion it was purely a faculty problem. It really didn't involve the students. A lot of us were just kind of like, 'What is this?' You pick up the paper and nine out of ten days there's West Charlotte on the front of the paper talking about these huge racial problems that they have. None of us were really aware of them." Students had known that West Charlotte had multiple academic tracks. But few saw the school as dominated by white interests or discouraging black achievement. Tori Scarborough, who came to West Charlotte through the open program, noted that her family was focused on the question: "Was I getting taught? That was the bottom line. 'How was your experience today at school, Tori? Did you learn? What do you want to do when you finish?' That was the conversation. Because that's what the civil rights movement was about. We want to be integrated. We want our kids to have the best education. I went to West Charlotte for the best education."

The school itself was living proof that black students could succeed. Clinton Blake's picture presided over the front office, and members of the National Alumni Association were a constant presence at the school, reminding students of its distinguished African American heritage. "What was seeped through the foundation, especially as an African American, you knew there was black excellence," Scarborough explained. "You knew the history. You knew walking down the hallway. Going to West Charlotte was not just going to a high school. It was going to a legacy that was longstanding. So you understood what that meant. Especially being an African American."

As adults battled, students sought to recapture the school's spirit. "Maybe if we try to bring the students together, everything else will fall into place and turn everything back into a family," Karen Neckyfarow suggested. "I really think that students and teachers and the administration should all have a say and work together."[49]

Eric Smith, who had succeeded John Murphy as superintendent, promised "decisive action to make sure that West Charlotte continues in a very positive direction next year."[50] He then acted swiftly. On June 10, 1997, in front of a standing-room-only audience, he announced that he was replacing Simmons with Terry Cline, a newcomer to the district. The next day, in a meeting with West Charlotte staff, he added that he had also seen "situations among faculty members that were highly unprofessional," and announced that all teachers who wanted to stay at the school would have to reapply for their jobs. Staff members who wanted to remain, from custodians to lunchroom employees to administrative assistants, were required to sign a "letter of intent" indicating that they were fully committed to "serve all the children" at the school. "There is a need to ensure that all employees are committed to the future of that school," Smith stated.[51]

The multiple changes had dramatic effects. West Charlotte was already facing heightened competition, not only from the Myers Park IB program but from two brand-new high schools were scheduled to open that fall. The closest of those, Vance High School, offered a high-tech curriculum, had a workplace magnet program, and was led by one of the district's most respected principals. A number of West Charlotte's departing teachers moved to Vance. Some West Charlotte students were reassigned to the new school, and others used the workplace magnet program to join them there. Still others headed elsewhere. When classes started at West Charlotte in the fall of 1997, it was a different place. Two-thirds of the staff members were new to the school. A third of the teachers were in their first year of teaching. The percentage of African American students had risen from 55 to 64.[52]

The 1998 yearbook captured the unease that pervaded the year. Editors noted that the yearbook had gone without an advisor for the first quarter, requiring them to take on new responsibilities. Participants in the renowned drama department dealt with a rotating series of substitutes. Students coped with the loss of friends and teachers who had left for other schools. Still, they carried on. "West Charlotte is on Road Back," an *Observer* article trumpeted that fall, citing praise for Terry Cline and the energetic spirit he had brought to the campus.[53] Many white as well as black families remained loyal to the school. Students studied, attended school events, applied to college. The women's volleyball team won the state championship, cheered on by a proudly multiracial crowd.

Yearbook editors predicted a bright future. "Last year was filled with political controversy that put the school in the local spotlight," they announced. "This year presented the fearless lions with many changes including a staff that was 66 percent new, a different principal, and three additional administrators. They have reformed various aspects of the school focusing on respect and discipline in an attempt to take the mighty lions back to the top. As the lions strive to regain the pride they pull together and help each other when needed. The focused lions have not let their goal to reign at the top once more fall from their sights as they roar . . . The Pride is BACK."[54]

"There is a genuine love for this school," noted Patsy Rice Camp, who had started teaching at her alma mater in 1980. "And that's not only from blacks. There are people who just love the school and want to see that it is maintained, and that its traditions are maintained and that it has an opportunity to always be rated among the excellent. That the goal of excellence will always be there."

West Charlotte's supporters, however, would not have much time to regroup. Even as the school's struggles unfolded, the forces set in motion during the Reagan era were starting to coalesce, pressing toward far more wrenching change. In October of 1997, for the first time in more than thirty years, the *Swann* case returned to court, spurred by a lawsuit filed by sub-urban parent William Capacchione. Capacchione's daughter had failed to win a seat at a popular magnet school — seats that were allocated through a race-based lottery. With the help of the Campaign for a Color-Blind America, a Houston-based group that was becoming known for "matching plaintiffs, money and attorneys in a campaign to end race-based laws," Capacchione filed a lawsuit that challenged Charlotte-Mecklenburg's use of race in stu-dent assignment.[55]

By 1997, legal challenges to school desegregation plans had become increasingly common across the country. In its 1968 *Green* decision, the Supreme Court had required school systems to actively desegregate until they reached "unitary status" — which meant that they had remedied all the inequalities produced by decades of separate and unequal systems. While the term "unitary" was vague and difficult to define, by the mid-1980s districts began to successfully claim that they had met its requirements.

The new flurry of activity reflected changes in legal circumstances, as well as within school districts. Realizing that many of the social and political trans-formations of the 1960s had been spurred by court decisions, conservatives had planned a counter-strategy that focused on appointing conservatives to federal judgeships and on laying legal groundwork to challenge race-based policies in areas that ranged from college admissions and public school as-signment to the makeup of congressional districts. In 1986 Norfolk, Virginia, became the first public school district to win release from a court-ordered plan. The number of districts seeking to end court orders quickly multiplied.[56]

The Charlotte-Mecklenburg school board would take a different tack. Shortly after the suit was filed, the board voted 6–3 to defend its desegrega-tion plan. That decision set up a countywide confrontation. Several white parents added their names to the *Capacchione* suit, and a number of local lawyers joined the legal team. Opposition came from groups that included the NAACP, the Black Political Caucus, and the League of Women Voters. Although Julius Chambers had left town to become the president of North Carolina Central University, James Ferguson and his colleagues petitioned to reopen the *Swann* case. The day he filed the petition, Ferguson led a dem-onstration on the courthouse steps. "We know from the past that separate cannot be equal," he announced, arguing that if the *Capacchione* plaintiffs prevailed, it "would mean a return to neighborhood schools and, inevitably, a return to racially segregated schools." He was joined by members of the Swann Fellowship, an interracial group of longtime Charlotte residents that had formed several months earlier to advocate for a continued focus on full desegregation.[57] Students from West Charlotte came as well. "You can teach students about racial harmony," Justin Perry told the gathering. "But they will never understand it until they experience it."[58]

The case was assigned to Judge Robert Potter, who began hearings in April of 1999. During two months of testimony, experts for the school board focused on the unmistakable racial inequalities that remained in the system, echoing many of the concerns that had been voiced in the 1980s. They pointed to persisting gaps in performance between black and nonblack students, even when economic status was taken into account. They demonstrated that schools with particularly large numbers of black students lagged in class offerings, teacher experience, classroom resources, faculty quality, and student achievement. "Charlotte-Mecklenburg Schools do not provide equal educational opportunities to African American students," expert Robert Peterkin flatly stated. "This is evidenced by a persistent pattern both in access to adequate educational resources and to advanced educational programs."[59]

Experts for the plaintiffs took a different tack. They did not deny the differences between the experiences of black and white students. Instead they argued that those differences were not related to "past or present school discrimination." Rather, they attributed the divides to families' choices about which neighborhoods to live in and to "socioeconomic factors — such as lower average family incomes and higher poverty rates in black households."[60] They did not address the question of whether unequal schooling under segregation had contributed to persisting economic inequalities. The plaintiffs' lead lawyer, Atlanta-based A. Lee Parks, was practiced in this line of argument, having represented clients seeking to overturn a range of racial preference programs.[61]

On September 9, 1999, Judge Potter issued his ruling. He declared the Charlotte-Mecklenburg system unitary and ordered the district to design a new assignment plan that did not take race into account. While racial inequalities were still present, Potter wrote, he judged that the school system's efforts had overcome the damage done by legal segregation "to the extent practicable."

Few observers were surprised. Robert Potter was a conservative judge. Back in the 1970s, he had helped opponents of the *Swann* decision frame their arguments against the original busing plans. Ronald Reagan had nominated him to the federal bench in 1981. Still, Charlotteans who had spent decades championing school desegregation found the verdict deeply disappointing. "I knew that we were fighting an uphill battle with Judge Potter,"

James Ferguson explained. "But even knowing that, I felt that the facts were so strong and there was enough sentiment in the community and the need was apparent to continue it. That even Judge Potter would see that it would not be good for our community, would not be good for the school system, to retreat. But I was wrong."

News of the end of *Swann* spread around the country, sparking multiple reactions as well as various predictions about its effects. One expert judged it "the end of an era in American social policy."[62] The parents who had filed the suit rejoiced — one called it "a grand slam." Those who opposed it spoke of "a sad, dark and dreary day." Jay Robinson, who had led the system during its glory days, was worried. "I believe we are a much better country because we've demanded . . . that schools stop relegating their underprivileged people to a second-class education," he stated. "It appears to me that we're going back to where we were 30 years ago. And that's frightening." County commissioner Parks Helms was more optimistic. "I think this community is going to change on its own, and I think in time the school system will be integrated naturally, normally," he said. "I see that within the next decade."[63]

School board members were split as well. A few weeks after Potter announced the decision, the board voted 5–4 to appeal. The vote showed a clear racial divide — all four African American board members voted to appeal the decision, while four of the five white members opposed it.[64] Desegregation's backers took heart when a three-judge committee from the Fourth Circuit U.S. Court of Appeals voted in the district's favor. In September of 2001, however, the full Court of Appeals upheld the bulk of Potter's ruling. While the board could have appealed to the Supreme Court, the possibility of victory seemed slim. Board members decided to let the matter rest.

The situation marked a dramatic reversal from the time when Judge James McMillan first ruled in *Swann*. In the late 1960s, supporters of busing for desegregation had legal but not political power. While the courts ruled in their favor, a school board dominated by busing opponents did its best to block the process. Three decades later, they had political but not legal power. The school board majority supported busing. A court order forced them to stop.

The school board could have turned to an assignment plan based on income instead of race. While racial discrimination was covered by the Fourteenth Amendment to the Constitution, socioeconomic status had no such protection. Families could not sue school districts over socioeconomic discrimination, and they could not legally challenge assignment plans based on economic status. A number of districts across the country, including

North Carolina's Wake County Schools, had adopted this approach. But the Charlotte-Mecklenburg board decided to focus on choice. They instituted a "Family Choice Plan" that gave each school a home attendance zone, then grouped schools into four racially balanced "choice zones"—purple, green, blue and gold. Students were guaranteed a seat at their home school. They could also apply to any school in the county—as long as that school was not already filled with home-zone students. Transportation was guaranteed to schools within a student's choice zone.

No one doubted that the plan would produce greater racial and economic segregation. The question was how the community would tackle the divides, as well as the challenges they posed for higher-poverty schools and their students. "Make no mistake, right now educational opportunities are not equal," *Observer* editorial writers noted. "[The] challenge before the school board and this community remains clear: We must provide the resources and environment to ensure all children access to an equitable and quality education."[65] That would prove a daunting task.

RESEGREGATION

In the fall of 2002, Mecklenburg County families began to make the decisions that would reshape their school system. Choice and competition were the watchwords of the day. "YOU'RE IN CHARGE," the *Charlotte Observer* reminded parents as the "choice period" opened. "While capacity and transportation may limit your choices, remember it's ultimately up to you, the parent, to find out the information you need to make a good choice for your child. Don't be passive." Every family received a 72-page information booklet that described the complex application process and introduced the county's 148 schools. In November, the district staged an elaborate, daylong "Showcase of Schools." Individual schools selected themes, created promotional materials, designed tours, and scheduled open houses. Some made videos that stressed their virtues; others mailed recruitment letters to potential students. As the deadline drew near, district, school, and PTA workers staffed phone banks and traversed neighborhoods, knocking on doors of families who had not yet submitted choices. Pastors reminded their congregations to fill out their forms. Schools offered pizza parties, ice-cream sundaes, and extra recess to students who returned applications.[1]

By the time the process ended, more than 100,000 families had officially chosen schools. When the results were released, it became clear that families across the district had scrambled for spots at higher-wealth, higher-performing institutions. It was also clear that the process had worked better for some families than others. White families were more than twice as likely as black families to choose the guaranteed spots at their home schools. Many African American families who reached beyond their home schools were disappointed—African Americans made up 41 percent of the "choice pool" as a whole, but 57 percent of those who did not get any of the schools they chose. Suburban schools were packed with students, while some center-city schools filled less than half their seats. "It doesn't take a genius or a rocket scientist to see that we're going to have resegregation," commented parent Terry Belk. "Would you want your kids going to a subpar school? They know the center-city and inner-city schools are going to receive less resources."[2]

The lottery results underscored the limits many African American families faced under this new version of "choice." In the 1950s and 1960s, black families' efforts to exercise "freedom of choice" by sending their children to predominantly white schools were blocked by district officials seeking to shore up racial segregation. In 2003, families' choices were approved or rejected by a computer program rather than human beings. But the system's rules, which gave priority to families living in a given school's home zone, meant that low-income families were effectively shut out of schools in neighborhoods where they could not afford to live. Because the county's wealth remained concentrated among white families, the resulting racial and economic divides would prove nearly as dramatic as those produced by legal segregation. Anticipating the gaps the new assignments would create, school board members had approved an "equity" plan designed to direct additional resources to high-poverty schools. But the school board lacked taxing authority and depended on the county commission and the state legislature for most of its funding. In the end, limited funds and political resistance meant the plan would fall far short of its goals.[3]

The return to home-zone schools solidified patterns that had been forming across the county for several decades. While better-off families moving to the growing suburbs had drawn the bulk of public attention, plenty of working-class families had come to Charlotte as well, filling low-wage jobs and taking posts in the booming construction industry. These new arrivals included immigrants and refugees as well as U.S. families — Charlotte's Hispanic population increased nearly tenfold between 1980 and 2000.[4] Many of these new families settled in aging "middle-ring" neighborhoods that had been built to accommodate the growth of the 1960s and 1970s, and where homes and apartments had become increasingly affordable. As a result, the new plan created a curving swath of high-poverty schools that filled the neighborhoods around Beatties Ford Road and continued both east and west of the Myers Park corridor. The area held two magnet high schools — Harding High, which had become an International Baccalaureate magnet, and Phillip O. Berry, a brand-new career and technical school. It also included four home high schools — Garinger, West Mecklenburg, newly opened E. E. Waddell, and West Charlotte.

West Charlotte became a classic example of the effects of the choice plan. Less than a third of its home-zone students put the school as their first choice, opting instead for other choice-zone schools, or for magnet programs. The school was scheduled to open at only 90 percent of capacity. The percentage of African American students had risen to 85 percent, and the percentage of whites had dropped to 6 percent. The school's estimated poverty rate — 56 percent according to the number of students who qualified for free or reduced-price lunch — marked it as the poorest high school in the system. Its actual poverty rate was considerably higher, as high school students were notorious for failing to apply for lunch assistance, preferring hunger to the stigma of free lunch.[5]

Rather than helping balance West Charlotte's population, the choice component of the plan raised the school's percentage of disadvantaged stu-

As Charlotte-Mecklenburg Schools moved away from busing, the number of white students at West Charlotte dropped dramatically. *The Lion*, 2001. Courtesy of West Charlotte High School.

dents. Many of the west side's more ambitious families pushed to get their children into other choice-zone schools, or into magnet schools such as Harding and Berry. Faced with this harsh reality, the school board sought to make West Charlotte more competitive by creating an International Baccalaureate program at the school. It had limited effect. By 2005, the school enrolled about 1,500 students. More than 900 students from its attendance zone attended other city high schools.[6]

West Charlotte had spent its first three decades as a successful, all-black school. But circumstances had changed dramatically since then. During segregation, West Charlotte employed an exceptionally talented corps of African American teachers for whom it offered the most prestigious jobs available. It enrolled a sizeable group of students from well-educated, economically successful families. Students and teachers lived in the same communities, bound together by ties of family, neighborhood, and church. While the bulk of students came from modest backgrounds, the rise of the civil rights movement and the postwar economic boom were expanding ambitions and opportunities for African Americans across the nation, creating a palpable sense of optimism. By 2002, in contrast, middle-class black families were nearly as likely as middle-class white families to live outside West Charlotte's attendance zone and to set their sights on more conspicuously successful schools. Not only did top teachers have many schools eager to hire them; their pay

Resegregation

had long been losing ground to salaries in other fields, and growing numbers were deciding to take better-paying jobs outside of education. Few educators, black or white, still lived in the communities that housed West Charlotte's students, and gaps between rich and poor were widening, both in the city and around the nation.

In addition, West Charlotte faced a new, harsher set of standards. Previously, it had been judged largely in terms of its successes: the grades, scholarships, and jobs claimed by its top students. In the new climate, it would be assessed primarily by the areas in which it fell short: the numbers of students who did not pass state tests, or who failed to graduate. These assessments were powered by the growing significance of state standardized tests. In 1998 North Carolina launched a widely publicized set of ratings based on standardized test scores—schools received official designations that included "School of Excellence," "School of Distinction," and "Low Performing." In 2001 a bipartisan Congressional majority added additional weight to test performance with a sweeping education bill dubbed "No Child Left Behind." The bill, which President George W. Bush signed in early 2002, mandated a new set of annual tests, along with increasingly severe sanctions for schools where proficiency levels did not improve from year to year.

The new emphasis on test-focused accountability, one observer predicted, would accelerate the divides opening up between resegregating schools. Because low-income students rarely scored well on standardized tests, high-poverty schools almost always had low proficiency levels, University of North Carolina law professor Jack Boger pointed out in a 2003 essay. While the new accountability programs were designed to identify problems and direct resources towards low-performing schools, they were also likely to drive parents of means to higher-performing schools in better-off parts of town. "What school accountability—with its annual test scores and its annual information about school performance trends—adds to this general tendency toward neighborhood stratification is its aura of concrete certainty," Boger wrote. "While neighborhood ambiance or the economic profiles of a community may be more intangible, comparative public school performances are now available on the Web, accurate to the decimal point."[7] In addition, he continued, the heightened focus on tests and sanctions was likely to drive experienced teachers away from challenged schools, prod struggling students to drop out, and burden many schools with the demoralizing label of "failing." Schools such as West Charlotte would struggle mightily under this new regime.

West Charlotte remained a popular school in many west side communi-

Although few white students went to West Charlotte after busing ended, the ESL and
IB programs continued to draw immigrants from many backgrounds. *The Lion*, 2005.
Courtesy of West Charlotte High School.

ties. Joe Hamilton, who grew up just off Beatties Ford Road, recalled a youth
filled with events and celebrations, many of which were tied to the school.
"As far as Beatties Ford Road goes, there was always a great sense of pride," he
explained. "From the people that had come before us, and the things that you
saw. . . . Parades. The football games. West Charlotte homecoming." Among
longtime Charlotte families, attending West Charlotte remained a cherished
tradition. "It was a rite of passage for a lot of people," explained Hamilton,

Resegregation

who became a West Charlotte freshman in the fall of 1998. "Like the baton is passing. . . . You feel like someone's handing the baton back and you're ready to take it."

Still, the neighborhoods themselves offered few opportunities for aspiring young people. "We were always told — my generation — 'You can be whatever you want to be,'" Hamilton said. "And people would tell us, 'Go to school, get you an education, get a good job and get out of here.' Instead of 'Go to school, get an education, get a good job and carry on a legacy.'" Tammy Hill, who returned to the west side after graduating from Bennett College in 1989, echoed that sense. "Even when a lot of people from West Charlotte graduated, if they came back to Charlotte they didn't come back to the community," she said. "They went out. That's one reason why I stayed. Everybody was always saying 'Why do you live over here?' Because I choose to live over here. Why do I have to run? If everybody runs, who's going to be left over here to fight? That's one reason why I did not run, and I stayed."

The community to which Hill returned, and in which Hamilton grew up, was not, in fact, what it had once been. Many longtime residents remained — Hamilton lived with his grandparents, who had bought their home in 1959. But the exodus of young people to other neighborhoods made it difficult to maintain the social fabric that once stretched across the area. As homes emptied, they often became inexpensive rentals, temporary stops for people who could not afford to live anywhere else. "I think it turned from being 'this is a community' to 'this is a place: I'm having a hard time in my life right now, and this is where I'm going to be until I can get back on my feet,'" Hamilton said. "And I think that's what it ended up being ultimately for a lot of people. . . . I remember a lot of guys that I grew up with, we were friends for two years and then I don't know where they're at now, because they would come into the community for a little while and then they would be gone."

That transience made it difficult to maintain social ties. "We lost that family touch, the closeness, like you look after my child I look after yours," Hill said. "I think as the old people died out, the new people came in, we kind of lost that community touch and feel that we had when I was growing up." It also made it more difficult to advocate for city services — one reason she described her choice to live on the west side in terms of fighting. "The west side was always dark," she said, referring to the dearth of streetlights. "The city didn't invest on the west side." The area's isolation, in Gerald Johnson's opinion, was a deliberate effort on the part of city leaders to hide low-income communities. "When I was coming up, I-77, I-85 split the black community," he explained. "Split it and redirected traffic so that you would never be able to see the heart of the west side and see what's going on in some of the impoverished communities."[8]

Neighborhoods also saw fallout from the spread of drugs, particularly crack cocaine. Starting in the 1970s, the empty buildings that dotted the remains of the Genesis Park neighborhood, a handful of streets sandwiched between Fairview Homes and I-77, became the focus of an especially notorious drug "supermarket." Gunshots, discarded needles, and long lines of cars driving slowly in search of drugs became a familiar part of growing up in both Fairview Homes and Double Oaks.[9] The harsh federal sentencing laws that were part of the War on Drugs meant that many of the young men who became caught up in the trade served lengthy prison terms. A report compiled in 2016 would show nearly 17,000 black men between the ages of twenty and fifty-four "missing" from Charlotte's neighborhoods.[10] While the Beatties Ford Road area saw less direct drug dealing, the ravages of addiction and the crime it sparked made their marks. Hamilton and his friends spent much of their free time at the West Charlotte Recreation Center, just outside the West Charlotte campus. Walking to the Center was a sobering experience. "We would leave out of our street and we would go up this street, Garnette Place, and kind of cut through this little path," Hamilton explained. "And there'd be a lot of guys that were back there, a lot of guys and women that were back there and we knew what they'd been doing. We knew why they were asleep back there. We knew what was wrong with them."

Amid the challenges that west side families faced came the rise of hip-hop, a dynamic, astutely marketed collection of cultural endeavors that spoke eloquently to the experiences of young African Americans and that often proved far more attractive than academic pursuits. "There were so many distractions in the neighborhood," Hamilton recalled. "We would be more focused on when shoes were coming out, and clothes and stuff like that, than what was going on in the school. . . . I think there was more studying of movies than anything else. Stuff like *Juice*—that movie *Juice* was kind of big. *Menace II Society*."

Hamilton's grandparents provided a counterweight to those distractions. "I was lucky to get what my grandparents passed on from the generation that came before," Hamilton said. "A lot of my friends would look to my grandfather and other people in the neighborhood as people that you listen to. Guys that were kind of lost." For other young men, however, popular culture became all-absorbing. "A lot of people tell me, they say music is art and art is a reflection of your environment," Hamilton continued. "Well I go back to it now, and I say no, not really, I say now the way things are is it's like life is imitating art. . . . And then not only is life imitating art, it's mostly a lot of people trying to fake it until they make it. So they act in a certain way until people believe that that's exactly what they are."

By the end of Hamilton's second year at West Charlotte, two of his close friends had dropped out of school, and he had started to get into trouble "hanging around the guys I'd been hanging around." His family responded by arranging for him to go live with his mother and attend Myers Park High for his junior year. Other young men, however, did not have that kind of intervention: "Nobody was there to tell them 'Hey that's stupid. Don't do that. . . . That ain't the way this works.'" Several years later, a study of the effects of Charlotte's school resegregation linked growing racial isolation to both a drop in academic performance and a significant increase in crime among the city's young black men.[11]

As in the past, West Charlotte's staff sought to counterbalance the temptations of youth culture and the underground economy and to help students cope with the even greater challenges posed by poverty and instability—challenges that could include hunger, homelessness, and violence. "There were a lot of good teachers," Hamilton recalled. "I think they were in the mind-changing and the life-changing business." Spencer Singleton, who had become a history teacher at the school and who had taken over the reins of the chess club, recalled that many teachers took "extraordinary measures" to help students succeed. "After-school offerings, a chance for them to beef up after school," he noted. "Talking to them every chance you get, trying to motivate them. They need that constant motivation to keep them directed. Because a lot of their focus is elsewhere because of things that are going on back home."

These new demands made teaching at the school especially challenging. "It's work," Singleton continued. "Because these kids are dealing with so much other stuff. And the teacher could say 'I don't have time for that, I'm just going to teach.' But you're not going to teach them anything—they're not going to learn anything if their mind is not there. So you've got to take your time out to listen to these kids. Sometimes a class—you may spend 30 minutes or so just dealing with whatever issues they're dealing with. Get it out."

Not everyone, however, was up to those challenges. Staff turnover and academic struggles made stability elusive, weakening the school at a time when its students needed it more than ever. In the spring of 1999, West Charlotte had the lowest state test scores of any high school in Mecklenburg County.[12] That summer, principal Terry Cline was replaced with West Char-

History teacher and chess coach Spencer Singleton with student Jarris McGhee-Bey, 2001. Photograph by Gayle Shomer, courtesy of the *Charlotte Observer*.

lotte graduate Venton Bell, who had overseen the transformation of Harding High School into a successful International Baccalaureate magnet. The next spring, however, scores fell further, making West Charlotte the second-lowest performing high school in the state, and triggering a state intervention team. That September, Bell abruptly retired, citing troubles with his health. Delores Lee became West Charlotte's sixth principal in eight years.

The principal turnover further stretched the school's staff. "Every principal does something different, and every principal has a different philosophy," explained Robert Yost, one of the few teachers who held on during the shifts. "And you come in and you adjust to a certain philosophy and a certain way of doing things. And then another principal comes in and does it the opposite way. It is really difficult." Few experienced teachers applied to the school during those years. Many of the new hires were young teachers getting their first jobs, and many of those left as quickly as they could. "Every year there would be new faces and old faces gone," Singleton noted. "Because the work is hard. It's very challenging. So some people are: 'I didn't get in for this. This is above what I bargained for.'" In the 2001–02 school year, only 58 percent of the school's teachers were fully licensed, compared to 88 percent at Myers Park High. Teacher turnover that year was 39 percent, compared to 10 percent at Myers Park.[13]

Resegregation

Students appreciated the teachers who made serious efforts to work with them. But they had little trouble recognizing a low-skilled teacher, or one who had burned out. One year, for example, students in a precalculus class found their teacher could not explain the subject. If students couldn't figure out the problems on their own, one student explained to a reporter, the teacher's advice was to "put your head down and just go to sleep." When the teacher was put on an action plan—the first step on the path to being fired—the students did not hide their satisfaction. "You're getting fired 'cause you can't teach," they told him. He quit soon afterward.[14] Parents regularly demanded that the district assign a corps of skilled, experienced teachers to the school. But while district leaders had the power to reassign teachers, they balked at the idea, fearing that reassigning teachers against their will would prompt a general exodus from the district.

The growing inequalities did not go unnoticed. The concentration of low-income students in high-poverty schools, along with federal requirements that schools report test performance scores by categories such as race and economic status, publicly highlighted dramatic gaps between better-off students, most of whom were white, and lower-income students, most of whom were not. In response, Charlotte's volunteer and philanthropic organizations expanded programs designed to assist struggling students, and scoured the nation for ideas and inspiration. But while such efforts made significant differences in many individual students' lives, observers warned that Charlotte-Mecklenburg was becoming a system with "one set of schools for the haves and one set for the have-nots."[15]

The divisions that school resegregation opened between schools and in the community as a whole also helped spark a public resurgence of old racial stereotypes, images that gained new force from the era's political realignments. Champions of markets, choice, and competition often spoke in strong moral tones and regularly attributed poverty to personal shortcomings. Political leaders such as Ronald Reagan had adopted race-neutral language, in keeping with their argument that old racial divisions had been overcome and race-based policies should be eliminated. At the same time, however, they also proved adept at channeling old fears and prejudices into images that raised particular alarm about low-income African Americans living in inner cities. Condemnation of "ghetto culture" had started in the 1960s, sparked in part by the urban rebellions that shook so many major American cities during that tense era. It reemerged with force during the 1980s, often through loaded terms such as "welfare queens" and criminal "predators."[16]

In a resegregating Charlotte, the visible struggles of high-poverty, high-minority schools sparked new levels of public criticism — often coming from elected officials who resisted spending additional dollars on those schools. In 2004, the head of the Mecklenburg County Commission proposed creating a high school challenge fund that would seek to improve performance at the city's four lowest-performing high schools — Garinger, West Mecklenburg, Waddell, and West Charlotte. Commissioner Bill James, who represented the southernmost suburbs, loudly proclaimed that the funds would do no good. In contrast to the color-blind language that had prevailed in previous decades, he cast his opposition in openly racial terms.

"The education problem at CMS is mostly a black problem and specifically a moral problem with behavior in the black community," James wrote.[17] African American communities, he continued, were beset by "rampant immorality — and in particular promiscuity and the willingness to have sex with pretty much anyone, creating babies out of wedlock while expecting someone else (taxpayers) to take care of the mess." He closed his diatribe with a sweeping statement: "To paraphrase a movie line — 'most blacks think monogamy is some kinda wood.'"[18] While many public officials, including a considerable number of chagrined fellow Republicans, denounced James's rhetoric, his suburban constituents continued to elect him year after year.

In this increasingly critical atmosphere, uneasiness about being seen as a "black" school spilled over into many areas of West Charlotte life. One such arena involved the school's prized marching band. When Jeff Black entered West Charlotte in the fall of 1996, he had been especially excited about joining the band. But longtime band director Marvin Davenport retired in 1997, the same year Kenneth Simmons was removed. The next year, as West Charlotte struggled to recover, the band's style came under fire — from the school's own leadership.

"It seemed like people were like: 'We have to change this. This isn't right,'" Black explained. "We used to do breakdowns and dances on the field all the time. . . . The administration came down and was like: 'Look. You are not going to do that. . . That's not proper. That's not West Charlotte.' . . . We did a field show this year. It wasn't even a high step routine. It was just like corps-style marching. That's good that the band knew how to do that, but people didn't want to see that. That's not what West Charlotte's known for." Black then pointed specifically to concerns about the school's image. "It's like people are thinking we're a ghetto school. People are thinking that all we do is dance. But some things are just tradition, and that's what concerns me.

The type of changes that are being made just strictly based on perception instead of what West Charlotte has always been about."

One reason for the administrative angst about the band came clear when West Charlotte's performance in the Thanksgiving Carrousel Parade became the target of highly public condemnation. In 1999 a complaint about the band "parading half dressed and dancing provocatively in the streets" sparked an angry exchange of disagreements about performance style. In 2002, the dispute escalated to a formal rebuke, when Carrousel Parade president Les Miller required the West Charlotte and Harding bands to alter their performances in order to participate. "We feel like we have a responsibility to the folks in the community that the parade is in good quality, good fun, and not offensive in any way," Miller told the press. In addition, the parade's executive director warned that "counter marching, reverse marching, and/ or stopping the forward motion of the parade without specific instructions to do so is prohibited."[19]

Few African Americans were surprised by the critique. "It was predictable," Gerald Johnson noted. "Because of the labeling and all of that. [The band] was a crowd-pleaser, but everybody wanted to put a negative spin on it because of the area and because of what was going on with the schools." West Charlotte's supporters leaped quickly to the defense of their band and its traditions. "If you see pornography and lust in rhythmic dance movements, then it's your thoughts that need to be 'toned down,'" one band parent wrote. But the conflict did nothing to lift school spirits or make students feel welcome outside their own communities.[20]

Along with the band controversy, the principal churn and the dismal test score results, West Charlotte staff and students had to contend with a string of highly publicized incidents that involved only a handful of individuals but reinforced a full range of stereotypes about black urban life. In July of 2000, West Charlotte's recently hired band director was charged with statutory rape for having sex with a fifteen-year-old female student in his band office. The next April, the *Charlotte Observer* greeted readers with a front-page story that featured eight mug shots of young black men, beneath the headline "Students among 8 Charged in 5-Week Robbery Spree." Five of the men, the article explained, were students at West Charlotte High. That September, shots were fired in the West Charlotte parking lot as a crowd left a West Charlotte–Garinger football game, wounding two people and leading to four arrests.[21]

These incidents sparked further public criticism. "West Charlotte High

The West Charlotte band performs at the Carrousel Parade, 2002.
Photograph by Jeff Siner, courtesy of the *Charlotte Observer*.

School has made a lot of news this year," one Charlotte resident wrote to the *Observer* in July of 2001. "Sex offenders on staff; five student bank robbers; end-of-grade test failures. Ask any conscientious WC student about the learning climate, the behavior problems and the teachers who are leaving. Why don't we end the misery now? Let's take this beast off the endangered species list. Just kill it."[22]

The steady beat of criticism and bad publicity wore on the community and its students. West Charlotte's academic struggles, and the widespread publicity they gained, battered student morale. "It really made us feel like we were dumb," student Vaisha Gregory noted of the persisting public focus on the school's low scores.[23] West Charlotte supporters were "furious" about the football game shooting, the *Observer* reported. "They said hundreds of students and adults had a great time at the game and their team won, but the evening was ruined by the senseless violence." Student-body president Darius Graham wrote the paper that next week. "I'm so tired of opening the newspaper and seeing negative stories about my school," he said. "West Charlotte has given me opportunities and experiences I wouldn't give up for the world. As student council president, I try hard to get out positive news. But someone always messes it up."[24]

Such stereotyping, Gerald Johnson observed, cut more deeply in the twenty-first century than it had back in the 1950s, when west side residents lived within a supportive, economically integrated, and largely self-contained community. "We were self-sustaining," he noted. "We knew we couldn't do what we wanted to do, in terms of where we wanted to go, where we wanted to eat. But what we couldn't do going out, we built it in. And so we built our own theaters, we built everything we wanted to do within our own community, what we could afford to do. We did whatever we needed to do to sustain ourselves." When that world broke up, he continued, so did the cushion it had provided. "Now the labeling is much more painful, much more hurtful."

As Darius Graham's letter made clear, turmoil and criticism did not keep West Charlotte's staff from nurturing students. While some faltered, many soared. Isaiah Scott, who arrived as a freshman in 2003, described his experience in terms that echoed the stories told by generations of his predecessors. "First time I went to West Charlotte, I was still in middle school, and I went to a football game," he explained. "My brother Matthew was on the football team. It was incredible. The band was playing and the music was going and the crowd was just so lively and it was just so much energy and the football team was really good. They had a fish fry, and it was great. I had a ball. I loved it."

Scott started out as a shy student, in the shadow of two successful older brothers. Then he found a home in the ROTC program, presided over by Lieutenant Colonel Kenneth Love. While Love was strict — "I've never been yelled at so much by a teacher" — he was also fully devoted to his students. He picked cadets up before school, drove them home, found them jobs, and advised them on everything from dress to romance. "He has a way of just taking us under his wing," Scott said. "He mentors us and lays a path out for us and supports us." Scott drew additional strength from supporters such as math teacher Deborah Kellogg, who brought breakfast to class, held study sessions in her home, and "made me love math." He got help and advice from several members of the West Charlotte National Alumni Association, most notably 1952 graduate Mable Latimer, who had become one of the school's most steadfast supporters.

Like many families, the Scotts had ended up on the west side during a bout of financial trouble — one that in their case left them temporarily homeless. Once their finances stabilized, they could have moved to a different part of town and sought out a different school. But they had found a home at West Charlotte. Between 2001 and 2013 all seven Scott children attended the school, excelling in class, on sports teams, and in student government. After graduation, they enrolled in some of the nation's top colleges, including Davidson, Spelman, and Dartmouth. "If you were motivated, and if you tried, you got so much support," recalled Scott, who went on to graduate from Morehouse. "All the scholarships and support and opportunities they could find, they opened up to us. The reason we are who we are is because we were able to benefit from a community that was there to support us."

Still, the Scotts and their peers also dealt with challenges that few of their predecessors had confronted. Like earlier generations, they reveled in the warm, celebratory atmosphere of football games and other school events. Academically, however, they often felt more the exception than the rule. "It was very easy to find the group of kids who wanted to learn and who were passionate about being successful, because it was a small group of us," Scott explained. "If you were one of the motivated students you all studied together and you succeeded and you moved on."

Students also chafed at the distance between community perceptions and their own experience, especially when people seemed surprised that students at such a maligned school could reach high levels of accomplishment. "I always say the opposite: I accomplished this *because* I went to West Charlotte," Scott emphasized. But the criticism was almost impossible to avoid. "When you come from West Charlotte, it comes with a stigma," he continued. "That's always been something we've combatted." For him, that stigma was closely twined with race: "I always felt that because it was segregated, the 'black, bad school' was the typical stereotype."

As west side residents struggled with the new assignment plan, a different dilemma unfolded in the city's suburbs, where families flocked to neighborhoods served by high-performing schools. Charlotte's realtors had been among the strongest supporters of the plan, predicting that it would "boost home values and ensure healthy appreciation in the years ahead." Guaranteed seats in home-zone schools mattered a great deal to many real estate transactions. "I have a set of clients who're very particular about schools," one realtor stated. "They're shopping for a home based on schools, especially high schools."[25]

The rush to popular schools and the neighborhoods that served them produced significant school overcrowding, and led suburban residents and their representatives to advocate for expanding popular schools and building new ones nearby. Advocates for the inner city, in contrast, argued that crowding should be addressed by reassigning students from overcrowded suburban schools to underfilled inner-city schools. The diverging concerns of suburbs and inner city translated into a contentious and deeply divided school board, and into dropping confidence in the district's ability to effectively educate its students.

In their efforts to deal with the new economic divisions, district leaders looked to the courts—this time for added resources. North Carolina had rarely been generous with public-school funding, and a group of rural counties had sued the state over its funding formula in 1994. In the lawsuit, *Leandro v. State*, districts claimed that state funding levels were too low to give students in low-wealth counties the "sound, basic education" required by the state constitution (while wealthier districts supplemented state school funds with local money, low-wealth districts could not). Several urban districts, including Charlotte-Mecklenburg, joined the suit, arguing that state funding was also inadequate for low-income students in urban areas.

Superior Court Judge Howard Edwards Manning Jr. oversaw the long-running case. In 2005 he scheduled hearings on high school performance. A group of Charlotte students took the opportunity to argue that resegregation was central to the problem. While they were keenly aware that simply desegregating schools had failed to provide all black children with an equal education, the concentration of African American students in schools that were not only overwhelmingly black, but also overwhelmingly poor, seemed a recipe for disaster. Represented by Julius Chambers, who was deeply troubled by resegregation, the students made an official request to join the *Leandro* litigation. The concentrated poverty produced by Charlotte's new assignment plan, their request contended, "creates high school environments that discourage recruitment and retention of effective teachers and administrators . . . reduces the odds students will experience a safe and orderly school environment, and . . . discourages—rather than encourages—student achievement."[26]

There was plenty of evidence for the students' position. The large majority of Charlotte's high-poverty schools were struggling academically—two years earlier only four of thirty high-poverty elementary and middle schools had met federal performance standards.[27] That year, a *Charlotte Observer* analysis of test scores at the system's schools showed clearly that students at high-poverty schools, regardless of income, were less likely to do well than their counterparts at lower-poverty schools. "The high-poverty handicap shows up at every level, from elementary reading to advanced high school courses," the *Observer* noted. Those results reflected similar findings from across the nation. "The numbers don't lie, and they don't vary," commented John Dornan, director of the Raleigh-based Public School Forum. "Low-income students do benefit when they're in schools that are economically balanced. When you put them all together, it's just the opposite."[28]

Howard Manning, however, would not venture onto the treacherous ground of school assignment. While he allowed the Charlotte students to join the lawsuit, he set strict limits on their participation. The students and their representatives could challenge "the failure of the CMS district to provide sufficient human, fiscal, and educational resources to its central city and high poverty schools." He would not, however, hear arguments about possible relationships between student assignment and the students' "right to a sound basic education under *Leandro*."[29]

Manning was far from impressed by the material presented at the hearings. In May of 2005, he officially declared that many of the state's high school students were being denied their educational rights. His report, titled "The High School Problem," singled out Charlotte high schools for particular criticism. At six of the city's schools, Manning noted, less than half the students had passed state tests. West Charlotte, with a 31 percent pass rate, sat at the bottom of the list. Manning did not mince words. "The most appropriate way for the Court to describe what is going on," he wrote, "is academic genocide."[30]

Shortly after "The High School Problem" was issued, principal Delores Lee retired. Lee had stuck it out for four hard years — the longest tenure since Barbara Ledford a decade before. Students admired her. "She has a unique sense of humor, an exhaustive energy level and she is fast-paced," yearbook editors wrote in 2003. "Students and staff read her well for to know her is to experience her body language. When she is pleased, we know it. When she isn't pleased, we know it. The students and staff truly like her frankness, personality and charisma. We feel blessed to have such an inspirational leader."[31] But while Lee was an experienced administrator, the challenges the school faced, amplified by the barrage of public criticism that it endured, had taken its toll. Her replacement, John Modest, found the school profoundly demoralized, in part because of the years of negative attention. "You hear it, and you're going to internalize some of it," he explained. There were "pockets of excellence" — a number of fine programs and many students who were determined to succeed. But there was "a lot of work to do."

SEPARATE
AND
UNEQUAL

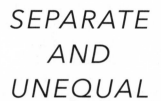

A year after Howard Manning accused Charlotte high schools of "academic genocide," sweeping change descended on West Charlotte once again. "CMS Board Backs Major Shakeup," the *Observer* informed readers in late September, 2006. Newly hired superintendent Peter Gorman had set his sights on the district's lowest-performing high schools, proclaiming that genuine improvement would require a "significant number" of staff members to go. Principals and teachers at West Charlotte and the three other targeted schools would undergo intense evaluation. Those who did not measure up would lose their jobs. It would be a painful but necessary process. "Dramatic reform," Gorman stated, "means dramatic changes."[1]

The school board had hired Peter Gorman with dramatic change in mind. The young superintendent, who held an MBA as well as a doctorate in education, was a rising star in what was becoming known as the "corporate reform" movement. This powerful coalition of politicians, philanthropic organizations, and proponents of private enterprise had built on the concerns raised in *A Nation at Risk* to gain enormous influence in political and intellectual circles. Wealthy foundations such as the Eli and Edythe Broad Foundation and the Bill and Melinda Gates Foundation financed studies that looked for ways that schools could operate more effectively and efficiently, and offered generous grants to districts willing to test out their ideas. Supporters of "charter" schools—privately run schools financed with public funds—argued that charters would lift student performance not only by offering alternatives to traditional public schools, but also by forcing traditional schools to compete for students.[2]

Low-income children of color became a central focus of this endeavor. The barrage of testing made it clear that black and Hispanic students, the bulk of whom came from low-income homes, generally scored far below white and Asian students, who tended to come from better-off families. This looming gap led some reformers to call their efforts "the civil rights movement of our time."[3] "We are failing a generation of kids," Gorman said. "We are sentencing them to a lifetime of poverty. I'm trying to stop that."[4] In a departure from condemnatory rhetoric such as that used by Bill James, reformers championed students' abilities, proclaiming that "every child can learn." The main obstacle for struggling students, they argued, was a system of schooling that did not meet their needs.

This approach, espoused by a charismatic superintendent, had broad appeal in Charlotte. Not only did corporate reform mesh neatly with the community's business-focused outlook, it promised to mitigate the divisions created by the new assignment plan. If focused and efficient effort could uplift students regardless of their backgrounds or their schools' demographics, then there would be no need to tinker with school assignment—or with the economic system that had fueled the city's growth. Effective application of the new approach would also put Charlotte-Mecklenburg back on the map as a cutting-edge school system, in line with the city's sterling reputation as a good place to do business. "This community has had a 2010 plan in place for business development for a while," *Observer* editors wrote in response to Gorman's initial proposals. "A 2010 plan for educating our children is long overdue."[5]

Peter Gorman filled this role with flair. "We want to educate our children so they are competitive locally, nationally and internationally—so that they can compete with anyone in the world," he stated as he unveiled a five-year plan that November. These efforts, he made clear, would center on what happened inside individual schools. "The classroom is the focal point of our reforms," he wrote. "We will refine and enhance our classroom teaching at every level—boosting our instruction in reading, math and science by strengthening the curriculum and training our teachers. . . . We will aggressively recruit good teachers and principals and work to retain them with salary incentives, professional development and leadership training."[6]

As Gorman's words emphasized, most of the new reform efforts focused on teachers. Too many teachers, the nationwide reform movement claimed, lacked either the skills or the determination to make a real difference in struggling students' lives. Many reformers accused teacher unions of protecting the interests of the adults they represented at the expense of schoolchildren. Popular reform efforts included a number of programs designed to make schools more "businesslike," among them intensive analysis of teacher effectiveness as measured by standardized test data, proposals to shift teacher salaries from an emphasis on seniority to "pay for performance," and the elimination of tenure. In keeping with their interest in sweeping change, reformers often championed hard-nosed determination over traditional educational experience or expertise. They recruited school and district leaders with business or military backgrounds, and supported organizations such as Teach for America, which signed up newly minted college graduates, Peace Corps style, for two-year stints of teaching in low-income communities. Peter Gorman's promise to clean house at the district's low-performing high schools fit neatly into that matrix.[7]

John Modest, who was starting his second year as West Charlotte's principal, had significant reservations about the value of the new emphasis on standardized test data. But he welcomed the opportunity to overhaul his

John Modest with students, 2008. Photograph by Todd Sumlin, courtesy of the *Charlotte Observer.*

staff. Years of struggle and instability had left West Charlotte with an inexperienced and demoralized teaching corps that was not up to the challenges the school faced. When Modest arrived at the school, he found a number of dedicated, top-notch teachers. But many were burnt out or disillusioned, and were "just collecting paychecks." He took Gorman's mandate and went to work. Along with a central office team, he observed, evaluated, and critiqued every teacher at the school. It was a dramatic period. "At one point I had 60 people on action plans," he recalled. Absenteeism soared, and by the end of the year, a third of the faculty had left.[8]

Still, Modest knew that rebuilding West Charlotte would require far more than improving classroom instruction. He needed to create an atmosphere that helped his most challenged students feel that they belonged, that they mattered, and that they could succeed. To that end, he expanded extracurricular activities, to give a broader range of students a connection to the school. He worked with alumni to organize leadership and mentoring programs. He regularly checked on students that he knew belonged to gangs, "just touching base" and waiting for them to respond. While "education is the game-changer," he explained, school climate was the key. "If we could become a beacon, a light for the kids, it didn't matter where they came from. If they could come to our school and feel safe, nurtured, encouraged, we could help them put some dreams together. Help them realize that they could dream and they could have hopes."

Separate and Unequal

Modest's focus on hope targeted one of the greatest challenges West Charlotte faced: hope was in short supply on the west side. In the fall of 2008, west side residents had rejoiced when Barack Obama became the nation's first African American president. But the Great Recession that took hold that year bit deep into west side communities, sparking soaring unemployment and widespread housing foreclosures. North Carolina's unemployment rate in February of 2009 was double what it had been the year before. These new hardships followed years of stagnant opportunities for the city's lower-income residents. In 2013, a major study of social mobility conducted by Harvard University researchers examined the likelihood that young people born in the early 1980s would move from the bottom to the top of their community's income ladder. Of the nation's fifty largest urban centers, Charlotte ranked dead last.[9]

Many of the students who reached West Charlotte in the fall of 2006 had been struggling for years—67 percent of ninth graders showed up reading below grade level.[10] While Modest firmly believed that all his students were fully capable of learning, he also knew that they would only make the effort if they saw a reason. Abstract praise for hard work and success would get him nowhere. "For so long and for most of their life experiences they've been rejected and they've been told essentially that they're nothing, and so they're very wary of adults," he explained. "So I think there's almost a metamorphosis that the students have to go through, to find out: 'This man, is he crazy, or is he for real? Is he just getting a paycheck, does he really care?' They have to realize that you do sincerely care about their well-being and their education, their community where they're living, and their families. They've got to realize that. Once they realize that, though, you've got them."

The transience created by Charlotte's dearth of affordable housing made this relationship building into a never-ending effort. The city's need for low-cost housing continued to outstrip the supply—a situation that intensified as public housing officials began to demolish complexes such as Fairview Homes. The housing shortage sent the number of homeless children soaring—in 2006, nearly 2,000 of the district's students officially lacked homes.[11] Many low-income families ended up moving from neighborhood to neighborhood, staying sometimes in low-rent houses or apartments, sometimes with family members, sometimes in shelters. When living situations changed, schools often did as well. West Charlotte enrolled so many transfer students that Modest eventually decided to schedule a regular monthly orientation for new students and their families. The process was hard on students as well as schools. "When kids change schools, that's a big ordeal," Modest noted.

"Especially when they're in adolescence. That can be a very traumatic experience for them."

Unlike in earlier years, staff and students also had to build school loyalty. While most of West Charlotte's students were African Americans living in west side communities, many rooted their identities not in the west side as a whole, but in family networks and the scattered neighborhoods and public housing projects that fed the school. "They have neighborhoods and that's where their turf is. And that's where you get a lot of the gang stuff going on, too, the neighborhoods," Modest noted. "So then when you get them all in one school, my thing was you leave all that at the door. When you come into this school, we're West Charlotte. We've got to be one. Sometimes that would spill over into the school, the turf issues. . . . But again, you had the West Charlotte turf, too. The school could be the focal point—the opportunity to try to get rid of some of that."

Helping students through those adjustments could be a lengthy process. Mable Latimer learned about the challenge first hand when she retired and began to volunteer at the school. She found it hard to fathom the difference between many of the students she met and her memories of West Charlotte in the far more sheltered post–World War II era. "There are some kids here, I call them off the hook because they are loud, boisterous, disrespectful, use terrible language and it's unbelievable," she explained. Unlike in the past, when a punishment at school automatically meant a second punishment at home, some hard-pressed parents did not trust school staff. "When the mother comes in, she's using the same thing," Latimer continued. "Some of them are coming from the shelter and they don't know how they're supposed to act."[12] Still, she sympathized. "A lot of these children that's all they know and old habits are hard to break," she explained, telling a reporter that "the children now, they carry the weight of some adults." What they needed was "a confidante, someone who understands that they are scared, that they don't grasp their lessons, that they need help."[13]

Latimer became one of West Charlotte's staunchest advocates, coming to the school so often that Modest eventually decided to put her on the staff. When students acted out, she kept her cool. "I'll just look at them and say, 'Well you need to calm down because it doesn't call for all of this,'" she explained. "My whole tone of voice changes, my attitude changes and nine times out of ten the ones that I talk to do calm down." She backed up her stern statements with unmistakable devotion. She came to school almost every day. She attended football and basketball games, and sometimes trav-

And The Award Goes To...

Mrs. Mabel Latimer

Showing Lion Pride
during Spirit Week 2009.

Mrs. Latimer
graduating from
West Charlotte
at the age of 17.

Each year the staff of *The Lion* selects one special individual who exhibits all the qualities of a true Lion. Courage, diligence, love and compassion are just a few of the many wonderful attributes exhibited each day by West Charlotte Lions and the recipient of this year's dedication honor, Mrs. Mabel Latimer.

Mrs. Latimer has been a dedicated member of the West Charlotte High School family starting with her graduation from this very school in the prestigious class of 1952. Her love for West Charlotte caused Mrs. Latimer to return to West Charlotte in 1997 to work as a volunteer. In 2005, she was asked to become a full-time staff member, and she has been a dedicated Lion ever since. Her passion for education and love, not only for her school community but the greater city of Charlotte, makes Mrs. Latimer deserving of this honor.

Whenever someone enters the front doors of West Charlotte High School, they are greeted by the love and Lion's spirit that Mrs. Mable Latimer has shown West Charlotte for over 50 years. Many students consider her a part of their families and endearingly call her "Grandma Latimer".

When asked what she loved the most about West Charlotte she said: "Besides the love for my school, I really embrace the kids because I know the hug I give them may be the only they will get. Whatever I can do to make this a better school I will do it."

Inspiring her 2100
Grandchildren at
2009 Pride Rally

Students paid tribute to West Charlotte's most steadfast volunteer in the 2010 yearbook. *The Lion*, 2010. Courtesy of West Charlotte High School.

eled with the teams. She loaned students lunch money. "West Charlotte is my passion," she noted. "This is my school."[14]

Some staff members weathered the changes as well, most notably Jade Harris. Her job had changed dramatically since she started in the 1980s. "I didn't have to build up the kids at the beginning," she noted. "Because they had parents building them up. But now, we're social workers here and we're nurses—everybody else's hats. . . . You have to get through all of that, before you get to academics." Like Mable Latimer, she saw a dramatic difference between the experiences of the students she was working with and those of earlier generations. "It starts with the other experiences that they've had, coming from places where they've had no success," she said. "We've always had poor kids. Everybody's had poor kids. We have had economically challenged kids over the years who have succeeded and done well." Now, however, "we have kids whose spirits have been broken. Who just feel like there's absolutely no hope. . . . If that's all you see, you don't see anybody else who's succeeding or has hope, that's hard to come up out of."

Colleagues at other schools sometimes questioned Harris's commitment to West Charlotte. "I've had comments like, 'Oh, you're wasting your master's degree over there,'" she noted. But she never seriously considered leaving. "I'm dedicated to teaching," she said. "And teaching kids. Kids are kids. They bring to you their best. Black, white, Asian, Latino, whatever. Kids are kids. And it's the adults that have the problems. It's not the kids." To meet the challenge, she fell back on the teaching experience and community connections that played such an important role in the school's earlier years. "My experience has helped me," she continued. "And then coming from a family of teachers. Being from the area. Knowing them already. That's also a plus on my side. I've taught their parents. Or their aunts and uncles. Or we went to school together. Or we go to church together. They've had me in Vacation Bible School."

Modest looked for teachers with a similar balance of sympathy and determination. "Once students realize that the teacher truly does want to help them learn, the teacher has them," he explained. "You just have to do that, if you're an educator in a school that hasn't experienced much success you have to have those qualities, help kids believe in success and hang in there with them. They want to reject you, but you just have to hang in there. But not every teacher can do that." Harris sympathized with teachers who were overwhelmed. "Some people want it easier," she noted. "And that's fine. I get it. I get it."

One teacher who decided to move on was Robert Yost, who with Jade

Separate and Unequal

Harris was one of the few remaining staff members from the desegregated era. Yost had been at West Charlotte for nearly two decades, teaching hundreds of students even as his chess club became noted both for its diversity and its multiple state championships. He had stuck with the school through all the previous turmoil. But his experience had also made him keenly aware that he had limitations. "I've had an impact on a lot of lives," he had explained a few years earlier. "But I've also had a lot of kids that I just can't reach. No matter how smart I am, how good a teacher I am, how witty I am, there are some kids that I'm just incapable of reaching. So I've learned that I'm not God's gift to everybody." The new pressures proved more than he was willing to handle. After several months on an action plan, Yost learned he had won the right to be rehired. But the tense atmosphere had exacerbated an ongoing health problem. He took medical leave, and did not return.

Replacing teachers who left was a huge challenge. In the new, results-focused climate, teachers at high-poverty schools operated in difficult situations, under great pressure, and with the eyes of districts and communities fixed on their students' performance. The press to raise math and reading scores eroded teacher autonomy and narrowed the scope of instruction, leaving many teachers feeling unable to do their best work. Yet greater pressure and responsibility rarely came with greater funding, higher pay, or genuinely effective new approaches to teaching or learning. As a result, many teachers were reluctant to take on the endeavor. In the spring of 2006, the district offered a $10,000 bonus to teachers who agreed to transfer to low-performing high schools. Few teachers took the offer. Not a single one agreed to move to West Charlotte.[15]

The school board, Gorman, and his staff worked to address this challenges in several ways. The district already directed more resources to higher-poverty schools, so per-pupil funding was generally higher at high-poverty schools than low-poverty ones. Gorman added a program called "strategic staffing," which was designed to move teachers to struggling schools in groups, rather than as individuals. He personally asked some of the district's most successful principals to move to high-poverty schools, and allowed each to recruit five top teachers to bring with them.[16]

John Modest used all his connections and abilities to convince strong teachers to join him at West Charlotte. Even as he did the best he could with what he had, however, he was also frank about the challenge posed by West Charlotte's economic segregation. Modest had long experience with economically and racially integrated schooling. When he was growing up in Schenectady, New York, his mother drove him across town every day to attend what his family believed was a better school. In the 1970s he oversaw a program that sent African American students out of Boston and into wealthy, predominantly white suburban schools. "Young people made tremendous sacrifices and parents made tremendous sacrifices," he noted. He came to Charlotte from Raleigh, where the student assignment plan was based on economic integration, and where he had led a racially and economically integrated magnet school with a strong reputation for helping black students succeed. He did not approach the touchy issue of West Charlotte's attendance zone, or the question of racial integration. But he frequently pointed to the hundreds of students assigned to West Charlotte who had chosen magnet schools instead. "Those are the middle-class kids leaving us," he told one group of supporters. "I need some more middle-class kids. I don't care if they're black or white."[17]

West Charlotte's demographics did not change, and the school continued to struggle with high rates of transfer and dropout—of 500 freshmen who started in the fall of 2005, only 250 graduated in 2009. For those who stayed, however, the systematic work made a difference. The percentage of West Charlotte students who passed state tests rose steadily, reaching 69 percent in the spring of 2009.[18] For the first time in many years, West Charlotte's African American students were scoring above the district average. Teacher turnover rates dropped. Modest found the accomplishments tremendously satisfying. "I feel like all my prior experiences had prepared me for the West Charlotte experience," he later explained. "I had started out with a group of kids who started out at the bottom, and when they graduated they weren't at the bottom any more." At the same time, however, four years of strenuous effort had tired him out. "It was a lot of heavy lifting," he noted. In the summer of 2009, he left West Charlotte for an administrative job in a nearby district.

Charlotte-Mecklenburg's efforts at school reform drew nationwide attention. Gorman's strategic staffing plan earned him praise from national publications such as the *New York Times* and *Time* magazine—the latter headlined an article on the program "How One District Fixed Its Failing Schools."[19] West Charlotte gained notice as well, particularly for a "groundbreaking" data analysis program sponsored by the high-profile Bill and Melinda Gates Foundation. The program's lofty goals included using "high-quality student performance data to strengthen and accelerate improvement and guide classroom instruction," as well as deploying test results "to develop effective approaches that ensure all students graduate on time and prepared for the challenges of college, work, and life."[20] When Modest left the school,

Gorman replaced him with the administrator who had been managing the Gates grant. While Shelton Jeffries's only hands-on school experience had been in elementary schools, Gorman expressed confidence in his abilities, terming him "the most competent young administrator in all of CMS."[21]

In the fall of 2009, the Gates themselves came to West Charlotte. "Billionaire philanthropists Bill and Melinda Gates spent five hours at West Charlotte High on Wednesday, checking out the investment their foundation has made in helping Charlotte-Mecklenburg Schools use data to boost learning," the *Observer* reported. "The Gateses and their foundation have made quite an investment in Charlotte-Mecklenburg Schools — and some of the fruits are visible at West Charlotte," the editorial page added.[22]

Plans were also underway for an additional effort at the school, spearheaded by 1980 graduate Anna Spangler Nelson, whose father, former school board member C. D. Spangler Jr., had used shrewd investments to build the Spangler family businesses into a multibillion-dollar fortune. The C. D. Spangler Foundation had already funded a handful of West Charlotte endeavors, including a scholarship program, and the Spanglers were anxious to find other ways to help improve the school. The spring after the Gateses visited Charlotte, community leaders brought to town superstar reformer Geoffrey Canada, who had created the cradle-to-college "Harlem Children's Zone." Canada had gained national renown for his expansive approach to educational improvement, which in the eyes of many had "proven that intense attention starting at birth can help kids thrive in even the toughest circumstances."[23] Nelson and other philanthropic leaders launched an aggressive fundraising effort that convinced local foundations to contribute $55 million toward a Harlem Children's Zone–style project, eventually dubbed Project LIFT (Leadership and Investment for Transformation). No one was surprised when the group decided to focus on West Charlotte and its feeder schools.

Steady progress, however, remained elusive. Even as West Charlotte's supporters raised funds and monitored programs, other factors heightened the challenges the school faced. Both Charlotte and North Carolina were hit particularly hard by the Great Recession, which sent tax revenues plummeting. The drop led to deep cuts in state programs, including education budgets, and school systems across the state scrambled to find ways to save money. The path that Peter Gorman chose featured a massive disruption of west side schools.

In September of 2010, Gorman presented the school board with a plan to close three of the west side's four middle schools and transform eight ele-

Yearbook staff, 2006. *The Lion*, 2006. Courtesy of West Charlotte High School.

mentary schools into K–8 schools. The plan also recommended changing some school boundaries, ending several magnet programs and closing the struggling E. E. Waddell High, whose building would be given to a popular language immersion magnet. While the plan did not directly address West Charlotte High, it would have profound effects on the neighborhoods served by the school, most of whose students would be assigned to the new K–8s.

K–8 schools had become a popular tool of reform efforts. "As the gap between the more advantaged and disadvantaged students within the United States has widened . . . many large-scale and high-resource reform efforts have been undertaken over the last decade with the direct aim of improving student achievement," noted an *American Journal of Education* article that Gorman circulated in support of his proposal. "One of the more popular reforms currently sweeping across the educational landscape is a policy of converting middle schools into K–8 schools, with the belief that the latter are more effective at nurturing student achievement." K–8s, the article explained, had been lauded for eliminating the often-difficult transition from elementary to middle school, while providing a more intimate environment for struggling students.[24]

Closing schools had also become a hallmark of corporate reform. Struggling schools were often portrayed as hopelessly broken — "factories for failure" became a familiar term for high schools in particular. Under the No Child Left Behind legislation, two of the approved remedies for addressing

Separate and Unequal

chronically low-performing schools were to close them or turn them over to charter-school management. Peter Gorman was far from alone in choosing to close schools. Between 2004 and 2010, for example, Chicago Public Schools closed dozens of inner-city schools, arguing that the move would both save money and give students better opportunities. In 2009 Barack Obama appointed Chicago superintendent Arne Duncan to be U.S. Secretary of Education.[25]

On the ground, neither K–8 conversions nor school closings had lived up to their promises. The article that Gorman circulated in support of K–8 schools raised questions about the value of shifting from high-poverty elementary schools to K–8s, noting that changes in student test scores at most new K–8 schools were small at best, and cautioning that "administrators must ask themselves if such a massive reform is truly worth the resources given the likely impacts."[26] In 2009 a study of Arne Duncan's Chicago closings indicated that most students from closed schools were moved to schools that performed little better than the ones they had left, and that most showed no academic improvement as a result of the change. But Gorman pressed ahead.[27]

As elsewhere in the country, the prospect of school closings prompted sharp reaction in Charlotte. Hundreds of parents and activists made the trek to the next school board meeting to fight for their schools, filling the meeting room with signs and angry words. "We're losing jobs. We're losing our homes. Now we're going to lose our schools?" asked parent Niksa Balbosa. "It's time to stop losing. We need to stand up and fight for what's ours." Speaker after speaker denounced the plan. At 8:00 P.M. the scool board chairman cut off comments, and called for the room to be cleared. NAACP president Kojo Nantambu and high school teacher Hans Plotsender did not leave, and were arrested. More protestors showed up at a Saturday rally, where Waddell teacher Erlene Lyde spoke of children "being taken out of their schools and tossed to the wind."[28]

The K–8 component of the proposal caused particular controversy, in part because it was limited to schools on the historically black west side. The move from elementary to middle school had advantages as well as disadvantages. It was a major rite of passage that presented young people with the challenges and possibilities of a larger world. Middle schools required their students to develop greater responsibility. They offered a broader range of classes as well as more activities that ranged from sports teams to band and orchestra. As soon as the plan was announced, west side parents began to ask why theirs were the only schools being forced to change. "If that is so good, then why don't we do it at all schools?" asked longtime school activist Blanche Penn.[29]

Concerns about the limited opportunities available at K–8 schools spoke to a larger dissatisfaction with the education provided at Charlotte's high-poverty schools, in part because of the intensive focus on student test scores. Across the country, a drive to raise scores on the reading and math tests monitored by the No Child Left Behind legislation often meant taking time from other endeavors, such as science, art, or recess. Gorman promoted that approach as well. His initial plans required elementary school students who struggled with reading to spend the entire school day on that subject, while offering high-performing schools more flexibility in their instruction. Middle school students who were behind in math and English had to take extra classes in those subjects, at the expense of electives.[30] It also became increasingly clear that students at higher-wealth schools were offered a richer and more varied range of experiences than their low-wealth counterparts, both in classrooms and in extracurricular opportunities. To many advocates, the switch to K–8s put an official stamp on those disparities.

As parents from across the county began to rally behind their schools, the proposal also came to symbolize the uneven distribution of political power. Initially, Gorman had recommended closing several popular magnet schools, and making boundary changes at two suburban schools. But less than a week after the plan was officially presented to the school board, members voted to eliminate most of those changes. Board members explained that they did not want to tamper with schools they considered to be successful. "We have some major problems that we need to solve in this district," stated member Trent Merchant. "For God's sake, leave these people alone and let's go fix something that needs our attention."[31] West side residents, however, saw the quick decision as evidence of the political clout wielded by well-off parents. "They're not targeting the schools that have these giant PTAs," stated Tasha Houston, a parent at one of the middle schools slated to be closed. "They're targeting our children because we are who we are."[32]

A press release from Save Our Schools, an organization of African American teachers, students, and community members that formed to fight the closings, made it clear that members were "frustrated with the lack of rationale for the proposed closure of high-minority and high-poverty schools," and "perplexed why this community wants to force the burden of change on the backs of its poorest children and parents." The process, the report asserted, was doing more harm than good. "We stand unconvinced that any of these proposed changes will increase academic achievement. No board member has demonstrated to us that they will. Teachers in these targeted schools are depressed, demoralized, devastated, confused and hurt about the uncertainty of their professional future."[33]

Just before the vote, attorney James Ferguson called on the board to reject the plan. "Quite apart from its profound racial implications, the proposal appears to be unfair, unprincipled and unnecessary," he wrote in the *Observer*. "Unfair in that it places an inexplicable onus on schools with a certain demographic make-up; unprincipled in that no objective criteria have been articulated for the choices of which schools to close and which programs to shift; unnecessary in that the projected savings are at best meager and no showing has been made that this is the only or best way to cut projected costs." The negative effects on community trust, he continued, were obvious. "Against this background, it is no surprise that the local NAACP president and others would view the board's proposal as highly racially suspect. The only surprise is that the community reaction was not even stronger.... If we are to move beyond our sorry racial past, we must be willing to have an honest discussion about race, something we have never had as a community."[34]

Gorman and the board majority, however, were determined to move ahead. They scheduled a vote for November 9, 2010. The emotion-packed meeting drew an overflow crowd, with chanting protesters and more than 100 speakers. In the early hours of the morning, after the speakers had finished, board members voted 5–4 to close the three middle schools and create the K–8 schools. In separate votes, Waddell High School and four other high-poverty elementary schools were also closed. The five members who voted for all the closings lived in or represented wealthy parts of town.[35]

The vote sparked anger and despair. "The African-American community is more disturbed by the action of the board last night than I've seen them since the lifting of the desegregation order," James Ferguson stated the next day. "The scars run deep, and the board has exacerbated the wounds." Tammy Hill concurred. "A lot of parents, they just gave up," she said later. "We felt like the parents over here, a lot of them were angry, frustrated. 'They just don't care about our children, they treat our children like nothing.' The kids were angry. Some of my daughter's friends, they would say 'Ms. Hill, why do they think we're not nothing?' And we kept saying 'You can't lose hope. You can't lose hope.'"

Descriptions of the vote underscored the vastly different perspectives that prevailed in different parts of town. Gorman and the board members who voted for the closings denied that race had anything to do with the decisions, focusing on their intentions rather than the results of their actions.

"We didn't target any one group," Gorman said. "What we're doing is targeting problems, and our problem is the financial challenge." The school board chairman, who represented affluent Myers Park, defended the vote in similar terms. "Most of the schools we closed are in the African-American community. That's factually accurate," he said. "We didn't close them because they're in the African-American community."[36] Those explanations, however, did little to quell community anger.[37]

In the fall of 2010, when the new K–8s opened, Peter Gorman was gone— he had resigned that June to take a job with an education company founded by media tycoon Rupert Murdoch. The school year got off to a rocky start. Enrollment surged beyond expectations at all of the K–8 schools, with several swelling to 140 percent of capacity. Students packed into every corner of the buildings as district officials scrambled to install mobile classrooms. The existing buildings had not been retrofitted to accommodate middle school students, Tammy Hill noted, and "a lot of the eighth grade boys, they felt humiliated. They said the toilets were too small. You're talking eighth grade boys using these little elementary school toilets." Resentment and instability boiled over into fights, and suspensions rose dramatically among elementary as well as middle school students.[38] "It was just too many kids to keep track of," Hill surmised. "It wasn't a good choice at all, closing these schools like that."

While West Charlotte had not been directly affected by the school reshuffling, it faced challenges of its own. In the spring of 2012, just before state testing began, Shelton Jeffries abruptly resigned to take a job in a neighboring county. When that year's scores were released, it became clear that the young principal had been in over his head. Proficiency rates had plummeted more than twenty points. More than 200 students had not shown up for their exams, which made West Charlotte one of only three schools in North Carolina that had not met the federal mandate to test 95 percent of its students. Short-term suspension rates were nearly triple the district average. Another staff shakeup had sent twenty-one teachers packing, and others left on their own. The district scrambled to fill the vacancies. That fall, less than three-quarters of the school's teachers were fully licensed, and a third had less than three years of experience. Once again, staff and students faced the need to rebuild.[39]

Subsequent years made it clear that the school's challenges would not be overcome any time soon. Project LIFT debuted in the fall of 2012, with the ambitious goal of using the project's $55 million to help 90 percent of the West Charlotte corridor students reach state test proficiency. After a year of study, the project's leaders had adopted a program that included many of the most widely touted strategies of the reform movement. They invested the bulk of funds in teacher training and development. In an effort to lure and keep top teachers, they pioneered a new staffing structure known as "Opportunity Culture," which offered top-performing teachers substantial pay raises in return for taking on broader school responsibilities. They won approval from the state to extend the school year for several schools. They instituted their own set of tests. But progress proved slow.

The ongoing transience of area families created one challenge. Like the Harlem Children's Zone, LIFT sought to reach students at an early age, starting with prekindergarten programs and continuing through high school. But four years into the project, it became clear that less than 40 percent of the eighth graders who attended LIFT schools continued on to West Charlotte. The others either moved out of LIFT neighborhoods, or chose to attend magnet or charter schools.[40] Building teaching staffs also proved an enormous task. Across the nation, the expanded responsibilities that teachers had been given, combined with relatively low salaries, had made the profession far less attractive than it had once been. LIFT teachers, who worked in difficult situations and under an especially bright spotlight, felt even greater pressure to perform. Even teachers who did well often did not stay long. The LIFT goal of having a great teacher in every classroom "sounds so straightforward," Anna Nelson explained in an interview. "But it simply isn't."[41]

The program's most notable accomplishment came through an endeavor designed not to offer students an education that equaled the possibilities available in the county's top-performing high schools, but to provide an alternate route to a high school diploma. The program, known as LIFT Academy, placed students facing especially difficult challenges in small settings with skilled teachers who were able to provide one-on-one instruction and encouragement. The program operated in a separate building, and was open from 7:00 A.M. to 5:00 P.M. or later, so that students could fit classes into schedules that might involve full-time work or family responsibilities. Teachers and counselors kept students concentrated on the tasks at hand, aiming toward compiling enough credits for a diploma. "There's nothing else to think about except what we're focused on," administrator Timisha Barnes-Jones explained to the *Observer*. "We don't give them the opportunity to think about anything except their success and meeting their goals." The academy's success in raising West Charlotte's graduation rate led the district to lay plans for similar programs at other struggling high schools.[42]

To their credit, the LIFT funders did not pretend they had accomplished miracles. Four years into the project, an independently commissioned assessment cast LIFT not as a successful model to be followed, but as a starting point for broader discussions. "At a time when many Americans are wrestling with how to address entrenched issues of race and poverty," the report concluded, "funders, district leaders, and community members can use LIFT as a catalyst to initiate constructive community conversations about race, poverty, and equitable opportunities for students and families citywide."[43]

There was a lot to talk about. A decade and a half after busing ended, West Charlotte had come to occupy a position that in many ways resembled the one it held during the era of Jim Crow. While many students found ways to succeed, the school simply did not provide the level of opportunity found in schools that served the city's more prosperous neighborhoods. In 1948 a study by the NAACP had exposed dramatic differences between black and white high schools in facilities and academic offerings. In 2015 similar disparities were also evident. West Charlotte offered far fewer Advanced Placement classes than better-off schools such as Myers Park. Although West Charlotte was officially an International Baccalaureate school, it enrolled only about two dozen IB students per grade, its IB class offerings were limited, and its IB students only rarely earned IB diplomas.[44] Even in standard courses, there was a sharp contrast in achievement levels. In the spring of 2016, almost none of West Charlotte's students scored in the "superior" category on the state-required End of Course Tests. At Myers Park, in contrast, the percentage of students scoring in the "superior" category ranged from 18 percent in English to 35 percent in biology.[45]

West Charlotte's facilities also lagged behind, especially in comparison to the new high schools built to serve the wealthy suburban communities at the edges of the county. Not only did these schools have newer buildings, they incorporated the latest technology, which ranged from high-speed wireless networks to brand-new science facilities to artificial turf for football fields. As in earlier periods of growth, the district struggled to build new facilities while also bringing old ones up to new standards—a challenge that often left the older schools behind. Since older schools generally served far less affluent communities, parents also found it difficult to finance enrichment and extracurricular activities at similar levels. At the end of the 1990s, for example, West Charlotte's marching band uniforms wore out well before the district was scheduled to replace them, making "torn pants, missing buttons and soiled jackets" into "a fact of life" for band members. Students and parents launched a whirlwind of fundraising efforts that included raffles, car washes, and candy sales. But they fell well short of the $50,000 needed for the new attire.[46]

The combination of newer facilities and wealthier communities produced dramatic differences between schools across the district — differences that were often laid bare during athletic and other competitions. Michelle Kirby, whose son played in the West Charlotte marching band, recalled traveling to a football game at Ardrey Kell, one of the wealthiest high schools in the county and the first in North Carolina to have an artificial turf field. "It was astonishing to see what they had," Kirby noted. "Just the basic stuff, the condition of the field, the condition of the parking lot. The concessions. It was a clear distinction. So when we talk about separate but equal, not at all. It was very evident."

Earlier generations of West Charlotte students, who operated within a largely African American world, had rarely come face-to-face with the disparities between black and white schools — "We were separate and we were not equal, but I didn't know it, and I'm glad they didn't tell me," Madge Hopkins had recalled. Twenty-first-century students faced differences at every turn. "The kids see it," Michelle Kirby noted. "They see it in the uniforms. The coaching staff. The things that the teams have. Where we have maybe one or two coolers, they have a whole line of coolers for the team. It is a difference, and it's a difference that is unsettling to see. That we traveled thirty-five, forty minutes in the same school district and to see such a difference." Continual attention to the school's academic struggles also wore on students, particularly those who were doing their best to move ahead. "Nobody in the community believes in us," honors student Breonda Snead told a reporter in 2014. "Like, the whole city. Nobody thinks we're as great as we really are."[47]

There were plenty of bright spots as well. Every spring, West Charlotte sent a class of graduates into the world — many of whom had overcome great obstacles. Like many high-poverty schools, West Charlotte had a central core of dedicated, highly skilled teachers who could work wonders in a classroom. The West Charlotte National Alumni Association supplied mentors and volunteers. Although Spencer Singleton had retired, he still coached the chess team, and it continued to shine in competition. Staff members matched students with enrichment programs, wrote grants for take-home laptops and internet access, organized trips to look at colleges. All the while, the school and its supporters continued to bring west side residents together to affirm community bonds and carry on community traditions.

Some of West Charlotte's college-bound students, 2010. *The Lion*, 2010.
Courtesy of West Charlotte High School.

Michelle Kirby's son Jarrett chose West Charlotte because he fell in love with the marching band, like generations of young people before him. He first saw the Marching Lions when he was five years old, during a family excursion to the Carrousel Parade. "I was little, so everything was bigger than me," he explained. "So I see this big giant band full of people and they're dancing down the street, marching, playing music. Dancing and shaking and moving. It just caught me." Jarrett attended some of the district's most highly ranked elementary and middle schools, and his home high school had a strong academic rating. But when a friend called and told him the West Charlotte band was looking for musicians, he jumped at the chance.

Academically, the school was in turmoil—Shelton Jefferies had just left, test scores had plummeted and teacher turnover had risen once again. Still, Jarrett and his parents had confidence in his ability to navigate the situation. He joined the IB program, and found supportive teachers along with plenty of friends. He loved the energy of the band, the challenge of learning the complex rhythms of pieces such as "Battle Hymn Chorale" and the pleasures of setting the audience in motion by performing the latest dances, with a few "old school" tunes for the alumni so that "you wouldn't just be playing to one crowd." Between performances, band members regularly visited the area's middle schools to play for school events and build interest among future band members.

Through these experiences, he felt connections to history as well as community. "I looked into the history of West Charlotte, and saw everything about how it started the bus integration, and how it's the last historically black high school here in Charlotte," he said. "So it always made West Charlotte special. . . . It gives you a sense of pride to know that you're holding a torch and keeping the West Charlotte band going. A sense of responsibility, knowing that you can't slack off and let the band fall apart. It's a real positive feeling, to know that you're holding something up."

Michelle Kirby also reveled in the school's connections with the surrounding community and its traditions. "It felt welcoming," she explained. "It felt like a community. Just going to the football games and seeing the people that come back for the games. And clearly they don't have any children that go to school. But they were here just rooting for the school, just *invested* in the community. The community investment was big, and I enjoyed seeing that. . . . It felt you were a part of something. That you mattered."

Ongoing reminders of the school's African American past underscored the connections with the surrounding community's history. The National Alumni Association had installed a Wall of Fame, which featured a larger-than-life-sized photograph of Clinton Blake, just across from the school's main entrance. Thanks to Alumni Association lobbying, the school auditorium was named for Blake and the football field bore the name of coaching legend Thomas Martin. On most days, Mable Latimer staffed a table outside the main office, providing a living link to the school's past as she advised, joked with, and encouraged the students who passed by. Alumni Association members continued to speak at assemblies, finance scholarships, help with projects, and attend football games. Their efforts, Jade Harris noted, played a key role in building school loyalty. "We have a lot of kids who don't know the history of the school," she said. "But once they get here, by the time of their senior year, they're proud to be here."

West Charlotte's celebrated years of racial integration, in contrast, had faded to near-invisibility. The only physical evidence that white students had ever passed through the school's halls lay in a handful of photographs tucked into the back of the school's trophy cases.

When talking about the present-day West Charlotte, students, teachers, and parents mingled their love for the school with sober assessments of the challenges of economic and racial isolation. In Jarrett Kirby's senior year, when he was on the yearbook staff, he looked with envy at the yearbooks from the desegregated era, a time when the school was "like a big melting pot . . . and the whole community just rallied around." While he loved the West Charlotte of his era, he saw plenty of room for improvement. "I feel like having everybody from the same neighborhood isn't good for the school," he said. "I feel like it's taking them from the west side and keeping them there their whole life. And from a young age it's molding them to think that this is where they belong, and there's nowhere to go after. I know a lot of friends, when I try to talk to them about college, they just turn the other cheek. From their side, college is just something like a fairy tale. They hear about it, but they don't know anybody who's been to college, their parents don't know anybody who's been to college. Like everybody's from the same background. I think that people should go to other sides of town so they can see both sides of the world, instead of just being contained into this one mindset."

Kirby's assessment resonated with Charlotte's dead-last performance on the Harvard social mobility study, which underscored a developing consensus about the negative effects of growing up in neighborhoods of concentrated poverty. The set of factors that the study associated with low mobility was uncomfortably familiar: segregation, income inequality, school quality, social capital, and family structure.[48] "If you grow up poor in Charlotte, you are very likely to remain poor," *Charlotte Observer* editors noted of the study's conclusions. "It follows that Charlotte didn't score well," they continued, "given the extent of our segregation, the income chasms among our neighborhoods and the varying quality of our public schools."[49]

As throughout West Charlotte's history, however, challenge could also

Separate and Unequal

be opportunity, spurring students who had strong support networks to tap a different source of strength, one that did not rely on outside approval. The Kirby family worked hard on that project. The constant criticism that the school and surrounding neighborhoods endured, Michelle Kirby said, "was a frustration for Jarrett and then of course it made it a frustration for us, having to deal with that and tell him how to handle it and how to process it and not become resentful of how the school is portrayed. . . . Having to explain to him that it is unfair, but you just have to press on. Be that person who changes things."

Like so many of his predecessors, Jarrett Kirby developed not only a sense of achievement but an understanding of the value of persistent effort. "The school has been through a lot, and it's done a lot for the African American community, so I feel a connection to it because it's been through so much," he said. "The schools on the other side of town, they're always more looked after. And they're always sparkling and shining and West Charlotte is like the diamond in the rough. It's never too clean looking, but it has a lot of character. The fact that it has lasted this long, it has to be something pretty grand."

FINAL THOUGHTS

Past, Present, and Future

"You can't have a community unless it works for everybody."

SAM SMITH, 1977

On the afternoon of September 20, 2016, Charlotte-Mecklenburg police officers surrounded the Ford Explorer of Keith Lamont Scott, a forty-three-year-old black man waiting for his children to get home from school. The situation quickly escalated. A cell phone video made by Scott's wife, Rakeyia, showed officers circling the vehicle amid cries of "Hands up!" "Drop the gun!" and Rakeyia's desperate plea, "Don't shoot him!" One officer smashed a baton into a passenger-side window. Four rapid shots rang out. "He'd better not be dead!" Rakeyia shouted when she saw her husband lying on the ground. "He'd better not be dead!" But he was. Police reported that Scott had a gun and posed a threat; bystanders insisted he had been unarmed. As in other cities where black men had perished at police hands, outrage spread swiftly. That evening, an angry crowd marched from Scott's neighborhood onto nearby I-85, blocking the flow of traffic. For the next several days, marches and demonstrations filled the center city, while police and National Guard troops deployed riot shields, gas masks, and tear-gas canisters. Windows were smashed, protesters were arrested, and one young man was shot and killed.[1]

The contrast between the dramatic unrest and the image of New South prosperity that Charlotte's leaders had so carefully cultivated was lost on no one. The marches and confrontations topped national newscasts for days, and drew the attention of journalists from around the world. "The banking mecca—the Southeast's second-largest city—has tended to see itself as an avatar of modernity and moderation in a state where both are uneven," noted an article in the *Atlantic*. But although "gleaming skyscrapers and chain restaurants seem to suggest a city that is both without, and untethered from, history, the Queen City was built on slavery and its racial politics remain fraught, just like those of nearly every other city."[2]

As a shaken community assessed what activists called the Charlotte Uprising, the issue of separate and unequal schools came to the fore. "Charlotte is a city that has long had deep racial tensions, and frustration has been building for some time," a *New Yorker* article said. "There are many places one might look to find the catalyst of this resentment, nationally and locally. But one of the first places to look is Charlotte's public-school system."[3] Amid the clashes and clamor on the streets, a protester with a bullhorn put it more bluntly. "They got us in failing schools without adequate resources and then you don't have the education to get jobs," he announced to the surrounding crowd.[4]

The prominent role that schools assumed in the discussion was no surprise. As the training ground for youth, schools held the keys to the future as well as the present. The resegregation of Charlotte's school system, the highly visible struggles of high-poverty schools such as West Charlotte, and the heated political battles fought over student assignment had made schools into an especially visible example of the retreat from the civil rights movement's gains, and the city's willingness to tolerate glaring inequalities. Careful observers had been making those connections for some time. "West Charlotte tells you what can happen when you assume that we can continue along a path of progress, but we don't act to make sure that we stay there," James Ferguson noted in an interview two weeks before the Scott shooting. "Yes, we had an explosion of rights in the sixties. But it could go away. And we see it going away and it tells us what can happen to our society when we don't continue to focus on bringing people together and keeping people together for generations and generations and generations. The time may ultimately come when you don't have to wake up every day and say 'Oh my God, what do I have to do to maintain a desegregated society?' But we're not there."

The Charlotte Uprising prompted swift calls to action. At a meeting of Charlotte's powerful Chamber of Commerce, banking legend Hugh McColl called for an "action plan," and former mayor Harvey Gantt recommended a "reconciliation commission" that would discuss "the cancerous effects of racism."[5] The Charlotte-Mecklenburg Opportunity Task Force, a group that had been convened in response to the dismal findings of the Harvard mobility report, released a strong statement. "The anger and pain are real," it read. "The issues connected to the reality of racism are not new; The work requires change in systems and structures . . . The changes required will not be easy or comfortable; We must have the courage to listen, to respond and to act now." Within three months, the statement had gathered more than 2,000 endorsements, many from prominent religious groups, businesses, and civic leaders.[6]

There was a lot of work to do. Despite Charlotte's robust growth and rising national profile, the city's economic divisions were greater than any time since the era of Jim Crow, and low-income families were increasingly isolated in high-poverty neighborhoods.[7] School system leaders were especially aware of the challenges posed by these economic and physical divides. Spurred by the Harvard mobility report, and by the less-than-impressive results of efforts to build up the system's high-poverty schools, the Board of Education had spent most of 2016 looking for ways to follow the lead of other districts and reduce concentrations of school poverty.[8] But building consensus was proving as difficult as it had ever been.

Many residents and educators, especially those who lived or worked in neighborhoods around the center city, supported the endeavor. A newly formed community group, OneMeck, collected evidence of the unmistakable inequalities among the district's schools, and highlighted research that indicated students from all backgrounds could thrive in racially and economically integrated settings. "Our community's many high-poverty schools and neighborhoods undermine our nation's promise of opportunity for all," organizers wrote in the OneMeck platform, pledging to "challenge ourselves and our community to take responsibility for the ways in which we fail our children — especially children of color — who are separated and isolated in high-poverty schools and neighborhoods."[9]

Suburban parents, in contrast, quickly organized to defend the highly rated schools that they believed served the best interests of their children. In letters, articles, and presentations, they highlighted the logistical challenges of busing students across a district where high and low poverty schools generally sat far apart, and in which more than half the students qualified for free or reduced lunch. Rather than disrupting high-performing schools, many of these parents argued, the board and the community should work harder to improve high-poverty schools. A handful of African Americans made similar arguments, contending that low-income black students needed neighborhood-based strategies that included more black teachers and greater school autonomy.[10] In the end, the school board took its first steps in the less controversial realm of choice, expanding magnet programs and instituting new guidelines to ensure that magnet schools were economically integrated.

As the school board deliberated, west side residents were contending with yet another challenge — the nationwide phenomenon that some called "gentrification" and others termed "serial displacement."[11] Charlotte remained one of the nation's fastest-growing cities, and had become a magnet for young professionals of many backgrounds. This influx, along with a new taste for city living, was dramatically transforming the once-neglected neighborhoods around the city center. The west side's proximity to Charlotte's increasingly vital downtown culture, along with the area's older homes and tree-lined streets, made west side neighborhoods coveted destinations. A process that began with a few people renovating historic homes had become a full-scale transformation that filled neighborhoods with the racket of bulldozers and nail guns and dotted them with signs that announced "We Buy Houses."[12]

William Hughes Jr., who had graduated from West Charlotte in 1995 and who had become a mortgage banker, joined this trend in 2013, when he began to renovate the small, solid brick house his grandparents had built in Oaklawn Park in 1955. It was full of family memories. "My dad and uncle and cousins, everybody came through this home," he explained. It was also surrounded by neighborhood connections. The rows of neat brick structures that stretched along the hilly streets and looked out over the city skyline held many residents who had known his grandparents, and who still worked to maintain the social fabric that they had fashioned so effectively during the challenges of Jim Crow. They welcomed the latest generation of the Hughes family with open arms. "I love it where I live," Hughes explained, detailing the wide range of community projects in which he and his family had become involved. "I love the interactions of my neighbors. We always speak. You come out of the house, you see a neighbor, neighbors speak. My neighbors ask about my daughter, how's she doing. They ask about my wife. And it's a loving community in that way. So I really feel at home. I love it."

Hughes and other new west side residents arrived amid a flurry of public and private investments. In the 1980s, when Charlotte officials drew up plans to address the challenges of their rapidly growing city, projects slated for the west side languished. Now activities were picking up. A public-private partnership demolished the aging public housing complexes of Fairview Homes and Double Oaks, and replaced them with mixed-income developments that combined several hundred subsidized apartments with market-rate houses that sold for upwards of $400,000. Construction was scheduled to begin on a streetcar line that would once again run from the center of town up Beatties Ford Road. Johnson C. Smith was reaching beyond its campus to sponsor endeavors that included community gatherings, arts events, and a "Mosaic Village" that combined student housing with space for small businesses. A major grant from the wealthy Knight Foundation funded a strategic plan to strengthen local businesses and institutions and to examine ways to "honor and retain the historic, economic and cultural fabric of the area."[13]

As the focus on history suggested, west side residents looked to the past as well as the future. Many hallmarks of the nation's resurgent urban communities—locally owned and operated businesses, thriving entertainment venues, close community connections—recalled the culture fashioned by the west side's African American residents during Jim Crow. Like Oaklawn Park, most west side neighborhoods could still draw on the wisdom and experience of people and institutions who had persisted through the hard times of the 1980s and 1990s, holding onto history and community, working to fight off decline, and lobbying for investment and improvements. Civil rights icons such as desegregation pioneer Dorothy Counts Scoggins and sit-in leader Charles Jones, along with steadfast community leaders such as Mattie Marshall in Washington Heights and Martha McAfee in Enderly Park, played prominent roles in meetings and events, welcoming newcomers while also passing on the area's distinctly African American history.

William Hughes loved listening to family and neighbors tell stories of the time when the west side seemed like a world unto itself and "businesses were flourishing all up and down Beatties Ford Road." He was determined to see that history embodied in the new communities forming around him. "You're going to see an influx of different folks, different ethnicities," he predicted, promising that neighborhood activists would work to help new residents develop an appreciation "of the history, of the heritage, of everything that's so beautiful and rich, that they're moving into and are a part of now. I think that we'll continue to do that along the corridor. . . . The plan is to be part of the process of that reinvention as it takes shape."[14]

Within this expansive vision, it was also possible to imagine a vibrant and reintegrated West Charlotte High School, this time drawing on an integrated community. "I'd love to see my daughter see the same type of West Charlotte I saw," Hughes said. "I love everything about the West Charlotte I went to. It was the most phenomenal high school experience. I'm just so lucky and so blessed to have been able to have it. . . . We live in a world with all types of folks. In order to be able to be a productive citizen in that type of world, you need practice in that."

Still, residents who envisioned a thriving, integrated west side, as well as a reintegrated West Charlotte High School, faced powerful counter-trends. As the area's growing popularity boosted home prices and encouraged the demolition of low-cost rental units, neighborhoods saw white populations grow and black populations dwindle. (Charlotte was also a magnet for immigrants, with especially rapid growth in the city's Hispanic population, but most of those new residents settled in other parts of town.) The dramatic nature of the shift recalled the upheavals sparked by urban renewal. Back in the 1960s, for example, white homeowners in Seversville were besieged by real estate agents seeking to buy homes and turn them into rental housing for African American families displaced from the center city — efforts that transformed Seversville from a white community into a black one. Half a century later, as interest in the area grew, black Seversville homeowners began to receive similar solicitations — this time from buyers looking to create high-end opportunities for well-off families, most of whom were white.[15]

Change was also moving up Beatties Ford Road, reaching areas with deeper roots in the city's African American past. Biddleville was founded as a black community just after the Civil War, and remained entirely black until the first years of the twenty-first century. By 2016, however, a quarter of the community's residents were white, and the shift showed no signs of abating. Without strong measures to help lower-income residents stay in the changing neighborhoods — measures difficult to sell in a development-minded city — working-class black families faced the prospect of being scattered once again, scrambling to find new places where they could afford to live. When a reporter questioned Seversville resident J'Tanya Adams about the ongoing displacement, Adams minced no words. "Capitalism can be a beast," she said.[16]

A committed group of west side residents has devoted themselves to opposing this economic juggernaut. Community leaders participate in city planning endeavors, and study efforts to moderate gentrification's negative effects in communities around the nation. A group of longtime residents known as the Indaba Council of Elders hosts community forums and consults with developers and city officials. In the Enderly Park neighborhood, residents have appropriated the signs that read "We Buy Houses for Cash" and redesigned them with slogans such as "Don't Steal Our Neighborhood" and "We Cannot Be Bought." A multiracial group of older residents and new

Past, Present, and Future

arrivals advises homeowners, helps renovate houses, and has begun to organize a land trust designed to increase "community control over our actual geography." The group also presses for living wages, a key support for healthy families and communities.[17]

Residents have also begun work on the school front. In the spring of 2016, Greg Jarrell, a white minister who had been living and working on the west side for a decade, wrote an online article in which he advised new residents on how to be good neighbors. His list included "Support neighborhood businesses," "Fight for affordable housing," "Know the history," and "Send your kids to nearby public schools." He went on to emphasize the role that schools could play in creating connections among diverse groups of neighbors. "Kids are always learning, both in and out of school," he wrote. "Every morning as you drive your children by the kids waiting for the public school bus while taking them elsewhere to get educated, you'll be reinforcing the divisions that your kids see and are aware of. Teach them to be a part of the solution by using their bodies and their minds. We're only going to create the places—and the schools—we dream of by working together, and we'll only work well in places where we are fully invested."[18]

As new west side residents settle in and start families, they have begun to examine the area's public schools, especially elementary schools. At community meetings, in conferences with school and district staff, and in private discussions, young parents have weighed their options, and calculated odds. They have some precedents—a handful of schools, in Charlotte and around the country, where reintegration has brought positive results for all students. But it is a challenging endeavor. As west side residents have pointed out for years, the combination of resegregation, an intensive focus on standardized test performance, and the limitations of the K–8 model means that west side schools fall far short of offering the expansive range of academic and enrichment opportunities that middle-class families expect, and all children deserve. Refashioning them to expand those opportunities, and to serve all children equally, will require commitment, imagination, and a huge amount of work from parents, staff, district, and community.[19]

Efforts to reintegrate local schools are also complicated by the widespread promotion of school choice. In areas with high-performing schools, many families choose neighborhoods precisely for their schools. In areas where schools present more challenges, that connection weakens, in part because of the increasing number of magnet and charter options. While magnets were initially designed to promote desegregation, and while many of Charlotte's magnet schools are racially and economically diverse, they also serve more individualistic ends, providing opportunities for parents not only to select a distinctive curriculum but also to escape a low-performing neighborhood school or find a more socially comfortable environment. As John Modest noted during his West Charlotte tenure, magnets often draw especially ambitious and committed families out of a school's attendance zone, making it more difficult to build up neighborhood schools. Charter schools, which in Charlotte tend to be segregated by both race and class, magnify this fragmenting effect. While much of the recent charter-school push has been promoted as a way to help low-income children of color escape struggling schools, North Carolina charters enroll a disproportionate number of white students, and many have lower poverty rates than nearby traditional schools.[20]

In today's world, creating racially and economically integrated communities and schools requires deliberate action in multiple areas, from dedicated grassroots community-building to public policies that foster mixed-income housing and integrated schools. In Charlotte, in 2017, that possibility seems less than promising. Both state and federal governments are currently dominated by the ideology of competitive, profit-making individualism, making forceful public action unlikely. Charlotte's leaders have been historically reluctant to acknowledge the shortcomings of market economics and the limits of individual endeavor, preferring to celebrate advancements made rather than forcefully address work left to be done. In March 2017, when the Opportunity Task Force released its long-awaited report, it called for bold actions on the part of businesses, faith communities, and political leaders. But whether the hard truths in the Harvard mobility study, the furor over Keith Scott's death, or the task force recommendations will lead to the level of commitment that produces genuine transformation remains to be seen.

Still, if there is a place where it is possible to create a racially and economically integrated community, served by thriving, reintegrated schools, it should be the west side of Charlotte. The depth and strength of the area's African American history, the number of Charlotte leaders with west side connections, and the presence of institutions such as Johnson C. Smith offer a means for carrying that history forward. A significant number of young parents seems ready to embrace a different model of schooling, one that places less emphasis on test scores and more on a school's ability to impart broader lessons about living in a diverse society. As James Ferguson noted, "bringing people together and keeping them together" requires focused, persistent work. But on the west side of Charlotte, it has been done before.

West Charlotte band members, 2015. Photograph by Daniel Coston.
Courtesy of Daniel Coston.

While the paths traced by the past do not chart a clear direction for the future, they can provide guidance—illuminating themes and relationships, highlighting factors that contribute to successes and shortcomings, teaching, warning, and inspiring. Over more than three quarters of a century, West Charlotte's staff, students and community have weathered political and economic storms, confronted discrimination and disruption, learned how to work together, built on history while making their school anew. Amid dramatically shifting circumstances, they have fashioned and refashioned a place where a broad range of young people have been able to thrive, both individually and as part of a shared purpose that reaches beyond individual success to imagine a better, fairer city. As this present generation confronts its own challenges and seeks to shape schools that will address the present-day challenges of community, class, and race, the stories told about West Charlotte High School have much to offer.

"Our history is so important," said Tim Gibbs, one of the West Charlotte

National Alumni Association's most steadfast members. "To know where you're going, you need to know from whence you came. We've been an icon in that community for so long. And so many positive things have come out of it that you've got to say that somebody's done something right here. There were a lot of things that were done right, and for folk to be able to focus on that and study on that, I think, is a real good thing."

METHODS

Everybody's got their own different collage of stories.

WILLIAM HUGHES JR.

On May 12, 1998, I sat down with Saundra Jones Davis and asked the first questions of this project. It was a marvelous interview. Mrs. Davis had graduated from West Charlotte four decades earlier, and she talked with joyful enthusiasm about her days at the school, painting vivid portraits of classes, football games, teachers, and friends. Her voice grew sharper when the subject turned to busing, and she detailed the challenges the process created for African American families. It lightened once more as she began to talk about the long-term benefits of integrated schools, and the ways they had helped to dispel misconceptions and bring people together. As in so many of my West Charlotte interviews, the stories she told wove an intricate web of barriers and opportunities, failures and successes, good times and bad. What never wavered was her deep affection for her school. "I have loved West Charlotte all of my life," she said.

Stories such as those told by Saundra Davis lie at the heart of this book. Over a period of two decades, I recorded formal interviews with about sixty West Charlotte graduates, teachers, parents, and principals, seeking to include both blacks and whites from a range of backgrounds and economic circumstances. Students from oral history classes I taught at Davidson College and Johnson C. Smith University interviewed nearly two dozen others, and I held informal conversations with many, many more. The interviews ranged widely, following the paths that brought individuals to West Charlotte, exploring their activities at the school, and inviting reflections on the significance of those experiences. Rather than developing a standard set of questions, the students and I adopted a more free-form interview style, tracing the experiences of each individual while keeping key themes in mind. The interviews generally ranged from one to two hours in length. Many were both eloquent and emotional — testament to the significance that West Charlotte holds for so many of the people whose lives it has touched.[1]

I combined interview material with archival research to explore the interplay between the actions of individuals and large-scale historical shifts in legal, political, and cultural arenas. In so doing, I relied on the groundwork laid by a rich literature on schooling in Charlotte and North Carolina — detailed studies of the political and legal maneuvering that helped shape desegregation in city and state, as well as excellent accounts of Charlotte's physical development. Works that include Tom Hanchett's *Sorting Out the New South City*, Davison Douglass's *Reading, Writing, and Race*, Frye Gaillard's *The Dream Long Deferred*, Matthew Lassiter's *The Silent Majority*, and Stephen Smith's *Boom for Whom?* laid out the basic narrative and identified many of the forces — political, economic, and otherwise — that shaped the context within which West Charlotte's students, staff, and community created the school's history. With this framework in place, I was able to focus on the school itself.

As I noted in the introduction, the project shifted as integration gave way to resegregation. Initially, I focused on the work done by students, staff, and parents to build a successfully desegregated school. This effort, I believed, would add to the growing scholarship of what was coming to be called the Long Civil Rights Movement — helping extend the chronology of the movement past the legal and legislative victories of the 1950s and 60s and into efforts to fashion more equal institutions in the 1970s and 80s. When West Charlotte resegregated, however, the shift underscored the limitations of that approach. Rather than the culmination of decades of fighting for justice, desegregation now appeared to be simply one stage in a cycle of building, dismantling, and then rebuilding, as social and cultural circumstances changed. As a result, the period that was once my major focus ended up occupying a single chapter in the finished work.

That shift led me to focus more closely on African Americans. Because white Charlotteans have typically held the bulk of city and county power, previous accounts of desegregation have often focused on the motivations of white leaders, as well as the political calculations and often moving personal transformations that spurred many of them to support desegregation. But by the time I finished writing, West Charlotte's history had once again become primarily an African American story, with three decades of integration providing something of an interlude between three decades of segregation and nearly two decades of resegregation.

This project was also closely tied to my own life. I began researching West Charlotte history at the request of Jacquelyn Hall, director of the Southern Oral History Program at UNC Chapel Hill, where I had recently finished my Ph.D. The Program had received a grant from the Z. Smith Reynolds Foundation to conduct oral history interviews in several North Carolina locales, focusing on the era after World War II. I had been living and working in Charlotte for a number of years, and when Jacquelyn asked me to pick a Charlotte project, school desegregation came immediately to mind. At the time, desegregation was still hailed as a major community achievement. But its future was uncertain—the *Capacchione* lawsuit had been filed the previous year, and debates over desegregation's fate filled newspaper columns and public discussions. In the face of the move away from desegregated schools in Charlotte and many other communities—a move frequently accompanied by biting critiques of desegregation's unmet goals—it seemed worth looking closely at the school that epitomized that process, to examine what had and had not worked and why.

I completed my first series of interviews and curated a small museum exhibit on the school's history. Then my life—and my perspective on the project—changed dramatically. In December of 2000, my husband Peter and I welcomed our son Parker into the world. Our east side Charlotte neighborhood happened to be assigned to a high-poverty elementary school that contended with many of the same post-busing challenges West Charlotte faced. As Parker grew older, we confronted the decision of where he would go to school. Most of our neighbors avoided Shamrock Gardens Elementary, opting instead for magnet, charter, or private schools. But it seemed untenable to write about desegregation's accomplishments while personally contributing to its demise. In addition, my study of West Charlotte's remarkable history during both segregation and desegregation had given me a vibrant understanding of the strengths of schools where children came from many different backgrounds.

Parker started kindergarten at Shamrock in the fall of 2006, and we set about working to ensure that he and his classmates had the same educational opportunities as students in the county's wealthiest and most successful schools. It proved an immersive, highly instructive experience that vastly expanded our understanding of the broader community around us. Our efforts gave us first-hand experience with the strengths and challenges of schools that serve low-income children of color, the power parents can wield, the limits of even the best school's influence over students' lives, and especially the many shortcomings of a "data-driven" approach to schooling. I became an active participant in the district-wide politics described in this book's final chapter, although at that point I paid limited attention to West Charlotte itself. Not until Parker moved on to middle school — a magnet school outside our neighborhood — did I resume my research and begin to write.[2]

By then, some of the contours of West Charlotte's new reality had come into focus. Predictions that the end of busing would lead to widespread resegregation had come vividly true. Perhaps more significant, the many "reform" efforts devoted to West Charlotte, and the lurching patterns of improvement and decline that they produced, made it a prime example of the shortcomings of the constellation of testing, accountability, and choice that had come to dominate public policy and opinion. The renewed links between the school's fate and that of the neighborhoods surrounding it also underscored the importance of tracing the patterns of development that had sharpened the divides between different parts of town, even as children from many backgrounds attended school together.

Multiple pitfalls await the author of a history so closely linked to present-day issues, a history that through the years has been shaped in multiple ways and put to multiple ends. Those of us who write about the period of Jim Crow, for example, are regularly cautioned to fight against nostalgia, lest a portrait of the strengths developed in segregated African American communities obscure the evils of the system and contribute to arguments that resegregation is not really all that bad. Depictions of integration have similar political import: present-day supporters of integration efforts recount histories that focus on its accomplishments; opponents tend to highlight its many shortcomings. My own stance, as my actions show, is squarely on the side of integration, both because I think it benefits students and because my on-the-ground experience has helped me see the wisdom in Julius Chambers's half-century-old argument that schools will only be equal when the power and resources of parents are equally distributed. But, as with so many of the people I have interviewed, I am also keenly and sometimes painfully aware of ways in which desegregation has fallen short, and I have done my best to portray those fairly.

I cannot claim that the people and stories I have chosen for this work represent the only important aspects of West Charlotte's history. Nor can I claim that I have drawn a comprehensive portrait of such an extraordinary place. A high school is a remarkably complex entity, containing dreams as varied as the thousands of students who pass through its doors, as well as a dazzling multiplicity of relationships.[3] I have focused on characters and moments that I believe help illuminate the ways that West Charlotte has contributed to and been affected by the long and shifting struggle for racial equality, and which seem relevant to the present-day dilemmas faced by the school, the city, and public education as a whole. I have striven to retain thematic and narrative clarity, while also painting a portrait of the school that students, staff, and parents from its different eras would recognize as the place they love and remember. Much remains to be told. As William Hughes noted in the last interview I conducted for this project, everyone has a different collage of stories. This is mine.

ACKNOWLEDGMENTS

My first and greatest thanks go to the many people who so generously shared their memories of West Charlotte High School with myself, my students, and the other oral history researchers on whose work I have drawn. I only regret that I did not have time and space to interview more people and include more stories.

Members of the West Charlotte High School National Alumni Association, the able caretakers of West Charlotte's history, have helped me at every stage of the project. I am especially indebted to Ella Dennis and Tim Gibbs, who through the years have been steadfastly patient and encouraging, and always ready to engage in a discussion or help with anything I needed. I also owe much to the alumni of West Charlotte's great rival, Second Ward, and especially Vermelle Ely, longtime leader of the Second Ward High School National Alumni Association, who has worked tirelessly to ensure that Charlotte's first black public high school and the communities that nurtured it are not forgotten.

My steps were also guided by many other West Charlotte graduates, especially Stan Frazier, Malachi Greene, and Deacon Jones, whose interest in history matched my own, and who were willing to pursue wide-ranging conversations about their alma mater and the communities it served. Years of attending the Tuesday Morning Breakfast Forum, run by the luminous Sarah Stevenson, immersed me in community issues and concerns, and constantly reminded me that talk divorced from action is nothing more than words. I have also been aided by the work of Katherine Frye, a former West Charlotte teacher and filmmaker who has used her craft to keep the stories of West Charlotte and Second Ward alive, and who generously shared the interviews that made up her fine West Charlotte documentary, *The Mighty Lions*.

I have worked on this project so long that I have cycled through multiple archivists and media center specialists at many institutions, especially at West Charlotte and at the Robinson-Spangler Carolina Room of the Public Library of Charlotte and Mecklenburg County. From Pat Ryckman to Kristen Johnson, West Charlotte's media specialists have always taken time from their busy schedules to find materials I needed. I cannot count the number of times I visited the Carolina Room to look at their remarkable collections of photographs, annuals, clipping files, microfilmed newspapers, and census records. Sheila Bumgarner and Thomas Cole, two of the mainstays of the Carolina Room staff, have provided especially able assistance and support on many occasions over many years. The Beatties Ford Road Public Library was my go-to site for conducting oral history interviews, and the staff always made everyone feel welcome — an essential prerequisite to a good interview. Maria David at the *Charlotte Observer*, whose interest in history has greatly enhanced the paper's use of its historical photographs, helped me search out the *Observer* images.

I have also benefited from the work of several generations of *Charlotte Observer* reporters. The newspaper has covered the school system extensively through the years, and its well-researched stories not only offer statistics and analysis but help me hear voices from many different points in time. My journeys through back issues of the paper always remind me of the key role newspapers play in recording that first draft of history, and sharing it with a wide audience. In recent years, education reporter Ann Doss Helms has been a shining example of searching, responsible journalism, and education activists in Charlotte are envied by their counterparts across the country, whose local newspapers provide far less thorough coverage of educational issues. Conversations with former *Observer* reporter Pam Kelly, who shares my interest in the people and neighborhoods bypassed by Charlotte's economic growth, helped me refine numerous ideas during the final throes of writing.

In terms of Charlotte history, the Levine Museum of the New South has led the way, pursuing its mission of "Using History to Build Community" by combining pathbreaking exhibits with programs designed to draw people together and examine the lessons our area's past holds for the present day. The many national awards the Levine Museum has received testify to the quality and impact of that work. I was first introduced to West Charlotte and its graduates when I curated the museum's first major exhibit, *The Most Democratic Sport: Basketball and Culture in the Central Piedmont*. The museum also sponsored an exhibition of this project's early stages: *Carry-*

ing the Spirit: Voices of West Charlotte High School. The Levine has benefited from the passion and abilities of some of Charlotte's most remarkable residents, including founder Sally Robinson, longtime director Emily Zimmern, and historian Tom Hanchett, a graduate school classmate who introduced me to Charlotte and then happily chose to make his home here, becoming the Levine Museum's first full-time historian, and serving as a model of the engaged scholar.

Early in the project, Davidson College gave me the opportunity to teach two oral history classes, one of which included students from Johnson C. Smith. My students' interviews and projects contributed significantly to my own understanding of segregation and desegregation in this area, and this is the second book of mine in which their work figures prominently. I was fortunate to be able to hire former student, Davidson graduate, and champion for justice Jill Williams to do additional interviews.

My understanding of Charlotte-Mecklenburg Schools, and of the mix of policy and grassroots effort required for genuine school transformation was also aided by a decade of hands-on educational activism. I am eternally grateful to my mentor, former school board member Louise Woods, whose belief in and commitment to children from every background knows no bounds. Carol Sawyer and I worked closely and effectively together for many years, to the point where one school board ally jokingly dubbed us the "Gruesome Twosome" — a nickname I am proud to bear.

The state of North Carolina has nurtured generations of scholars and writers who have created a rich body of literature about the state — a trove of insights and information that made it possible to attempt a project of this scope. My initiation to this august group began at the Southern Oral History Program (SOHP) at UNC-Chapel Hill, where as a graduate student I honed my oral history skills and began to understand what it meant to be a responsible, committed scholar. Graduation did not end that process, as SOHP director Jacquelyn Hall drew me into "Listening for a Change," a project funded by the Z. Smith Reynolds Foundation that allowed me to work with an inspiring group of fellow scholars that included Spencie Love, Kelly Navies, Kathryn Newfont, and David Cecelski. I have also drawn on personal and intellectual support from many other North Carolina scholars, including John Kasson, Bob Korstad, Jim Leloudis, Lu Ann Jones, Tim Tyson, Roslyn Mickelson, Steve Smith, Amy Hawn Nelson, and most recently Charlotte native and newly minted Ph.D. Willie Griffin. The University of North Carolina Press has played an enormously important role in bringing many of these scholars' work to the profession and the public, and

I am proud to have this book included on their list. Special thanks to now-retired editor David Perry, who regularly encouraged me to keep going on the project, and to my editor, Mark Simpson-Vos, for doing the hard work of shepherding the book from rough draft to publication.

I have saved my most personal debts for last.

Being an independent scholar can be a lonely path. I would never have reached the end of this endeavor without the love and companionship provided by Jerma Jackson and Jill Snider. Our writing group has endured for well over a decade. Our meetings — daylong affairs in which we dive deeply into each other's work, break for lunch, and then resume — have been one of the highlights of my life. I hope we will carry on for decades to come. Barbara Lau, founder and director of the Pauli Murray Project in Durham, N.C., has been a true friend, generous host, and inspiring example of committed community work.

Successful independence is rarely truly independent — it requires significant support from family as well as friends and institutions. I was fortunate to have funding for this project not only from the Z. Smith Reynolds Foundation, but also from the ever-generous Spencer Foundation and from the National Endowment for the Humanities — funding that kept me going in the project's crucial, early stages. But at a recent forum, when a questioner asked about my strategy for building a public history career, I had to answer truthfully: I was lucky enough to marry the right person. I might also have added that I had the right parents. I could take risks, pursue interests, launch on a decades-long, at times all-consuming project with little hope of financial gain because I was surrounded by people who cared about me and my work. To my parents, Scott and Lois Grundy, and my boys, Peter and Parker Wong, thank you, thank you, thank you, thank you.

NOTES

CN   *Charlotte News*
CO   *Charlotte Observer*
CP   *Charlotte Post*
NCTR   *North Carolina Teachers Record*
WSJ   *Wall Street Journal*

INTRODUCTION

1. For an account of nostalgia in memories of black segregated schools, see Shircliffe, "'We Got the Best of That World.'"

2. For a detailed, thoughtful analysis of corporate reform, see Ravitch, *Death and Life of the Great American School System*.

3. For a similar discussion of character, citizenship, and the purposes of schooling, see Erickson, *Making the Unequal Metropolis*, 313–15.

CHAPTER 1

1. Blake, West Charlotte High School Report, 1939, box 10, High School Principals' Annual Reports, Division of Negro Education Records.

2. For the creation of west side black neighborhoods, see Hanchett, *Sorting Out the New South City*, 116–44. Johnson C. Smith was originally called Biddle Memorial Institute after a fallen Union soldier, but it was renamed in 1923 when the widow of Pittsburgh industrialist Johnson Crayne Smith became a major donor.

3. Ibid., 70–88. The best account of African American accomplishments in Charlotte following the Civil War is Greenwood, *Bittersweet Legacy*.

4. *CO*, 23 April 1937. In addition to her duties at Johnson C. Smith, Mary McCrorey had gained national prominence for her work with black women's service clubs. See Gilmore, *Gender and Jim Crow*, 192–202. Although the three black candidates trailed far

behind their white opponents, McCrorey won 1,313 votes and Alexander garnered 1,330. *CO*, 27 April 1937. For black voter registration numbers, see Newkirk, "Development of the National Association for the Advancement of Colored People," 78.

5. As late as 1950, more than 90 percent of Charlotte's employed African American men were manual laborers, and more than half of employed African American women worked as domestics. Douglass, *Reading, Writing and Race*, 55. For descriptions of the beatings routinely meted out by white Charlotte police in the 1920s and 1930s, as well as some of the disagreements between middle-class and working-class African Americans, see Newkirk, "Development of the National Association for the Advancement of Colored People," 45–82. One of Charlotte's first black policemen, James Ross, had a reputation for being equally brutal. "He was the kind of policeman that all black people hated," explained Mae Orr, who lived near Ross in Greenville. "He was mean." Orr interview by Howerton.

6. Frazier and Frazier, *T.D.'s Truths*, 54. In 1941, for example, although African American residents made up less than a third of Charlotte's population, more African Americans than whites died of tuberculosis, pneumonia, whooping cough, flu, kidney failure, strokes, and homicide. Charlotte's death totals for that year, as noted in the state's report, counted 437 African Americans and 471 whites. *Annual Report of the Bureau of Vital Statistics of the North Carolina State Board of Health*, 1941, 107.

7. Orr interview by Grundy.

8. *NCTR*, October 1947, 2.

9. Orr interview by Grundy.

10. The building of Second Ward High was not without controversy. A recent history of Dunbar High School in Washington, D.C., includes an intriguing family story about Samuel Banks Pride, a professor of mathematics at Johnson C. Smith, who was "known to stay up all night on the family porch because some local KKK members let it be known that they did not appreciate the fact that he and some like-minded individuals helped establish a high school for colored children in Charlotte." Stewart, *First Class*, 120–21.

11. *CN*, 4 September 1936. For more details on the development of African American schools in Charlotte and the South, see Anderson, *Education of Blacks in the South*.

12. *CN*, 4 November 1936.

13. Hanchett, "A Guided Tour of the Northwest Corridor." African American landowners often donated land for schools, and Tate was reportedly asked to do so, but refused.

14. Blake, West Charlotte High School Report, 1939, box 10, High School Principals' Annual Reports, Division of Negro Education Records. For figures on per-pupil expenditures, see Margo, *Race and Schooling in the South*, 21; and Theusen, *Greater Than Equal*, 49.

15. Randolph interview by Greesom.

16. Private conversation with Gloria Martin; *Star of Zion*, 18 March 2014; Charlotte Jazz Society newsletter I:1 (July 2009), 2. In author's possession.

17. *NCTR*, March 1936, 33.

18. For accounts of the culture of caring that prevailed in many segregated schools, see Walker, *Their Highest Potential*, and Fairclough, *A Class of Their Own*.

19. Randolph interview by Greesom.

20. Thomas Martin speech notes, in Gloria Martin's possession.

21. Orr interview by Grundy; Johnson interviews by Grundy and Waugh.

22. Orr interview by Grundy; Frazier and Frazier, *T.D.'s Truths*, 50.

23. J. A. Grigsby, Second Ward High School Report, 1938, box 9, High School Principals' Annual Reports, Division of Negro Education Records. For Caesar Blake's birth information, see *Tenth Census of the United States: 1880*, Township 4, Fairfield, South Carolina, ED 70, p. 125A. The Blakes were prominent members of Charlotte's African American society. Caesar Blake and Caesar Blake Jr. played key roles in the all-black National Alliance of Postal Employees, and Caesar Blake Jr. became one of the nation's most prominent black fraternal leaders as the Imperial Potentate of the Prince Hall Shriners. Griffin, "Courier of Crisis," 49–50, 57–62. For the challenges faced by railroad mail clerks, see Rubio, *There's Always Work at the Post Office*, 31. See also Glenn, *History of the National Alliance*.

24. Orr interview by Grundy.

25. *The Mirror*, 1941.

26. *NCTR*, March 1937, 21.

27. *The Mirror*, 1941.

28. Green, *A Southern Life*, 235–6; *Baltimore Afro-American*, 19 March 1940.

29. For more detail on the way that black coaches used athletics to help players meet the challenges of white supremacy, see Grundy, *Learning to Win*, 158–89.

30. Dropout rates calculated from reports in boxes 9–18, 24, High School Principals' Annual Reports, Division of Negro Education Records (1938–1948); boxes 89, 93, High School Principals' Annual Reports, Elementary and Secondary Education Section, Division of Instructional Services Records (1948–50); and box 14, High School Principals' Annual Reports, Supervision and Curriculum Section, Division of Instructional Services Records (1950–55). Post-1948 reports from white and African American schools are archived together. Given that the population around West Charlotte was growing during this period, the actual number of students who dropped out was probably somewhat higher. For a detailed discussion of the way that economic conditions made it particularly difficult to keep black males in high school across the state, see Theusen, *Greater Than Equal*, 71–88.

31. Latimer interview by Grundy.

32. Hanchett, "A Guided Tour of the Northwest Corridor." Druid Hills had begun as a neighborhood for whites, but as the city's black population grew, increasing numbers of black residents moved in.

33. *NCTR*, October 1955, 9.

34. For the successful campaign on the part of black Shriners, which was led by Clinton Blake's brother, Caesar, see Griffin, "Courier of Crisis," 59–61. For the dramatic events surrounding the murder trial of Clive Fowler and the successful campaign to build on the precedent of the Supreme Court ruling on jury selection in the famous Scottsboro case, see Newkirk, "Development of the National Association," 46–58; 75–81. For the ouster of postmaster Robin Yount following a campaign by Charlotte-based journalist and mail clerk Trezzvant Anderson, see Griffin, "News and Views of the Postal Service."

35. For details on a variety of Charlotte-based political endeavors in this era, see Griffin, "An Indigenous Civil Rights Movement."

36. The NAACP had a rocky history of starts and stops in the 1920s and 1930s, in part because many African Americans found the leadership too conservative. That changed when twenty-five-year-old Kelly Alexander reorganized the chapter in 1940 and began a rise to state leadership. See Newkirk, "Development of the National Association," 85–91.

37. Martin D. Jenkins, "A Survey of the Public Schools of Charlotte, North Carolina," May 1948. Legal Files, Group II, Box B-145, NAACP Papers, 1–2. Emphasis in original. Jenkins was a fascinating individual with a long career in higher education and a particular interest in gifted black children. See Davis, "Dr. Martin D. Jenkins."

38. Theusen, *Greater Than Equal*, 187.

39. Jenkins, "A Survey of the Public Schools," 11.

40. Ibid., 39. Jenkins was looking specifically at city schools; many of the rural African American schools in the Mecklenburg County system were in much worse shape.

41. *CO*, 11 July 1948.

42. *CO*, 28 September 1948. See also *CN*, 28 September 1948.

43. Quoted in Theusen, *Greater Than Equal*, 198. For a comprehensive and eloquent account of the NAACP's legal strategy, see Kluger, *Simple Justice*.

44. For a detailed description of the new building, see Architectural Record, *Schools for the New Needs*, 260–65. The book also contains a discussion of Myers Park High School, built in 1951. Ibid., 223–47.

45. Hanchett, "A Guided Tour of the Northwest Corridor." For redlining in Charlotte, see Hanchett, *Sorting Out the New South City*, 229–36. For the nationwide amalgamation of policies and practices that shut African Americans out of programs that promoted homeownership and neighborhood development, starting with the New Deal, see Rothstein, *Color of Law*.

46. Kluger, *Simple Justice*, 700–710.

47. *CO*, 18 May 1954.

48. Rosen and Mosnier, *Julius Chambers*, 16–17.

49. Randolph interview by Crawford.

CHAPTER 2

1. For the Greensboro sit-ins, see Chafe, *Civilities and Civil Rights*, 83–86.

2. Orr interview by Grundy.

3. Anderson, *Fifty Years Later*, 29. Statistics from U.S. Census.

4. *The Lion*, 1959.

5. Johnson interview by Waugh. The importance to young people's development of indirect lessons from schoolteachers who taught about human dignity and family members who stood up for it is discussed in many works on the civil rights movement, including Chafe, *Civilities and Civil Rights*, 23–28, and Payne, *I've Got the Light of Freedom*, 207–35.

6. Chafe, *Civilities and Civil Rights*, 48–52. The term "freedom of choice" gained widespread usage in the mid-1960s when many states enacted similar plans.

7. *State of North Carolina 1955 Session Laws and Resolutions*, 309–10. The transfer of authority from the state to individual districts made it much more difficult to challenge

pupil assignment plans; rather than filing a single, statewide lawsuit, an organization such as the NAACP had to challenge dozens of individual district plans. In 1956 the North Carolina legislature passed an even more comprehensive program called the Pearsall Plan after legislator Thomas Pearsall. The Pearsall Plan allowed districts to close schools rather than integrate them and authorized the payment of private school tuition for white students who did not wish to attend desegregated schools. The effectiveness of freedom of choice, however, meant that neither of those strategies was ever used in North Carolina. The success of the North Carolina approach drew praise from across the South. "You North Carolinians have devised one of the cleverest techniques of perpetuating segregation that we have seen," one Arkansas admirer famously wrote. Chafe, *Civilities and Civil Rights*, 48–70; quote is on 70.

8. *Mecklenburg Times*, 25 July 1957. The article noted that thirty-five other applications had been rejected.

9. Douglas, *Reading, Writing, and Race*, 44–45, 60.

10. Gaillard, *Dream Long Deferred*, 5–9.

11. In August 1960, the *Charlotte News* noted that in the four years between 1957 and 1960, a total of eleven black students had been admitted to white schools in Charlotte. The article also pointed out a steady drop in applications: fifty-eight in 1957, twenty-three in 1958, eight in 1959, and four in 1960. *CN*, 16 August 1960.

12. For more about Jones and his activities with SNCC, see the profile on the SNCC Digital Gateway. http://snccdigital.org/people/charles-jones/ (30 January 2017).

13. *West Charlotte Mirror*, December 1962.

14. For a more detailed description of this business-oriented outlook, see Douglas, *Reading, Writing, and Race*, 96–103.

15. Arsenault, *Freedom Riders*, 79–80. The arresting officer confronted Perkins after the acquittal, angrily telling him to "get the hell out of town," but took no further action.

16. Douglas, *Reading, Writing, and Race*, 96–99.

17. *CO*, 1 June 1963; 30 June 1995.

18. Douglas, *Reading, Writing, and Race*, 120–23.

19. Rosen and Mosnier, *Julius Chambers*, 97–102.

20. Johnson interview by Grundy. Johnson also described the way that school staff handled disorderly students. "I remember clearly one day . . . this big scuffle happened. Two gangs had started a war in the cafeteria, and I ran to pull up a chair to watch this, to get a ring-side seat. Chairs flying, fists flying, and I look around to my left and I saw Jack Martin coming to get one and Pop Miller from the other end and Earl Colston, who was another teacher who had a lot of respect on campus. They ran into the cafeteria. In five minutes, they had thrown kids everywhere. The fight had stopped and they had taken the guys who started the fight to the principal's office for discipline." Johnson interview by Waugh.

21. Grundy, *Lion Pride*, 24.

22. For a comprehensive account of Chambers's life and career, see Rosen and Mosnier, *Julius Chambers*.

23. Douglas, *Reading, Writing, and Race*, 108–9.

24. Rosen and Mosnier, *Julius Chambers*, 123–31.

25. Gaillard, *Dream Long Deferred*, 51–52.

26. Ibid., 52; Douglas, *Reading, Writing, and Race*, 109–11.

27. Gaillard, *Dream Long Deferred*, 52.

28. For an account of the regulations and lawsuits leading up to *Green*, see Douglas, *Reading, Writing, and Race*, 124–29.

29. Ibid., 138–39. Chambers also noted that the school board had chosen to close schools that bordered both black and white neighborhoods, which could have been easily integrated and which could have encouraged more mixed neighborhoods. See also Hanchett, *Sorting Out the New South City*, 252–53. For a detailed description of school board efforts to use assignment and school siting to minimize desegregation in the years that followed *Brown*, see Bundy, "A Community Worth Fighting For," 37–65. The work contains a particularly detailed description of struggles over the move of historically white Harding High School from an integrating neighborhood to an all-white neighborhood, and the conversion of Harding's old building into a predominantly black school called Irwin Avenue Junior High.

30. Douglas, *Reading, Writing, and Race*, 139–40.

31. For an excellent account of the multiple perspectives that African Americans held on schooling and equality, as well as the strategies that different groups of activists pursued, see Dougherty, *More than One Struggle*.

32. Douglas, *Reading, Writing, and Race*, 224; 316 n. 51.

33. For an account of black school closings across the South, and the story of a North Carolina African American community that fought successfully to keep its schools, see Cecelski, *Along Freedom Road*.

34. *CN*, 24 July 1969.

35. Douglas, *Reading, Writing, and Race*, 154.

36. *CN*, 1 August 1969.

37. Ramsey, *Second Ward and West Charlotte*.

38. *CO*, 13 July 1966.

39. Ramsey, *Second Ward and West Charlotte*.

CHAPTER 3

1. Douglas, *Reading, Writing, and Race*, 203–4.

2. *CO*, 6 June 1982.

3. Gaillard, *Dream Long Deferred*, 98–101.

4. Douglas, *Reading, Writing, and Race*, 197.

5. *Carolina Times*, 14 June 1969.

6. Patsy Sutherland, one of the young white teachers that Stroud hired, recalled the elaborate process she went through. "It was a very grueling interview, " she said. "I was interviewed by three principals. . . . I was interviewed individually by them. And then I had a group interview. And during the interview, they asked a lot of questions about how I might feel about working with black students. And at the end of the interview, I remember the principals walked me out to the hall and said to another group, 'I think we have one.'" Sutherland interview by Pamela Grundy.

7. Hanchett, *Sorting Out the New South City*, 249–51.

8. Simmons interview by Grundy.

9. Newsom, "Corridor's 'Color Line.'" By 1984, Seversville was more than 98 percent black. For descriptions of block-busting activities in other communities, see *CO*, 27 October 1965. For an account of the removals, see Douglas, *Reading, Writing, and Race*, 138.

10. Hanchett, *Sorting Out the New South City*, 246–53; Lassiter, *Silent Majority*, 126–28. As Hanchett notes, the policies that concentrated low-income housing west of the center city resulted from local zoning codes and loan policies that followed earlier federal guidelines which encouraged the development of homogenous suburban neighborhoods. While the Fair Housing Act of 1968 prohibited housing discrimination and called on communities to take steps to "affirmatively further" integrated communities, it would do little to change the massive shifts already in motion.

11. For an account of the lasting toll that the disruptions of urban renewal took on urban black communities around the country, see Fullilove, *Root Shock*.

12. Quoted in Douglas, *Reading, Writing, and Race*, 181–82.

13. "To the Members of the Charlotte-Mecklenburg Board of Education." Box 3, Folder 16, "January-June 1969." Chambers Papers.

14. Bundy, "A Community Worth Fighting For," 95.

15. Douglas, *Reading, Writing, and Race*, 226.

16. *Boston Sunday Globe*, 22 November 1970.

17. *CN*, 20, 27 February 1971.

18. Grundy, *Lion Pride*, 29.

19. *CO*, 8 February 1971. The unrest in Wilmington would lead to one of North Carolina's most prominent civil rights prosecutions, in which a group of ten black activists, known as the Wilmington Ten, would be given long prison sentences in connection with the arson shootings, despite dubious evidence. In 1972, Charlotte would have its own such case, the Charlotte Three, in which equally dubious evidence was used to convict three black Charlotte activists of burning down a horse barn at the Lazy B Stables. For a more comprehensive account of the cases and the forces that shaped them, see Janken, *Wilmington Ten*.

20. *CO*, 18 February 1971; 19 February 1971. For a brief account of the rise of interest in black studies among high school students, see Zimmerman, *Whose America?*, 119–24.

21. *CN*, 20 February 1971.

22. *CN*, 27 February 1971.

23. *CO*, 22 February 1971.

24. *CN*, 25 February 1971.

25. *CO*, 26 February 1971.

26. *The Lion*, 1971.

27. Lassiter, *Silent Majority*, 199. Crafting a busing plan for so many students across such a large area posed a tremendous logistical as well as political challenge. For a detailed account of the wrangling over different assignment plans and strategies, see Douglas, *Reading, Writing, and Race*, 141–234.

28. Gaillard, *Dream Long Deferred*, 78. See also Rothstein, *Color of Law*, 177–94.

29. Lassiter, *Silent Majority*, 140. Lassiter's work provides a detailed and insightful account of the development and dissemination of this focus on individual choice.

30. For a detailed account of Richard Nixon's involvement in the debates over busing, see Delmont, *Why Busing Failed*, 114–41.

31. Gaillard, *Dream Long Deferred*, 135.

32. Douglas, *Reading, Writing, and Race*, 228.

33. Lassiter, *Silent Majority*, 187.

34. *The Lion*, 1974.

35. *CO*, 20 June 1973. For a description of the behind-the-scenes discussions, see Douglas, *Reading, Writing, and Race*, 230–34.

36. *CO*, 12 February 1975.

37. For a description of the march and meeting, see *CO*, 20 February 1974.

38. *CO*, 26 February 1974. The *Observer* editorial staff also dismissed the suggestion that West Charlotte faced potential closure but in the same editorial expressed confidence that the board would eventually build the promised replacement for Second Ward — a promise that as of 2017 remained unmet. *CO*, 22 February 1974.

39. For a detailed description of the events leading up to the formation of the CAG, as well as the group's actions, see Gaillard, *Dream Long Deferred*, 101–52. See also Lassiter, *Silent Majority*, 143–46, 193–97.

40. Gaillard, *Dream Long Deferred*, 135.

41. *Philadelphia Inquirer*, 23 April 1989.

42. Lassiter, *Silent Majority*, 202–10.

43. *CO*, 10 July 1974.

44. *The Lion*, 1976.

45. For an account of the Boston busing crisis and the way it was dramatized on national television news, see Delmont, *Why Busing Failed*, 190–207.

46. Haywood interview by West.

CHAPTER 4

1. *WSJ*, 8 May 1991.

2. *The Lion*, 1985.

3. Haywood interview by Grundy.

4. Haywood interview by West.

5. Simmons interview by Grundy.

6. Haywood interview by West.

7. *The Lion*, 1986.

8. Gaillard, *Dream Long Deferred*, 181.

9. Haywood interview by Grundy.

10. For a description of Robinson and his tenure in Charlotte, see Gaillard, *Dream Long Deferred*, 179–200.

11. LaBorde interview by Cottrell.

12. LaBorde interview by Grundy.

13. *The Lion*, 1984.

14. In 1993, for example, a community study showed that the University Park neighborhood remained 99 percent black, with 11 percent college graduates and 37 percent of households in the study's top income bracket — earning more than $35,000 a year. Tryon Hills was 95 percent black, with 3 percent college graduates and 14 percent of households in the top bracket. Eastover was 1 percent black, with 69 percent college

graduates and 77 percent of households in the top bracket. Cotswold was 11 percent black, with 33 percent college graduates and 38 percent of households in the top bracket. Oakhurst was 6 percent black, with 19 percent college graduates and 25 percent of households in the top bracket. Charlotte-Mecklenburg Planning Commission, *City Within a City Neighborhood Assessment*, 93, 123, 131, 145, 159.

15. *The Lion*, 1982. For descriptions of racial patterns in cafeteria seating and other school activities, see Baxter interview by Williams; Nelson interview by Grundy; and Simmons interview by Grundy.

16. *CO*, 24 April 1988.

17. Ibid.

18. "West Charlotte Senior High School Class of 1958, 50th Anniversary Program," 4–5 July 2008, in author's possession.

19. West Charlotte High School National Alumni Association, Inc., "Thirtieth Anniversary Founders' Day Awards Luncheon Program," 5 November 2011, in author's possession.

20. Nelson interview by Grundy.

21. LaBorde interview by Grundy.

22. *CO*, 2 March 1980.

23. A sociological study of the class of 1980 at several desegregated high schools, including West Charlotte, argues that the schools generally adhered to a "color-blind" ideology in which race was rarely discussed. See Wells et al., *Both Sides Now*, 115–54. This account differs from that one at several points, in part because it carries on into the 1980s, when the initial challenge of simply bringing different groups of students together had lessened and direct discussion of racial issues seems to have become more prevalent, and in part because it attributes more agency to African Americans—*Both Sides Now*, for example, tells Sam Haywood's story of removing trophies and pictures from the segregated era without recounting Mertye Rice and Marge Belton's admonitions to put them back. Ibid., 95–96.

24. Smith, *Boom for Whom?*, 82.

25. *The Mirror*, 22 November 1989.

26. *WSJ*, 8 May 1991.

27. *The Lion*, 1986.

28. Gaillard, *Dream Long Deferred*, 186

29. Smith, *Boom for Whom?*, 25–26, 71–72; Gaillard, *Dream Long Deferred*, 176; personal communication from Gaillard.

30. Gaillard, *Dream Long Deferred*, 177.

31. Smith, *Boom for Whom?*, 1.

CHAPTER 5

1. *CO*, 9 October 1984.

2. *The Lion*, 1985.

3. Johnson interview by Waugh.

4. Douglas, *Reading, Writing, and Race*, 197.

5. *CO*, 13 September 1987.

6. *CO*, 30 May 1989.

7. Hannah-Jones, *Living Apart*.

8. Smith, *Boom for Whom?*, 45–46.

9. U.S. Census; Kendi, *Stamped from the Beginning*, 424–30.

10. For an account of changing housing and employment patterns in the decades between 1970 and 2000, see Katz et al., "The New African American Equality."

11. For the growth of mass incarceration and its effect on African American communities, see Alexander, *New Jim Crow*; Kohler-Hausman, "Guns and Butter"; Thompson, "Why Mass Incarceration Matters."

12. Smith, *Boom for Whom?*, 46–55.

13. For figures on black students, see Lassiter, *Silent Majority*, 215; for figures on white students, see *WSJ*, 8 May 1991. See also Rothstein, *Color of Law*.

14. *CO*, 23 April 1988.

15. Ibid.

16. *CO*, 25 April 1988.

17. National Commission on Excellence in Education, *Nation at Risk*.

18. Lassiter, "Schools and Housing in Metropolitan History," 195–204. See also Dougherty, "Shopping for Schools."

19. Smith, *Boom for Whom?*, 92–99.

20. *CO*, 8 June 1994. A school board call for a housing policy task force that year was quickly dismissed by then-mayor Richard Vinroot, who championed "free choice and economics." *CO*, 17, 19 June 1994.

21. *CO*, 28 January 1988; Smith, "Price of Success," 24.

22. Smith, *Boom for Whom?*, 103–5. For a similar shift among business elites in Nashville, and resulting debates over desegregation and school quality, see Erickson, *Making the Unequal Metropolis*, 286–94.

23. Smith, *Boom for Whom?*, 107–10.

24. *CO*, 10 February 1991.

25. *CO*, 30 March 1994.

26. *CO*, 12 March 1992.

27. *CO*, 31 March, 8 December 1992.

28. *CO*, 24 September 1995.

29. Smith, *Boom for Whom?*, 115–16.

30. *The Lion*, 1995.

31. Simmons interview by Whitten.

32. Simmons interview by Grundy.

33. Ibid.

34. Simmons interview by Whitten. An earlier study found West Charlotte with the system's second-highest percentage of black juniors and seniors in advanced classes—17 percent. But those numbers were dwarfed by the 43 percent of white students in those classes. Smith, *Boom for Whom?*, 82. Longtime teacher Betty Seizinger also talked about tracking's negative effects. See Seizinger interview by Williams.

35. *CO*, 26 November 1991.

36. Brown and Donnor, "Toward a New Narrative," 20.

37. *CO*, 28 April 1995. By 1995, SAVE had chapters in forty-eight states as well as Canada, Zaire, and New Zealand.

38. *CO*, 25 February 1990.

39. *CO*, 18 February 1990.

40. *CO*, 30 May 1989.

41. Malkins, "Black Teacher Shortage."

42. *CO*, 5 June 1997.

43. Simmons interview by Whitten.

44. *CO*, 5 June 1997.

45. *CO*, 31 May 1997.

46. Ibid.

47. *CO*, 5 June 1997.

48. Ibid.

49. *CO*, 6 June 1997.

50. *CO*, 31 May 1997.

51. *CO*, 12 June 1997.

52. *CO*, 16 October 1997.

53. Ibid.

54. *The Lion*, 1998.

55. For a summary of the case, see Smith, *Boom for Whom?*, 159–71. For a description of the Campaign for a Color-Blind America and its founder, Houston stockbroker Edward Blum, see *Washington Spectator*, 15 November 2012.

56. Orfield and Eaton, *Dismantling Desegregation*, 116–21.

57. For a description of the Swann Fellowship, see Bush interview by Grundy.

58. *CO*, 26 October 1997.

59. *CO*, 5 January 1999.

60. Ibid.

61. *New York Times*, 11 September 1999.

62. Ibid.

63. *CO*, 11 September 1999.

64. The 5–4 vote was on whether to appeal the most crucial issue—Judge Potter's finding of unitary status. The board left some of the ruling unchallenged, and voted 6–3 to appeal other aspects of the decision, including Judge Potter's order that the school system pay the plaintiffs' legal fees. Smith, *Boom for Whom?*, 175–79.

65. *CO*, 2 August 2001.

CHAPTER 6

1. *CO*, 28, 29 November, 23 December 2001; 19 January 2002.

2. *CO*, 20, 23, 24 February, 20 March 2002.

3. The equity plan included bonuses for teachers at high-poverty schools, oversight of school facilities and extracurricular offerings, and extra staff in areas that included health, social work, and gifted education. *CO*, 28 March 2003. The board also commissioned a citizen-led "Equity Committee" charged with monitoring the educational opportunities

available across the system. Almost immediately, however, the Equity Committee began to warn that funding shortfalls were helping to create "a dual system." *CO*, 13 February 2004.

4. Center on Urban & Metropolitan Policy, "Latino Growth," 6.

5. *CO*, 18 August 2002.

6. *CO*, 24 January 2007. For projected IB enrollment numbers for 2017–18, see http://cmschoice.org/wp-content/uploads/2017/03/Magnet_School_Results_2017_18_Round1.pdf (20 March 2017).

7. Boger, "Education's 'Perfect Storm?,'" 1443.

8. Johnson interview by Grundy.

9. *CO*, 26 March, 22 April, 7 August, 7 September 1989; 25 March 1991.

10. Nichol and Hunt, *Economic Hardship*, 15–16. The number of "missing" men is calculated by comparing the number of men and women in different age cohorts. In Charlotte's 2016 19-and-under cohort the number of black men and women was roughly equal, but in the 20–54 cohort there were 17,000 more women than men.

11. Billings, Demings, and Rockoff, "School Segregation," 435–476.

12. The state of North Carolina began issuing high school evaluations in 1998, but that first year too few West Charlotte students took the tests to qualify for an official evaluation. http://www.ncpublicschools.org/abc_results/results_98/hsnot.htm (28 February 2017).

13. North Carolina School Report Card, West Charlotte High, 2001–02; North Carolina School Report Card, Myers Park High, 2001–02. http://www.ncreportcards .org/src/schDetails.jsp?Page=4&pSchCode=576&pLEACode=600&pYear=2001 –2002 (28 February 2017); http://www.ncreportcards.org/src/schDetails.jsp?Page=4 &pSchCode=466&pLEACode=600&pYear=2001–2002 (28 February 2017).

14. *CO*, 21 January 2007.

15. *CO*, 11 February 2004. The Equity Committee also observed that budget pressures, along with a clamor to build schools in suburban areas, threatened equity efforts. *CO*, 31 January 2004. Full Equity Committee reports, which document persistent inequalities, are available at http://swannfellowship.org/cms-equity-reports/ (3 March 2017).

16. Kendi, *Stamped from the Beginning*, 394–98; Alexander, *New Jim Crow*, 48–49; Kohler-Hausmann, "Welfare Crises."

17. *CP*, 10 June 2004.

18. *CP*, 1 July 2004.

19. *CO*, 12 November 2001. For the description of another controversy over the performance of another band from an all-black high school, see Stewart, *First Class*, xv–7.

20. *CO*, 28 November 2002.

21. *CO*, 25 July 2000; 26 July 2000; 15 August 2000; 26 June 2001; 7 April 2001; 27 March 2002. The band director and the students were convicted.

22. *CO*, 3 July 2001.

23. *CP*, 11 April 2001.

24. *CO*, 12 September 2001.

25. *CO*, 15 June 2002.

26. *Charlotte Students Reply*, 1 August 2005.

27. *CO*, 23 July 2003.

28. *CO*, 24 August 2003.

29. Manning, Order: Hoke County v. State, 19 August 2005.

30. Manning, *Report from the Court.* While the original *Leandro* lawsuit involved rural schools in low-wealth counties, it had been expanded to include high-poverty schools in other areas, including Charlotte. For a more detailed description of *Leandro,* see Dorosin and Largess, "Pursuing School Diversity," 157–172.

31. *The Lion,* 2003.

CHAPTER 7

1. *CO,* 27 September 2006.

2. Ravitch, *Death and Life of the Great American School System,* 195–222.

3. Ravitch, *Reign of Error,* 55.

4. *CO,* 29 November 2006.

5. Ibid.

6. Ibid.

7. Ravitch, *Death and Life of the Great American School System,* 169–94. The issue of teacher unions was less prominent in North Carolina, where state law had long forbidden public employees to unionize.

8. *CO,* 21 January 2007; 13 December 2008.

9. Chetty et al., "Where is the Land of Opportunity?"

10. *WP,* 15 May 2007.

11. *CO,* 11 June 2006.

12. Latimer interview by Reed.

13. *CO,* 14 October 2007.

14. Ibid.

15. *CO,* 13 December 2008.

16. *Time,* 12 October 2010.

17. *CO,* 14 October 2007. The diverging strategies of North Carolina's two largest school districts — Mecklenburg County and Wake County — have been the focus of several studies, including Clotfelter et al, "Charlotte-Mecklenburg Schools in Context," and Parcel et al., "A Study in Contrasts." See also Grant, *Hope and Despair in the American City.*

18. While the rise in test scores may have been helped some by an increased dropout rate — more than 400 fewer students took the battery of state tests in 2009 than in 2005 — overall growth remained significant even when that drop was taken into account. North Carolina School Report Cards, West Charlotte High, 2004–05, http://www.ncreportcards.org/src/schDetails.jsp?Page=2&pSchCode=576&pLEACode=600 &pYear=2004-2005 (20 March 2017), and North Carolina School Report Cards, West Charlotte High, 2008–09, http://www.ncreportcards.org/src/schDetails.jsp?Page=2&p SchCode=576&pLEACode=600&pYear=2008-2009 (20 March 2017).

19. *Time,* 12 October 2010.

20. www.gatesfoundation.org/Media-Center/Press-Releases/2008/03/CMS-Unveils -Groundbreaking-Initiative-to-Transform-Teaching-and-Learning-in-Achievement-one -Schools (3 March 2017).

21. Peter Gorman e-mail to Pamela Grundy, 19 June 2009, in author's possession.

22. *CO,* 27 September 2009.

23. *CO*, 14 March 2010. For a more comprehensive account of Canada and his educational philosophy, see Tough, *Whatever It Takes*.

24. Byrnes and Ruby, "Comparing Achievement," 101–2.

25. de la Torre and Gwynne, *When Schools Close*.

26. Byrnes and Ruby, "Comparing Achievement," 133.

27. de la Torre and Gwynne, *When Schools Close*.

28. *CO*, 17 October 2010.

29. *CO*, 7 November 2010.

30. *CO*, 29 November 2006.

31. *CO*, 5 October 2010.

32. *CO*, 13 October 2010.

33. *CO*, 24 October 2010.

34. *CO*, 6 November 2010.

35. *CO*, 11 November 2010.

36. Ibid.

37. *Education Week*, 8 December 2010.

38. *CO*, 17 January 2012.

39. *CO*, 9 February, 15 August 2012. West Charlotte's score plunge in 2011–12 took place amid relative stability; neither Charlotte-Mecklenburg or North Carolina scores changed much that year.

40. Kim and Ellison, *Project L.I.F.T. Story*, 20.

41. Nelson interview by Grundy, 11 March 2016.

42. *CO*, 7 June 2015.

43. Kim and Ellison, *Project L.I.F.T. Story*, 56.

44. In 2016, for example, West Charlotte advertised nine different Advanced Placement courses, while Myers Park advertised twenty-one. http://mphsap.weebly.com/courses .html (3 March 2017); http://schools.cms.k12.nc.us/westcharlotteHS/Pages/AboutOur School.aspx (3 March 2017).

45. Figures come from North Carolina School Report Cards, 9-12 School Snapshot, West Charlotte.High, 2015–16, https://ncreportcards.ondemand.sas.com/src/reports /600576_2016_High.html (20 March 2017), and North Carolina School Report Cards, 9–12 School Snapshot, Myers Park High, 2015–16, https://ncreportcards.ondemand.sas .com/src/reports/600466_2016_High.html (20 March 2017). The exact number of West Charlotte students who scored in the "superior" category cannot be calculated because the school report cards do not specify numbers for categories where percentages fall below 5 percent of the student body.

46. *CO*, 15 October 2000.

47. *Charlotte Magazine*, 20 August 2014.

48. *CO*, 8 May 2015.

49. *CO*, 24 November 2014.

FINAL THOUGHTS

1. The video can be seen on the *New York Times* website, https://www.nytimes.com /2016/09/24/us/charlotte-keith-scott-shooting-video.html?_r=0 (25 September 2016).

The link also includes an article that describes aspects of the shooting. For a series of images about the marches, see https://nyti.ms/2lEvElk (3 March 2017).

2. *Atlantic*, 22 September 2016.

3. *New Yorker*, 3 October 2016.

4. *CO*, 17 October 2016.

5. *Charlotte Business Journal*, 5 October 2016.

6. http://www.opportunitycharmeck.org/thisisourcharlotte (3 March 2017).

7. In 2014 a living wage for a Mecklenburg County family of three was three times the minimum wage, and county poverty rates were higher than they had been since the 1960s. While apartments for the young and prosperous multiplied, housing for low-income families lagged far behind—estimates showed a need for more than 35,000 additional affordable units. Class divides were magnified by race. Across Mecklenburg County, the median white household income remained nearly double the median black income. The poverty rate for African Americans was three times higher than for whites, and more than a third of black children lived in families whose income fell below the poverty line. Between 2000 and 2014 the percentage of low-income families living in high-poverty areas nearly doubled, reaching 64 percent. Figures from Nichol and Hunt, "Economic Hardship."

8. For an analysis of the assignment plan in Wake County, North Carolina, which focused on economic integration, see Parcel et al., "A Study in Contrasts."

9. http://www.onemeck.org/platform/ (3 March 2017). For a more detailed account of the 2016 debates, see Rhew, "Swann and Public School Segregation."

10. See, for example, the group of editorials on school assignment published by the *CO*, 26 February 2016. See also the account of a proposal for strengthening predominantly black schools made by a group of African American educators, including former West Charlotte principal Kenneth Simmons, in *CO*, 24 September 2015. For a thoughtful assemblage of varying perspectives on the value of desegregation from Louisville, Kentucky, a community whose story in many ways resembled Charlotte's, see K'Meyer, *From Brown to Meredith*, 149–79.

11. *Charlotte Agenda*, 28 December 2015. https://www.charlotteagenda.com/31336/stop-talking-about-gentrification-in-west-charlotte/ (3 March 2017).

12. *Creative Loafing Charlotte*, 2 November 2016.

13. Charlotte Center City Partners, *Historic West End Initiative*. Accounts of several West End efforts can be found in Stodghill, ed., *Let There Be Light*. For subsidized apartment numbers, see *Charlotte Agenda*, 17 March 2017. https://www.charlotteagenda.com/84527/charlottes-newest-affordable-housing-projects-gorgeous/ (20 March 2017).

14. As residents of the Shaw/U Street neighborhood in Washington, D.C., learned, however, a strong black history did not necessarily keep a neighborhood from being overwhelmed by an influx of wealthy outsiders; new nonblack residents could in fact be attracted to both the history and the "edginess" of an urban black neighborhood. Hyra, *Race and Class and Politics*, 75–104.

15. Mary Newsom, "Corridor's 'Color Line.'"

16. *CO*, 20 March 2016. Across the county, the demand-supply gap for affordable housing was enormous; while the estimated need topped 30,000 units, the Charlotte City Council was struggling to fulfill a pledge to build 5,000 units over three years.

17. *Creative Loafing Charlotte*, 2 November 2016.

18. *Charlotte Agenda*, 23 May 2016. https://www.charlotteagenda.com/50717/moving -against-gentrification-charlotte/ (3 March 2017).

19. For an example of a successful effort to reintegrate one high-poverty Charlotte elementary, see Nelson, "Long Path to Success." For a description of some of the pitfalls of reintegration, particularly the tendency of middle-class arrivals to take charge of school affairs, see Posey-Maddox, *When Middle-Class Parents Choose Urban Schools*.

20. Rhew, "Swann and Public School Segregation."

METHODS

1. Because the interviews did not follow a standard format, and because they were conducted by a variety of individuals over a long period of time, it is difficult to formulate much in the way of comprehensive analysis. All the interviews I cite use the speakers' real names — with their permission — and the bulk of them have been deposited in the Southern Oral History Program's archives at UNC–Chapel Hill. This follows standard practice in the field of oral history, as well as my own convictions about my responsibility as a researcher and writer. Using real names honors the people who have made history. It respects them as thoughtful human beings who are fully capable of deciding whether or not they wish to be identified. It also places writers under what I believe are useful constraints, requiring them to pay particular attention to accuracy, fairness, and the perspectives of the people whose voices they include in a work. There are of course specific cases in which pseudonyms are necessary, but I avoid them whenever possible.

2. For an account of these efforts, see Nelson, "Long Path to Success." For a description of one of the advocacy movements in which I was involved, see Grundy, "Fighting Testing Madness." That my husband and I chose to send our son to a magnet middle school and then to a magnet high school, rather than to the schools to which our neighborhood was assigned, speaks to the challenges of working with high-poverty schools. We had put a great deal of energy into Shamrock, and while we were elated by our successes, we were tired. It was also hard to envision a path to success at these higher levels — middle and high schools are tougher to transform than elementary schools. By happy coincidence, Parker's high school — Northwest School for the Arts — was located in the Beatties Ford Road building built for West Charlotte High in 1938, and he walked some of the corridors trod by West Charlotte's earliest students.

3. Perhaps the most notable omission involves the experiences of the many immigrants from Latin America, Asia, and Africa, who in recent decades have dramatically transformed Charlotte's population — nearly one in five of Charlotte's current residents was born outside the country. This recent wave of immigration poses intriguing dilemmas for Southern historians such as myself: it has profound effects on the present-day South, but rarely figures into the historical developments that we are used to tracing when we examine the history of race. In an effort to keep an already unwieldy narrative coherent, and because few of Charlotte's recent immigrants have settled on the west side, I reluctantly set that particular subject aside.

BIBLIOGRAPHY

INTERVIEWS

If the person interviewed graduated from West Charlotte High, the graduation year is noted in parentheses. All interviews took place in Charlotte, N.C.

Abramson, Carrie Culp (1988). Interview by Pamela Grundy. 21 February 1999. Southern Historical Collection, Wilson Library, University of North Carolina at Chapel Hill.

Alexander, Agnes (1974). Interview by Amanda Lauria. 13 February 2001. Southern Historical Collection, Wilson Library, University of North Carolina at Chapel Hill.

Alexander, Kelly, Jr. (1966). Interview by Pamela Grundy. 24 March 2013. Southern Historical Collection, Wilson Library, University of North Carolina at Chapel Hill.

Anderson, Edward, Jr. (1964). Interview by Pamela Grundy. 9 June 2015. Southern Historical Collection, Wilson Library, University of North Carolina at Chapel Hill.

Babb, Jim and Mary Lou. Interview by Jill Williams. 14 July 1999. Southern Historical Collection, Wilson Library, University of North Carolina at Chapel Hill.

Barbee, Amantha (1984), and Mary Helms (1984). Interview by Pamela Grundy. 14 November 2015. Southern Historical Collection, Wilson Library, University of North Carolina at Chapel Hill.

Baxter, Andrew (1988). Interview by Jill Williams. 29 June 1999. Southern Historical Collection, Wilson Library, University of North Carolina at Chapel Hill.

Black, Jeff (1999). Interview by Pamela Grundy. 29 March 1999. Southern Historical Collection, Wilson Library, University of North Carolina at Chapel Hill.

Bradley, Mary Anna Neal (1958), Joanna Neal Dowling (1959), and Barbara Funderburk (1958). Interview by Pamela Grundy. 1 August 2012. Southern Historical Collection, Wilson Library, University of North Carolina at Chapel Hill.

Bush, Lucy. Interview by Pamela Grundy. 11 July 2016. Southern Historical Collection, Wilson Library, University of North Carolina at Chapel Hill.

Camp, Patsy Rice (1962). Interview by Pamela Grundy. 23 March 1999. Southern Historical Collection, Wilson Library, University of North Carolina at Chapel Hill.

Coleman, Sarah Moore Armstrong (1941). Interview by Pamela Grundy. 9 April 2015. In author's possession.

Culp, William. Interview by Pamela Grundy. 19 February 1999. Southern Historical Collection, Wilson Library, University of North Carolina at Chapel Hill.

Davis, Barbara Wellborne. Interviews by Pamela Grundy. 14 and 21 November 2000. In author's possession.

Davis, Sandra Jones (1958). Interview by Pamela Grundy. 12 May 1998. Southern Historical Collection, Wilson Library, University of North Carolina at Chapel Hill.

Dean, Curtis (1997), and Tori Scarborough (1997). Interview by Pamela Grundy. 26 September 2016, Southern Historical Collection, Wilson Library, University of North Carolina at Chapel Hill.

Dennis, Ella (1966). Interview by Pamela Grundy. 9 November 2012. Southern Historical Collection, Wilson Library, University of North Carolina at Chapel Hill.

Dowling, Joanna Neal (1959), Mary Anna Neal Bradley (1958), and Barbara Funderburk (1958). Interview by Pamela Grundy. 1 August 2012. Southern Historical Collection, Wilson Library, University of North Carolina at Chapel Hill.

Elder, Thereasea (1944). Interview by Leslie Brown. 15 June 1993. Duke University Libraries.

Enloe, Alma (1965). Interview by Pamela Grundy. 15 May 1998. Southern Historical Collection, Wilson Library, University of North Carolina at Chapel Hill.

Ferguson, James and Barbara. Interview by Pamela Grundy. 6 September 2016. Southern Historical Collection, Wilson Library, University of North Carolina at Chapel Hill.

Frazier, Stan (1971). Interview by Pamela Grundy. 23 March 2012. In author's possession.

Fritz, Angela Wood. Interview by Pamela Grundy. 6 November 2000. Southern Historical Collection, Wilson Library, University of North Carolina at Chapel Hill.

Foxx, Anthony (1989). Interview by Pamela Grundy. 11 November 2012. Southern Historical Collection, Wilson Library, University of North Carolina at Chapel Hill.

Funderburk, Barbara (1958), Mary Anna Neal Bradley (1958), and Joanna Neal Dowling (1959). Interview by Pamela Grundy. 1 August 2012. Southern Historical Collection, Wilson Library, University of North Carolina at Chapel Hill.

Gibbs, Timothy (1978). Interview by Pamela Grundy. 27 May 1998. Southern Historical Collection, Wilson Library, University of North Carolina at Chapel Hill.

Graham, Amanda (1948). Interview by Pamela Grundy. 4 March 2012. In author's possession.

Greene, Malachi (1960). Interview by Pamela Grundy. 8 April 2015. In author's possession.

Griffin, Arthur, Jr. Interview by Pamela Grundy. 7 May 1999. Southern Historical Collection, Wilson Library, University of North Carolina at Chapel Hill.

Hamilton, Joe (2003). Interview by Pamela Grundy. 27 April 2016. Southern Historical Collection, Wilson Library, University of North Carolina at Chapel Hill.

Hamlin, William (1965). Interview by Pamela Grundy. 29 May 1998. Southern Historical Collection, Wilson Library, University of North Carolina at Chapel Hill.

Harris, Jade. Interview by Pamela Grundy. 31 October 2016. In author's possession.

Hawkins, Reginald. Interview by Melinda Desmarais. 11 June 2001. J. Murrey Atkins Library, University of North Carolina, Charlotte.

Haywood, Andrew "Sam." Interview by Pamela Grundy. 15 November 2000. Southern Historical Collection, Wilson Library, University of North Carolina at Chapel Hill.

Haywood, Andrew "Sam." Interview by Matt West. 27 March 2001. Southern Historical Collection, Wilson Library, University of North Carolina at Chapel Hill.

Helms, Mary (1984), and Amantha Barbee (1984). Interview by Pamela Grundy. 14 November 2015. Southern Historical Collection, Wilson Library, University of North Carolina at Chapel Hill.

Hill, Tammy (1985). Interview by Pamela Grundy. 17 March 2016. Southern Historical Collection, Wilson Library, University of North Carolina at Chapel Hill.

Hipp, Elliott (1975). Interview by Pamela Grundy. 29 November 2016. Southern Historical Collection, Wilson Library, University of North Carolina at Chapel Hill.

Hopkins, Madge (1960). Interview by Pamela Grundy. 17 October 2000. Southern Historical Collection, Wilson Library, University of North Carolina at Chapel Hill.

Howard, David (1988). Interview by Pamela Grundy. 9 February 2016. Southern Historical Collection, Wilson Library, University of North Carolina at Chapel Hill.

Hughes, William, Jr. (1995). Interview by Pamela Grundy. 8 December 2016. Southern Historical Collection, Wilson Library, University of North Carolina at Chapel Hill.

Irons, Ned (1999). Interview by Pamela Grundy. 16 March 1999. Southern Historical Collection, Wilson Library, University of North Carolina at Chapel Hill.

Johnson, Gerald (1967). Interview by Dwana Waugh. 24 May 2008. Southern Historical Collection, Wilson Library, University of North Carolina at Chapel Hill.

Johnson, Gerald (1967). Interview by Pamela Grundy. 14 March 2016. Southern Historical Collection, Wilson Library, University of North Carolina at Chapel Hill.

Jones, J. Charles. Interview by Debbie Howard. 18 May 2005. J. Murrey Atkins Library, University of North Carolina, Charlotte.

Jones, Leonard "Deacon" (1967). Interview by Pamela Grundy. 20 April 2005. In author's possession.

Kirby, Jarrett (2016). Interview by Pamela Grundy. 19 July 2016. Southern Historical Collection, Wilson Library, University of North Carolina at Chapel Hill.

Kirby, Michelle. Interview by Pamela Grundy. 7 July 2016. Southern Historical Collection, Wilson Library, University of North Carolina at Chapel Hill.

LaBorde, Charles. Interview by Auda Cottrell. 22 March 2001. Southern Historical Collection, Wilson Library, University of North Carolina at Chapel Hill.

———. Interview by Pamela Grundy. 19 October 2000. Southern Historical Collection, Wilson Library, University of North Carolina at Chapel Hill.

Latimer, Mable Haynes (1952). Interview by Lynn Reed. 18 April 2005. J. Murrey Atkins Library, University of North Carolina, Charlotte.

———. Interview by Pamela Grundy. 9 May 2005. Southern Historical Collection, Wilson Library, University of North Carolina at Chapel Hill.

Ledford, Barbara. Interview by Jill Williams. 17 July 1999. Southern Historical Collection, Wilson Library, University of North Carolina at Chapel Hill.

Love, Harriet Gentry (1962). Interview by Pamela Grundy. 17 June 1998. Southern Historical Collection, Wilson Library, University of North Carolina at Chapel Hill.

Love, John, Jr. (1980). Interview by Pamela Grundy. 17 February 1999. Southern Historical Collection, Wilson Library, University of North Carolina at Chapel Hill.

McAllister, Latrelle (1978). Interview by Pamela Grundy. 25 June 1998. Southern Historical Collection, Wilson Library, University of North Carolina at Chapel Hill.

McCullough, Charles (1951). Interview by Pamela Grundy. 20 and 26 October 2015. Southern Historical Collection, Wilson Library, University of North Carolina at Chapel Hill.

McMillan, William B., Jr. Interview by Pamela Grundy. 26 October 2000. Southern Historical Collection, Wilson Library, University of North Carolina at Chapel Hill.

Meeks, Rosalie Davis (1945). Interview by Matt West. 27 February 2001. Southern Historical Collection, Wilson Library, University of North Carolina at Chapel Hill.

Miller, Leroy "Pop." Interview by Pamela Grundy. 8 June 1998. Southern Historical Collection, Wilson Library, University of North Carolina at Chapel Hill.

Modest, John. Interview by Pamela Grundy. 13 March 2013. In author's possession.

Nelson, Anna Spangler (1980). Interview by Pamela Grundy. 11 March 2016, Southern Historical Collection, Wilson Library, University of North Carolina at Chapel Hill.

Nelson, Anna Spangler (1980), and Abigail Spangler (1983). Interview by Pamela Grundy. 15 February 1999. Southern Historical Collection, Wilson Library, University of North Carolina at Chapel Hill.

Orr, Mae Clark (1946). Interview by Steven Howerton. 8 April 2004, J. Murray Atkins Library, University of North Carolina at Charlotte.

————. Interview by Pamela Grundy. 6 May 2005. Southern Historical Collection, Wilson Library, University of North Carolina at Chapel Hill.

Perry, Justin (1999). Interview by Pamela Grundy. 7 March 2016. Southern Historical Collection, Wilson Library, University of North Carolina at Chapel Hill.

Pharr, Eunice. Interview by Amanda Lauria. 12 April 2001. Southern Historical Collection, Wilson Library, University of North Carolina at Chapel Hill.

Pharr-Smith, Emille (1988). Interview by Amanda Lauria. 19 March 2001. Southern Historical Collection, Wilson Library, University of North Carolina at Chapel Hill.

Randolph, Elizabeth Schmoke. Interview by Jennifer Greesom. 16 June 1993. J. Murrey Atkins Library, University of North Carolina, Charlotte.

————. Interview by Vickie Crawford. 21 August 1996. J. Murrey Atkins Library, University of North Carolina, Charlotte.

Ray, Maggie. Interview by Pamela Grundy. 9 November 2000. Southern Historical Collection, Wilson Library, University of North Carolina at Chapel Hill.

Scarborough, Tori (1997), and Curtis Dean (1997). Interview by Pamela Grundy. 26 September 2016. Southern Historical Collection, Wilson Library, University of North Carolina at Chapel Hill.

Scott Isaiah (2007). Interview by Pamela Grundy. 2 March 2012. Southern Historical Collection, Wilson Library, University of North Carolina at Chapel Hill.

Seizinger, Betty. Interview by Jill Williams. 22 June 1999. Southern Historical Collection, Wilson Library, University of North Carolina at Chapel Hill.

Simmons, Kenneth (1970). Interview by Jacqueline Whitten. 15 March 2001. Southern Historical Collection, Wilson Library, University of North Carolina at Chapel Hill.

————. Interview by Pamela Grundy. 27 May 2016. Southern Historical Collection, Wilson Library, University of North Carolina at Chapel Hill.

Singleton, Spencer. Interview by Pamela Grundy. 24 August 2016. Southern Historical Collection, Wilson Library, University of North Carolina at Chapel Hill.

Spangler, Abigail (1983), and Anna Spangler Nelson (1980). Interview by Pamela

Grundy. 15 February 1999. Southern Historical Collection, Wilson Library, University of North Carolina at Chapel Hill.

Stroud, Gerson. Interview by Pamela Grundy. 26 May 1999. Southern Historical Collection, Wilson Library, University of North Carolina at Chapel Hill.

—————. Interview by Pamela Grundy. 24 October 2000. Southern Historical Collection, Wilson Library, University of North Carolina at Chapel Hill.

Sutherland, Patricia. Interview by Pamela Grundy. 6 December 2000. Southern Historical Collection, Wilson Library, University of North Carolina at Chapel Hill.

Tarr, Brian. Interview by Pamela Grundy. 27 April 1999. Southern Historical Collection, Wilson Library, University of North Carolina at Chapel Hill.

Tarr, Jeremy (1994). Interview by Pamela Grundy. 24 November 2000, Southern Historical Collection, Wilson Library, University of North Carolina at Chapel Hill.

Torrence, Rudolph (1946). Interview by Pamela Grundy. 27 May 1998. Southern Historical Collection, Wilson Library, University of North Carolina at Chapel Hill.

Van Hecke, Evelyn. Interview by Jill Williams. 20 June 1999. Southern Historical Collection, Wilson Library, University of North Carolina at Chapel Hill.

White, Gosnell (1973). Interview by Pamela Grundy. 29 March 1999, Southern Historical Collection, Wilson Library, University of North Carolina at Chapel Hill.

Yost, Robert. Interview by Pamela Grundy. 22 November 2000. Southern Historical Collection, Wilson Library, University of North Carolina at Chapel Hill.

MANUSCRIPT COLLECTIONS

Charlotte, N.C.
   Public Library of Charlotte and Mecklenburg County
        Robinson-Spangler Carolina Room
   University of North Carolina–Charlotte, J. Murrey Atkins Library
        Julius L. Chambers Papers
   West Charlotte High School
        Media Center Collections
Raleigh, N.C.
   North Carolina State Archives
        Department of Public Instruction
            Division of Instructional Services, Supervision and Curriculum Section
            Division of Negro Education
Washington, D.C.
   Library of Congress
        NAACP Papers

NEWSPAPERS AND JOURNALS

Atlantic

Baltimore Afro-American

Boston Sunday Globe

Charlotte Business Journal

Charlotte Magazine

Charlotte News

Charlotte Observer

Education Week

The Lion
The Mirror
Mecklenburg Times
New Yorker
New York Times
North Carolina Teachers Record

Philadelphia Inquirer
Star of Zion
Scalawag
Time
Wall Street Journal
Washington Post

BOOKS, ARTICLES, PAMPHLETS, VIDEOS, THESES, AND DISSERTATIONS

Alexander, Michelle. *The New Jim Crow: Mass Incarceration in the Age of Colorblindness.* New York: New Press, 2012.

Anderson, Edward M. Sr. *Fifty Years Later: The West Charlotte Senior High School Class of 1964.* Stone Mountain, Ga.: Your Family Research & Publishing, 2015.

Anderson, James. *The Education of Blacks in the South, 1860–1935.* Chapel Hill: University of North Carolina Press, 1988.

Annual Report of the Bureau of Vital Statistics of the North Carolina State Board of Health. Raleigh: Bureau of Vital Statistics, 1941.

Architectural Record. *Schools for the New Needs: Educational, Social, Economic.* New York: F.W. Dodge Corporation, 1956.

Arsenault, Raymond. *Freedom Riders: 1961 and the Struggle for Racial Justice.* Abridged ed. New York: Oxford University Press, 2011.

Billings, Stephen B., David J. Demings, and Jonah Rockoff. "School Segregation, Educational Attainment and Crime: Evidence from the End of Busing in Charlotte Mecklenburg." *Quarterly Journal of Economics* 129 (2014): 435–76.

Boger, John Charles. "Education's 'Perfect Storm'? Racial Resegregation, High-Stakes Testing and School Resource Inequities: The Case of North Carolina." *North Carolina Law Review* 81 (May 2003): 1375–1462.

Brown, Anthony, and Jamel K. Donnor. "Toward a New Narrative on Black Males, Education, and Public Policy." *Race Ethnicity and Education* 14 (January 2011): 17–32.

Bundy, Lauren. "A Community Worth Fighting For: African American Educational Activism in Charlotte, North Carolina, 1961–1974." MA thesis, University of North Carolina at Charlotte, 2008.

Byrnes, Vaughan, and Allen Ruby. "Comparing Achievement Between K-8 and Middle Schools: A Large-Scale Empirical Study." *American Journal of Education* 114 (November 2007): 101–35.

Cecelski, David S. *Along Freedom Road: Hyde County, North Carolina, and the Fate of Black Schools in the South.* Chapel Hill: University of North Carolina Press, 1994.

Center on Urban & Metropolitan Policy and the Pew Hispanic Center. *Latino Growth in Metropolitan America: New Patterns, New Locations.* Washington, D.C.: Brookings Institution, July 2002.

Chafe, William H. *Civilities and Civil Rights: Greensboro, North Carolina and the Black Struggle for Freedom.* New York: Oxford University Press, 1981.

Charlotte Center City Partners. *Historic West End Initiative: 2016 Tactical Plan.* Charlotte: Charlotte Center City Partners, 2016.

Charlotte-Mecklenburg Planning Commission. *City Within a City Neighborhood Assessment*. Charlotte: Charlotte-Mecklenburg Planning Commission, 1993.

Charlotte Students Reply to the Charlotte-Mecklenburg Board of Education's Opposition to Intervention. North Carolina General Court of Justice, Superior Court Division, 95 CVS 1158, Hoke County v. State, 1 August 2005.

Chetty, Raj, Nathaniel Hendren, Patrick Kline, and Emmanuel Saez. "Where Is the Land of Opportunity? The Geography of Intergenerational Mobility in the United States." National Bureau of Economic Research Working Paper 19843, January 2014.

Clotfelter, Charles T., Helen F. Ladd, and Jacob L. Vigdor. "Charlotte-Mecklenburg Schools in Context: Racial and Economic Imbalance at the District and State Level, 1994–2012." In *Yesterday, Today, and Tomorrow: School Desegregation and Resegregation in Charlotte*, edited by Roslyn Mickelson, Stephen Smith, and Amy Hawn Nelson, 69–84. Cambridge, Mass.: Harvard Education Press, 2015.

Davis, Joy Lawson. "Dr. Martin D. Jenkins: A Voice to be Heard (1904–1978)." In *A Century of Contributions to Gifted Education: Illuminating Lives*, edited by Ann Robinson and Jennifer Jolly. New York: Routledge, 2013.

de la Torre, Marisa, and Julia Gwynne. *When Schools Close: Effects on Displaced Students in Chicago Public Schools*. Chicago: Consortium on Chicago School Research at the University of Chicago, October 2009.

Delmont, Matthew F. *Why Busing Failed: Race, Media, and the National Resistance to School Desegregation*. Berkeley: University of California Press, 2016.

Dorosin, Mark, and Luke Largess. "Pursuing School Diversity and Equity in *Leandro's* Shadow." In *Yesterday, Today, and Tomorrow: School Desegregation and Resegregation in Charlotte*, edited by Roslyn Mickelson, Stephen Smith, and Amy Hawn Nelson, 157–72. Cambridge, Mass.: Harvard Education Press, 2015.

Dougherty, Jack. *More than One Struggle: The Evolution of Black School Reform in Milwaukee*. Chapel Hill: University of North Carolina Press, 2004.

———. "Shopping for Schools: How Public Education and Private Housing Shaped Suburban Connecticut." *Journal of Urban History* 38 (March 2012): 205–24.

Douglas, Davison. *Reading, Writing, and Race: The Desegregation of the Charlotte Schools*. Chapel Hill: University of North Carolina Press, 1995.

Erickson, Ansley T. *Making the Unequal Metropolis: School Desegregation and Its Limits*. Chicago: University of Chicago Press, 2016.

Fairclough, Adam. *A Class of Their Own: Black Teachers in the Segregated South*. Cambridge, Mass.: Harvard University Press, 2007.

Frazier, Stanley R., and Janice Frazier. *T.D.'s Truths*. XLIBRIS, 2013.

Frye, Katherine. *The Mighty Lions: A Story of West Charlotte High School*. Videorecording, North Carolina Center for Educational Films, 1996.

Fullilove, Mindy Thompson. *Root Shock: How Tearing Up City Neighborhoods Hurts America, and What We Can Do About It*. New York: One World/Ballantine, 2005.

Gaillard, Frye. *The Dream Long Deferred: The Landmark Struggle for Desegregation in Charlotte, North Carolina*. 2nd ed. Charlotte: Briarpatch Press, 1999.

Gilmore, Glenda. *Gender and Jim Crow: Women and the Politics of White Supremacy in North Carolina, 1896–1920*. Chapel Hill: University of North Carolina Press, 1996.

Glenn, A. L. *History of the National Alliance of Postal Employees, 1913–1955.* Washington, D.C.: National Alliance of Postal Employees, 1955.

Green, Paul. *A Southern Life: Letters of Paul Green, 1916–1981.* Chapel Hill: University of North Carolina Press, 2013.

Greenwood, Janette Thomas. *Bittersweet Legacy: The Black and White "Better Classes" in Charlotte, 1850–1910.* Chapel Hill: University of North Carolina Press, 1994.

Grant, Gerald. *Hope and Despair in the American City: Why There Are No Bad Schools in Raleigh.* Cambridge, Mass.: Harvard University Press, 2011.

Griffin, Willie J. "An Indigenous Civil Rights Movement: Charlotte, North Carolina 1940–63." MA thesis, Morgan State University, 2006.

———. "Courier of Crisis, Messenger of Hope: Trezzvant W. Anderson and the Black Freedom Struggle for Economic Justice." Ph.D. diss., University of North Carolina at Chapel Hill, 2016.

———. "'News and Views of the Postal Service': Trezzvant W. Anderson and Black Labor Journalism in the New Deal Era." In *Labor: Studies in Working Class History,* forthcoming.

Grundy, Pamela. "Fighting Testing Madness in Charlotte, North Carolina." In *Digital Networking for School Reform: The Online Grassroots Efforts of Parent and Teacher Activists,* edited by Alison Heron-Hubry and Melanie Landon-Hays, 48–60. New York: Palgrave Pivot, 2014.

———. *Learning to Win: Sports, Education and Social Change in Twentieth-Century North Carolina.* Chapel Hill: University of North Carolina Press, 2001.

———. *Lion Pride: West Charlotte High School, 1938–2013.* Charlotte: West Charlotte High School National Alumni Association, 2013.

Hall, Jacquelyn Dowd. "The Long Civil Rights Movement and the Political Uses of the Past." *Journal of American History* 91 (March 2005): 1233–63.

Hanchett, Thomas W. "A Guided Tour of the Northwest Corridor." In *Let There Be Light: Exploring How Charlotte's Historic West End Is Shaping a New South,* edited by Ron Stodghill. Charlotte: Johnson C. Smith University, 2014.

———. *Sorting Out the New South City: Race, Class and Urban Development in Charlotte, 1875–1975.* Chapel Hill: University of North Carolina Press, 1998.

Hannah-Jones, Nikole. "Living Apart: How the Government Betrayed a Landmark Civil Rights Law." *ProPublica,* 25 June 2015.

Hyra, Derek S. *Race, Class, and Politics in the Cappuccino City.* Chicago: University of Chicago Press, 2017.

Janken, Kenneth Robert. *The Wilmington Ten: Violence, Injustice, and the Rise of Black Politics in the 1970s.* Chapel Hill: University of North Carolina Press, 2016.

K'Meyer, Tracey E. *From Brown to Meredith: The Long Struggle for School Desegregation in Louisville, Kentucky, 1954–2007.* Chapel Hill: University of North Carolina Press, 2013.

Katz, Michael B., Mark J. Stern, and Jamie J. Fader. "The New African American Inequality." *Journal of American History* 92 (June 2005): 75–108.

Kendi, Ibram X. *Stamped from the Beginning: The Definitive History of Racist Ideas in America.* New York: Nation Books, 2016.

Kim, Juli, and Shonaka Ellison. *The Project L.I.F.T. Story: Early Lessons from a Public-Private Education Turnaround Initiative.* Chapel Hill: Public Impact, 2015.

Kluger, Richard. *Simple Justice: The History of Brown v. Board of Education and Black America's Struggle for Equality*. New York: Alfred A. Knopf, 1976.

Kohler-Hausmann, Julilly. "Guns and Butter: The Welfare State, the Carceral State, and the Politics of Exclusion in the Postwar United States." *Journal of American History* 102 (June 2015): 87–99.

———. "Welfare Crises, Penal Solutions, and the Origins of the 'Welfare Queen.'" *Journal of Urban History* 41 (June 2015): 756–71.

Lassiter, Matthew D. "Schools and Housing in Metropolitan History: An Introduction." *Journal of Urban History* 38 (March 2012): 195–204.

———. *The Silent Majority: Suburban Politics in the Sunbelt South*. Princeton, N.J.: Princeton University Press, 2006.

Leach, Damaria. "Progress under Pressure: Changes in Charlotte Race Relations, 1955–1965." MA Thesis, University of North Carolina at Chapel Hill, 1976.

Lowery, Wesley. *"They Can't Kill Us All": Ferguson, Baltimore, and a New Era in America's Racial Justice Movement*. New York: Little, Brown, and Company, 2016.

Lukas, J. Anthony. *Common Ground: A Turbulent Decade in the Lives of Three American Families*. New York: Vintage Books, 1986.

Malkins, Tia C. "The Black Teacher Shortage." *Journal of Negro Education* 80 (Summer 2011): 417–27.

Manning, Howard E. *Report from the Court: The High School Problem*. North Carolina General Court of Justice, Superior Court Division, 95 CVS 1158, Hoke County v. State, 24 May 2005.

———. Order. North Carolina General Court of Justice, Superior Court Division, 95 CVS 1158, Hoke County v. State, 19 August 2005.

Margo, Robert. *Race and Schooling in the South, 1880–1950: An Economic History*. Chicago: University of Chicago Press, 1991.

Mickelson, Roslyn, Stephen Smith, and Amy Hawn Nelson, eds. *Yesterday, Today, and Tomorrow: School Desegregation and Resegregation in Charlotte*. Cambridge, Mass.: Harvard Education Press, 2015.

National Commission on Excellence in Education. *A Nation at Risk: The Imperative for Educational Reform*. April 1983.

Nelson, Amy Hawn. "A Long Path to Success: Integration and Community Engagement at Shamrock Gardens Elementary School." In *Yesterday, Today, and Tomorrow: School Desegregation and Resegregation in Charlotte*, edited by Roslyn Mickelson, Stephen Smith, and Amy Hawn Nelson, 137–56. Cambridge, Mass.: Harvard Education Press, 2015.

Newkirk, Vann R. "The Development of the National Association for the Advancement of Colored People in Metropolitan Charlotte, North Carolina, 1919–1965." Ph.D. diss., Howard University, 2002.

Newsom, Mary. "The Corridor's 'Color Line': Devaluing Land and Community." In *Let There Be Light: Exploring How Charlotte's West End is Shaping a New South*, edited by Ron Stodghill. Charlotte: Johnson C. Smith University, 2014.

Nichol, Gene R., and Heather Hunt. *Economic Hardship, Racialized Concentrated Poverty and the Challenges of Low-Wage Work: Charlotte, North Carolina*. Chapel Hill: North Carolina Poverty Research Fund, Spring 2016.

Orfield, Gary, and Susan E. Eaton. *Dismantling Desegregation: The Quiet Reversal of Brown v. Board of Education*. New York: New Press, 1997.

Parcel, Toby L., Joshua A. Hendrix, and Andrew J. Taylor. "A Study in Contrasts: Race, Politics, and School Assignment Policies in Charlotte-Mecklenburg and Wake County, North Carolina." In *Yesterday, Today, and Tomorrow: School Desegregation and Resegregation in Charlotte*, edited by Roslyn Mickelson, Stephen Smith, and Amy Hawn Nelson, 85–100. Cambridge, Mass.: Harvard Education Press, 2015.

Payne, Charles M. *I've Got the Light of Freedom: The Organizing Tradition and the Mississippi Freedom Struggle*. Berkeley: University of California Press, 1995.

Posey-Maddox, Linn. *When Middle-Class Parents Choose Urban Schools: Class, Race, and the Challenge of Equity in Public Education*. Chicago: University of Chicago Press, 2014.

Ramsey, David. *Second Ward and West Charlotte*. Videorecording, Levine Museum of the New South, 1994.

Ravitch, Diane. *The Death and Life of the Great American School System: How Testing and Choice Are Undermining Education*. New York: Basic Books, 2010.

———. *Reign of Error: The Hoax of the Privatization Movement and the Danger to America's Public Schools*. New York: Alfred A. Knopf, 2013.

Rhew, Adam. "*Swann* and Public School Segregation in Charlotte." *Scalawag* 5 (Summer 2016): 38–48.

Rodgers, Daniel T. *Age of Fracture*. Cambridge, Mass.: Harvard University Press, 2011.

Rosen, Richard A., and Joseph Mosnier. *Julius Chambers: A Life in the Legal Struggle for Civil Rights*. Chapel Hill: University of North Carolina Press, 2016.

Rothstein, Richard. *The Color of Law: A Forgotten History of How Our Government Segregated America*. New York: Liveright Publishing, 2017.

Rubio, Philip F. *There's Always Work at the Post Office: African American Postal Workers and the Fight for Jobs, Justice, and Equality*. Chapel Hill: University of North Carolina Press, 2010.

Shircliffe, Barbara. "'We Got the Best of That World': A Case for the Study of Nostalgia in the Oral History of School Segregation." *Oral History Review* 28 (Summer/Fall 2001): 59–84.

Smith, Stephen Samuel. *Boom for Whom? Education, Desegregation, and Development in Charlotte*. Albany: State University of New York Press, 2004.

———. "The Price of Success: the Political Economy of Education, Desegregation, and Development in Charlotte." In *Yesterday, Today, and Tomorrow: School Desegregation and Resegregation in Charlotte*, edited by Roslyn Mickelson, Stephen Smith, and Amy Hawn Nelson. Cambridge, Mass.: Harvard Education Press, 2015.

Stewart, Alison. *First Class: The Legacy of Dunbar, America's First Black High School*. Chicago: Lawrence Hill Books, 2013.

Stodghill, Ron, ed. *Let There Be Light: Exploring How Charlotte's Historic West End Is Shaping a New South*. Charlotte: Johnson C. Smith University, 2014.

Theusen, Sarah. *Greater Than Equal: African American Struggles for Schools and Citizenship in North Carolina, 1919–1965*. Chapel Hill: University of North Carolina Press, 2013.

Thompson, Heather. "Why Mass Incarceration Matters: Rethinking Crisis, Decline, and Transformation in Postwar American History." *Journal of American History* 97 (December 2010): 703–34.

Tough, Paul. *Whatever It Takes: Geoffrey Canada's Quest to Change Harlem and America*. New York: Mariner Books, 2009.

U.S. Bureau of the Census. *Tenth Census of the United States, 1880: Census Reports, June 1, 1880*. Washington, D.C.: Government Printing Office.

Wake County Superior Court. *Report from the Court: The High School Problem*. 23 May 2005.

Walker, Vanessa Siddle. *Their Highest Potential: An African American School Community in the Segregated South*.

Watters, Pat. *Charlotte*. Atlanta: Southern Regional Council, 1964.

Wells, Amy Stuart, Jennifer Jellison Holme, Anita Tijerina Revilla, and Awo Korantemaa Atanda. *Both Sides Now: The Story of School Desegregation's Graduates*. Berkeley: University of California Press, 2009.

Zimmerman, Jonathan. *Whose America? Culture Wars in the Public Schools*. Cambridge, Mass.: Harvard University Press, 2002.

INDEX

60, 61; Nixon attack on, 74; one-way, 65, 74, 123; and parent choice, 123, 137, 140; Reagan attack on, 112; school board and, 78–79, 136; suburbs and, 72–73, 120–21, 123; Supreme Court *Milliken v. Bradley* decision on, 121; white resistance to, 60, 74, 88–89

Camp, Patsy Rice, 35, 38, 49, 133
Campaign for a Color-Blind America, 134
Canada, Geoffrey, 167
Capacchione, William, 133–34
Capacchione v. Charlotte-Mecklenburg Board of Education, 133–36, 193, 211n64
Carolina Times, 61
Central High School (Charlotte), 29, 42
Central High School (Little Rock), 43
Chambers, Julius, 134; civil rights litigation by, 47, 51–52, 53, 54, 155; on school desegregation and inequality, 31–32, 54, 58, 61, 79, 117, 194, 206n29
Charlotte, N.C.: black elected officials in, 29, 47, 55, 78, 108; bombings in, 47–49; city council of, 47, 107, 108, 215n15; civil rights movement in, 34, 44–46, 47; economic divisions in, 115–16, 178, 183, 215n7; Gantt as mayor of, 108, 115, 121; gentrification in, 184, 186; Hispanics in, 141, 186; housing in, 26–27, 30, 62–64, 107, 115, 161, 184–85, 215n15; illness among African Americans in, 11, 202n6; Jim Crow segregation in, 8–9, 10, 13, 37–38; "missing" black men in, 146, 212n10; music scene in, 37–38; Opportunity Task Force report on, 188; population growth in, 8, 14, 26, 108; progressive image of, 46, 78, 108, 112; protest marches and rallies in, 56, 65, 76, 169; Reagan speech in, 112, 114; residential segregation in, 26, 31, 63–64; school closings in, 55–56, 64, 65, 167–69, 170, 171–72; suburbs of, 63, 115, 120–21, 140–41, 150, 154–55, 174; uprising of 2016 in, 181–82
Charlotte-Mecklenburg Opportunity Task Force, 182–83

Charlotte-Mecklenburg Schools, 61, 65–66, 124, 140; and *Capaccione* suit, 134, 135, 136; and corporate reform movement, 158–59; equity plan of, 141, 211n3; inequality within, 116–17, 175; initial busing plan for, 60; and 1960 city-county merger, 40, 74; school assignment plans for, 42–44, 52–53, 60, 74–76, 78, 122–23, 134, 135, 136–37, 155, 156, 182, 205n11; and standardized testing, 122, 155–56. *See also* School board
Charlotte Observer, 10, 29, 97, 112, 121, 131, 133, 140, 173; editorials in, 137, 159, 167, 178, 208n38; on Gorman shakeup, 158, 159; on school board, 77, 79, 137, 171; on school performance by, 116–17, 120, 155–56; on student violence, 71, 151, 152; on West Charlotte High image, 102
Charlotte Post, 114
Charlotte Three, 207n19
Charlotte Uprising, 181–82
Charter schools, 158, 169, 188
Chavis, Benjamin, 65
Chess club, 92, 104, 147, 165, 175
Chicago Public Schools, 169
Chisholm, E. A., 14
Choice: and busing plan, 123, 137, 140; promotion of, 5, 120–21, 123–24, 187, 210n20; and resistance to desegregation, 41–42, 204–5nn6–7; school board focus on, 137, 183–84
Civil rights movement: Charlotte as fertile ground for, 45–46; Freedom Rides during, 46, 205n15; impact on West Charlotte High of, 49–51, 205n20; sit-ins during, 34, 44–45; struggles during previous decades, 27; voter registration efforts during, 10, 27, 47
Cline, Terry, 132, 133, 147–48
Coleman, Sarah Moore, 17
Coley, Te' Ali, 84
Color blindness, 5, 112, 114, 134, 150, 209n23
Colston, Earl, 205n20
Community, sense of, 36, 77; loss of, 127–28, 145–46, 153
Community Advisory Group (CAG), 78

Vance High School, 132–33
Vinroot, Richard, 210n20
Voter registration, 10, 27, 47

Waddell High School, 141, 150, 168, 171
Wall Street Journal, 84, 105, 109, 122
War on Drugs, 116, 146
West Charlotte community: borders of, 9–10; impact of Great Recession on, 161; loss of community feeling in, 127–28, 145–46, 153; sense of community in, 36; West Charlotte High connection to, 88, 144–45, 177
West Charlotte High School: advanced classes at, 19, 103, 126–27, 130–31, 174, 210n34, 214n43; African American history, significance of, 86, 88, 97–100, 132, 177–78, 189–90; basketball team at, 50–51, 91; black teachers at, 61–62, 87–88, 129, 130; black-white fights at, 69, 70–71; Blake as principal of, 14, 15, 19–22, 34, 38, 49; Boston students' visit to, 80; building school loyalty in, 133, 162, 164, 178; chess club at, 104, 147, 165; and civil rights movement, 34–35, 49–50, 51, 205n20; community's connection to, 88, 144–45, 177; construction of, 14, 30–31; as desegregation flagship, 81, 84, 108–9, 112, 124; desegregation's impact on, 69, 71–72, 74–75, 106–7, 112; disciplinary actions at, 17, 25, 205n20; diversity at, 92–97, 101–2; drama program at, 22, 91, 133; dropout rate at, 23, 97, 166, 203n30; effects of choice on, 124, 132–33, 141–42, 166; ESL program at, 84, 93, 101–2; extracurricular activities at, 17, 21–22, 105; football at, 25–26, 37, 90, 153; Haywood as principal of, 79, 85–86; IB program at, 142, 174; immigrants and refugees at, 93; marching band at, 37, 90, 99–100, 150–51, 174–75, 176–77; mascot of, 1; McMillan as principal of, 89, 90–91, 103–4; Modest as principal of, 159–62, 164–66; nurturing environment at, 17, 90, 127–28, 129, 153, 168; open-school program at, 76–77, 79, 84, 90, 100–101; percentage of black students at, 102, 124, 133, 141; pride in, 97–99, 125–26, 144–45, 179; racial and class divisions within, 18–19, 93, 94–95, 104–6, 126–27, 210n34; racial stereotyping of, 150–53, 154; resources and facilities at, 15, 18, 19, 28–29, 89–90, 174; and Second Ward High School, 26, 37, 56; Simmons as principal of, 129–32; sports programs at, 22–23, 25–26, 37, 50–51, 90, 91, 107; teacher diversity at, 96; teachers at segregated, 15, 17, 25; teachers' role at, 85–88, 91–92, 164, 175; teacher turnover at, 131, 148–49, 164–65, 166, 172, 177; test scores at, 130, 147–48, 161, 166, 172, 177, 212n12, 213n18, 214n38; *Wall Street Journal* article on, 84, 105, 109; white students at, 75–76, 89, 99–100, 103, 104–5; white teachers at, 62, 66, 67, 87–88, 206n6; youth culture at, 146–47
West Charlotte National Alumni Association, 99, 132, 153, 175, 177–78, 189–90
West Mecklenburg High School, 71, 117, 141, 150
White, Gosnell, 75, 79, 81
Williams, Frank, 91
Wilmington, N.C., violence in, 70, 207n19
Winston-Salem Journal and Sentinel, 30
Wright, Thomas, 45

Yost, Robert, 91, 104, 148, 164–65